Continuous Journey

A History of Canada's Peoples

Continuous Journey

A Social History of South Asians in Canada

Norman Buchignani
Doreen M. Indra
with Ram Srivastava

Published by McClelland and Stewart Ltd., in association
with the Multiculturalism Directorate,
Department of the Secretary of State
and the Canadian Government Publishing Centre,
Supply and Services, Canada.

Catalogue No. Ci 44-11/1985 E

McClelland and Stewart Limited
The Canadian Publishers
25 Hollinger Road
Toronto, Ontario
M4B 3G2

CANADIAN CATALOGUING IN PUBLICATION DATA
Buchignani, Norman, 1946-
  Continuous journey

(A History of Canada's peoples)
(Generations)
Bibliography: p.
Includes index.
ISBN 0-7710-1761-8

1. South Asian Canadians - History.* I. Indra,
Doreen Marie. II. Title. III. Series.
IV. Series: Generations (Canada. Multiculturalism
Directorate).

FC106.06B83 1985   971'.004914   C84-099727-2
F1035.06B83 1985

Printed and bound in Canada by John Deyell Company

Contents

Editors' Introduction

Canadians, like many other people, have recently been changing their attitude towards the ethnic dimension in society. Instead of thinking of the many distinctive heritages and identities to be found among them as constituting a problem, though one that time would solve, they have begun to recognize the ethnic diversity of their country as a rich resource. They have begun to take pride in the fact that people have come and are coming here from all parts of the world, bringing with them varied outlooks, knowledge, skills and traditions, to the great benefit of all.

It is for this reason that Book IV of the *Report of the Royal Commission on Bilingualism and Biculturalism* dealt with the cultural contributions of the ethnic groups other than the British, the French and the Native Peoples to Canada, and that the federal government in its response to Book IV announced that the Citizenship Branch of the Department of the Secretary of State would commission "histories specifically directed to the background, contributions and problems of various cultural groups in Canada." This series presents the histories that have resulted from that mandate. Although commissioned by the Government, they are not intended as definitive or official, but rather as the efforts of scholars to bring together much of what is known about the ethnic groups studied, to indicate what remains to be learned, and thus to stimulate further research concerning the ethnic dimension in Canadian society. The histories are to be objective, analytical, and readable, and directed towards the general reading public, as well as students at the senior high school and the college and university levels, and teachers in the elementary schools.

Most Canadians belong to an ethnic group, since to do so is simply to have "a sense of identity rooted in a common origin . . . whether this common origin is real or imaginary."[1] The Native Peoples, the British and French (referred to as charter groups because they were the first Europeans to take possession of the land), the groups such as the Germans and Dutch who have been established in Canada for over a hundred years and those who began to arrive only yesterday all have traditions and values that they cherish and that now are part of the cultural riches that Canadians share. The groups vary widely in numbers, geographical location and distribution and degree of social and economic power. The stories of their struggles, failures and triumphs will be told in this series.

As the Royal Commission on Bilingualism and Biculturalism pointed out, this sense of ethnic origin or identity "is much keener in certain individuals than in others."[2] In contemporary Canadian society, with the increasing number of intermarriages across ethnic lines, and hence the growing diversity of peoples ancestors, many are coming to identify themselves as simple Canadian, without reference to their ancestral origins. In focusing on the ethnic dimension of Canadian society, past and present, the series does not assume that everyone should be categorized into one particular group, or that ethnicity is always the most important dimension of people's lives. It is, however, one dimension that needs examination if we are to understand fully the contours and nature of Canadian society and identity.

Professional Canadian historians have in the past emphasized political and economic history, and since the country's economic and political institutions have been controlled largely by people of British and French origin, the role of those of other origins in the development of Canada has been neglected. Also, Canadian historians in the past have been almost exclusively of British and French origin, and have lacked the interest and the linguistic skills necessary to explore the history of other ethnic groups. Indeed, there has rarely ever been an examination of the part played by specifically British – or, better, specifically English, Irish, Scottish and Welsh – traditions and values in Canadian development, because of the lack of recognition of pluralism in the society. The part played by French traditions and values, and particular varieties of French traditions and values, has for a number of reasons been more carefully scrutinized.

This series is an indication of growing interest in Canadian social history, which includes immigration and ethnic history. This may particularly be a reflection of an increasing number of scholars whose origins and ethnic identities are other than British or French. Because such trends are recent, many of the authors of the histories in this series have not had a large body of published writing to work from. It is true that some histories have already been written of particular groups other than the British and French; but these have often been characterized by filio pietism, a narrow perspective and a dearth of scholarly analysis.

Despite the scarcity of secondary sources, the authors have been asked to be as comprehensive as possible, and to give balanced coverage to a number of themes: historical background, settlement patterns, ethnic identity and assimilation, ethnic associations, population trends, religion, values, occupations and social class, the family, the ethnic press, language patterns, political behaviour, education, inter-ethnic relations, the arts and recreation. They have also been asked to give a sense of the way the group differs in various parts of the country. Finally, they have been asked to give, as much as possible, an insider's view of what the immigrant and ethnic experiences were like at different periods of time, but yet at the same time to be as objective as possible, and not simply to present the group as it sees itself, or as it would like to be seen.

The authors have thus been faced with a herculean task. To the extent that they have succeeded, they provide us with new glimpses into many aspects of Canadian society of the past and the present. To the extent that they have fallen short of their goal, they challenge other historians, sociologists and social anthropologists to continue the work begun here.

Jean Burnet
Howard Palmer

[1] *Report of the Royal Commission on Bilingualism and Biculturalism.*
[2] Ibid. Paragraph 8.

Introduction

This is a book about Canadians of South Asian origin – those whose ultimate roots are in the peoples and cultures of India, Pakistan, Bangladesh, and Sri Lanka. Commonly called East Indians, they are easily Canada's most diverse ethnic population. Among them are recent immigrants from South Asia, East and South Africa, the South Pacific, and the Caribbean. Others are fourth-generation Canadians. Together, they represent over a dozen source countries and first languages, three world religions, and a score of ethnocultural and national groups. They are also one of Canada's largest ethnic populations, presently numbering about 310,000.

The history of South Asians in Canada divides itself into three distinct eras, and these are reflected in the three-part division of the book. Part One covers the 1902-1918 period. The first handful of South Asian men arrived in British Columbia in 1903. Within four years they were followed by over 5,000 others, attracted to Canada by high wages and available work. Chapter One describes the setting into which they came, their cultural origins and migration patterns, and initial reactions to their arrival. British Columbia had already put in place many social, legal, and economic restrictions on Chinese and Japanese immigrants and these, as outlined in Chapter Two, were quickly extended to South Asians. All South Asian immigration was banned, a deeply resented restriction that isolated men in Canada from their families overseas. Most immigrants were Sikh, and this provided them with the cultural tools to develop strong community solidarity in subsequent years; Chapter Three details the economic, social, and political development of the community subsequent to the ban on immigration. In addition, it charts the rise of a movement to get the ban removed. Continued lack of success in achieving this objective led community members to become increasingly involved in activities aimed at the elimination of British colonial rule in India. As seen in Chapter Four, this put them into direct conflict with the

1

British and Canadian governments and led to the rise of the Ghadar Party, an important early Indian revolutionary movement.

Part Two deals with the "quiet years" from 1919 to 1947. The ban on immigration was modified in 1919, allowing the entry of wives and children and the development of family life among Canadian South Asians for the first time. Hostility toward South Asians decreased and their economic security increased, as is illustrated in Chapter Five. However, all of the legal disabilities imposed on South Asians prior to World War I continued in effect. Chapter Six is concerned with the community's drive to remove these restrictions, which culminated in enfranchisement in 1947.

The year 1947 marked the beginning of a new era for South Asians in Canada, which is dealt with in Part Three. The immigration ban was removed in that year, and this led to a slow resumption of immigration. Chapter Seven outlines the exponential increase in immigration up to 1970 and presents some of its consequences for South Asian settlement and community development. With this increase in numbers came a parallel increase in the national, cultural, class, linguistic, and religious diversity of South Asian Canadians. Chapter Eight introduces the many sociocultural groups represented among South Asians in Canada, describes similarities and differences, and sketches the development of their communities.

The South Asian Canadian population has increased dramatically since 1961, when it stood at only 7,000. By 1971 it was close to 68,000 and it is presently over four times that. Consequently, immigration and settlement are an integral and important part of the experience of most South Asian Canadians. Chapter Nine deals with how the demands of immigration and settlement have affected South Asian individual and family life. It also discusses the impending changes signified by the rise of the second generation. The following two chapters extend this discussion to the development of informal social links with other community members and to the rise of South Asian community institutions.

South Asian immigrants typically come from places Canadians have had little contact with, places that are often thought to be exotic and culturally strange. Beyond this, many South Asians have been perceived by other Canadians as visibly distinct and Canadians have generally had little historical experience in dealing with visible immigrant groups prior to their arrival. As illustrated in the final chapter, the development of relations between South Asians and other Canadians has generally been smooth and reasonably trouble-free. This has not been uniformly so, however, for as South Asian immigration rose in the 1970's so also did a prejudiced minority opposed to it. The rise and recent abatement of these prejudices is also covered in Chapter Twelve.

Once a small and subordinate British Columbia minority group, South Asians are now active in every aspect of Canadian life. From Victoria to St. John's to Frobisher Bay, South Asians will be found in every occupation and station in life. Most have been Canadians for less than twenty years, yet already their contributions to Canada and their personal achievements are substantial. A vibrant cultural mosaic themselves, they are now an integral and valuable part of the greater Canadian mosaic of peoples and cultures.

Research and writing of this book took several years and it represents the contributions of hundreds of people. We would like to thank the many South Asian people and organizations across the country who provided much of the information for this book. We would also like to acknowledge the assistance of the staff at the Public Archives of Canada, especially Mark Hopkins; the Vancouver and Victoria City Archives; the British Columbia, Alberta, and Ontario Provincial Archives; the Cross Cultural Communications Centre in Toronto; the Multicultural History Society of Ontario; and the Special Collections Library at the University of British Columbia. Thanks also go to Dr. Howard Palmer, University of Calgary, and Dr. Jean Burnet, York University, for their editorial guidance and to Edna Wilson and Gail Irani for their work on manuscript preparation. Financial support for research and publication by the Multiculturalism Directorate, Secretary of State, is gratefully appreciated.

PART ONE

The Early Years, 1902-1918

ONE

Beginnings

THE SETTING

Few human sagas have been more dramatic than that of South Asians during their first two decades in Canada. Like that of so many immigrants, it is a story of transition, adjustment, and change. For South Asians, the intrinsic trauma of immigration was magnified by the strong reaction their arrival produced among the other Canadians. The kind of person who was a desirable immigrant was a contentious social issue at the turn of the century. The result was a compromising immigration policy that tempered common ethnic and racial biases with practical economic considerations: the "right kind" of British and Americans were best; Germans and Scandinavians were all right; eastern Europeans could be tolerated on economic grounds; southern Europeans were to be discouraged; and Asians and blacks should not come at all. During this turbulent period the first South Asian pioneers came to British Columbia, the province to which their destinies would be tied for the next fifty years.

It was an unsettled time, when the whole social and economic fabric of North America was changing. British Columbia exemplified these changes. The economy of British Columbia was becoming more complex, and the balance of power between workers and employers within it had not yet been struck. British Columbia was a new and in certain respects artificial society. Vancouver was less than twenty years old and was experiencing an explosive period of growth. It was a raw, newly formed settler society, largely established and defined by people born elsewhere, a rough, contradictory place where change was the normal order.

It was also a place where race and ethnicity were fundamental organizing principles.[1] British Columbia was categorically defined as "white man's country." Isolated from eastern Canada, it faced the Pacific with its "teeming millions." As one commentator of the 1920's put it:

4

British Columbia is one of the last frontiers of the white race against the yellow and the brown. It is a land where a hoary civilization meets a modern one, and where the swarming millions of ancient peoples, stung into restless life by modern events, are constantly impinging on an attractive land held by sparse thousands of whites. And here, the alarmed British Columbian, clamorous for Asiatic exclusion, feels that he is taking the long view . . . (British Columbia is) a community of half a million souls which stands in the sea gate of the northwest Pacific, and holds it for Saxon civilization.[2]

All white British Columbians of that era were by no means ethnically equal. British immigrants and Anglo Canadians set themselves up as the ethnic elite. Still, the major liabilities of ethnic origin fell squarely on those who were visibly different – the Chinese, Japanese, and native people. Discrimination against the Chinese and Japanese was profound. Both groups had been disenfranchised and otherwise legally restricted by the provincial government. On the job they were paid less than other workers and were denied positions of responsibility. No unions would accept them as members. Off the job they were socially isolated and not allowed access to many stores and other businesses. Highly stigmatic stereotypes of each contributed to little understanding and less sympathy for the Chinese and Japanese.

By the year 1900 virtually every sector of white British Columbia society was opposed to further Chinese and Japanese immigration. Under the British North America Act all matters dealing with immigration were a federal responsibility, but continual pressure by the provincial legislature had slowly brought the government in Ottawa around. In the late 1800's the federal government enacted a requirement that every arriving Chinese immigrant must pay a $50 tax in order to get into the country. This was increased to $100 in 1900. Strong pressure was being applied to achieve a similar restriction on Japanese immigration. Entering such a polarized racial situation, South Asians found themselves in the most difficult circumstances. Indeed, fighting against racial disabilities would be a central theme for the next twenty years.

THE BEGINNING

The first South Asian to come to Canada will probably never be known. In a token sense, Indian immigration to North America goes back to the 1640's, when a "Portuguese Indian" is mentioned as selling cloth to native people in Mexico City.[3] Visiting Indian dignitaries occasionally made Vancouver a port of call, especially after the construction of the Canadian Pacific Railway created an all-Canadian route to eastern ports. At the same time, visits to Victoria and Vancouver by Indian seamen must have been common.

Despite these contacts, immigrants did not begin to arrive in Canada before 1903.[4] What seems to have initiated South Asian immigration was the coronation of Edward VII in 1902. Following the pattern set by the celebration of Queen Victoria's Diamond Jubilee of five years before, representatives came to London for the ceremony from across the Empire.[5] Over 1,200 Indian troops alone went to London including the 10th Jats, the 15th Sikhs, and the 33rd, 20th, and 1st Punjab Infantries.[6]

Somewhat lost in this massive affair was a small contingent of eighty-three officers and men from the Crown Colony of Hong Kong. This multi-ethnic contingent was made up of forty-three members of the Hong Kong Volunteers, fourteen from the 1st Chinese, and either fifteen or twenty-three from the Hong Kong Regiment, Punjabis.[7] Together, they were among several military delegations from the Far East, including ones from Singapore, the Straits Settlements, and the Malay States.[8] What was unique about this Hong Kong contingent was that it came through Canada on its way to and from London. On June 3, 1902, they arrived in Victoria on the *Empress of Japan*.[9] After a short wait the ship sailed for Vancouver, where the men disembarked to a rousing welcome. The Punjabi contingent attracted the most attention, for by Vancouver standards they were the most novel. These men were officered by Sardar Major Kadir Khan Bahadur.[10] Khan and several other men in the contingent had distinguished themselves during the siege of Peking in 1900. Most of the contingent were Sikhs and the rest, Moslems. Following the British sepoy tradition, all of them were originally from the same area, in this case, Punjab.

During their brief stay in Vancouver Major Khan's men were very well treated and their newspaper coverage was positive:

TURBANED MEN EXCITE INTEREST
Awe inspiring men from India held the crowds[11]

On June 4 they were inspected by Major General Sir Charles Parsons, who was then head of the armed forces in Canada. They also went through drill exercises in front of an appreciative crowd in the drill hall of the 6th D.O.C. Rifles.[12] The next day they left by train for Montreal, from where they embarked for England with the Canadian contingent on June 14. While in England they were inspected by the King, who presented Khan with the Cross of India.[13] Upon their return to Canada they were inspected by Governor General Minto in Ottawa. From there they retraced their path through Vancouver and left for Hong Kong on September 8 on the *Empress of China*.[14] The Hong Kong Regiment, Punjabis was disbanded shortly after their return to Hong Kong.[15]

This event initiated South Asian immigration to Canada. At the turn of the century there were large communities of South Asians in a number of British possessions in the Far East and Southeast Asia, including Hong Kong, Singapore, Rangoon, and Shanghai. Most had initially moved there in British army detachments and had stayed on after leaving the army. Many were employed as watchmen, police, and dockyard workers. Indian troops used by the British in that part of the world were primarily from Punjab, which in turn largely determined the ethnic and religious makeup of these communities. Like Major Khan's coronation contingent, most people in these communities were Sikh, a religious group that arose in Punjab in the 1400's; most of the rest were Punjabi Moslems.

At the turn of the century these new Far Eastern communities were still in the process of developing substantial roots. In those days it was relatively inexpensive to take a train from Punjab to Calcutta and then to take passage on a ship to the Far East. Realizing this, many a brother, cousin, and nephew made the journey on the advice of their relatives who had already done so. In all these communities there were far more men than women and very few children, for few had yet decided to establish themselves permanently outside of India.

Once these small communities were established, the extension of the process to North America was only a question of time. Sikhs in particular have traditionally been extremely resourceful, independent, and unafraid of taking risks to better their situation. With their British army experience, migration to "British" Canada was a quite natural next step. The Hong Kong coronation contingent simply provided the initial inspiration. Without exception the first few hundred South Asian immigrants to Canada came from Hong Kong or one of the other British Far Eastern strongholds. Almost all of them were Sikhs.

No immigrants arrived before mid-1903, when five men landed in Vancouver and another five arrived in Victoria.[16] Altogether, about thirty men came in fiscal year 1903-04.[17] Thereafter, immigration increased rapidly:

TABLE 1

South Asian Immigration to Canada, Fiscal Years 1904-1907	
Fiscal Year	Number
1904-05	45
1905-06	387
1906-07	2,124
1907-08	2,623
TOTAL	5,179

SOURCE: "Hindoo Immigration to Canada," n.d., RG 76, #536999, pt. 1.

Until 1906 South Asian immigration received almost no governmental or press notice. The only exception was a brief flurry of private correspondence in the fall of 1904, which was prompted by an angry letter from Thomas McGuigan, Vancouver city clerk, to the federal superintendent of immigration, charging that South Asians had been lured to Vancouver by shipping companies.[18] According to him they were "led to believe that they can secure immediate employment at wages far beyond the dreams of an Oriental in his own country." In his official capacity, McGuigan expressed the city of Vancouver's opinion that these new immigrants were not wanted. He claimed that there was no work for South Asians and that they would be "unable to stand this climate which is so different from their own." In reply, the federal immigration official was surprised that people of Indian origin were coming to Canada.[19] Highly placed federal officials did not share McGuigan's concerns, citing the beneficial effect of South Asians in British Guiana, Trinidad, and elsewhere.[20]

McGuigan's complaint was full of inaccuracies. No shipping companies were offering inducements to South Asian immigrants at that time as far as the federal government could discover.[21] There was work available, at least in the summer months. Moreover, McGuigan's conviction that South Asian immigrants would be unable to stand Vancouver's climate was ridiculous: Vancouver winter temperatures are not much colder than those in Punjab. Still, these inaccuracies are relatively unimportant in respect to the more central point – that already South Asians were being defined as a distinct, non-European racial group. This foreshadowed the time a few short years later when South Asians would inherit the full force of racial hatred and discriminatory restrictions that were already the lot of the Chinese and Japanese.

By the end of 1905 a fundamental change in immigration was taking place. Now immigrants were starting to come primarily from India rather than the Far East, and in far greater numbers than previously. Several related factors contributed to this change. First, by 1906 an exclusionary $500 head tax placed on Chinese immigrants two years earlier was beginning to have its effects in the labour market; unskilled workers were becoming less plentiful and wage rates were rising. This directly benefited those South Asians already in Canada, for it was easier for them to find jobs and save money.[22] Economic prospects for the future brightened, and people began writing to their friends and relatives in India, encouraging them to come to Canada. These letters were widely circulated and generated an immigrant flow from the home villages of those who were already here. Chain migration became the rule, as it had been for many Chinese and Japanese.

No less important was another consequence of the $500 Chinese head tax. CPR shipping lines suffered a sharp decline in passengers making the trip from the Far East to Canada. From the company's point of view, what better way would there be to restore flagging revenues than to solicit immigrants from India? At that time passage from India to Vancouver was traditionally from Calcutta to Hong Kong to Vancouver, and the last leg of the trip was the one hurt by the decrease in the number of Chinese passengers. Although the CPR continually denied doing so, it is clear that by early 1906 their agents were circulating posters in the port of Calcutta and in Punjab advertising the benefits of coming to Canada.[23]

Feeble attempts were also made in Vancouver by a Dr. Davichand to develop a system of contract South Asian labour in British Columbia similar to the systems already established with the Chinese and Japanese.[24] It was his unrealistic hope that South Asian workers would supplant the Chinese and Japanese in the British Columbia economy.

Canada offered substantial economic rewards to prospective Indian immigrants, but such "pull" factors alone do not fully explain the subsequent explosion in immigration nor do they account for why some types of people came while others did not. Indian "push" factors primarily determined this, especially considerations of ethnicity, religion, class, and degree of contact with the British. Then as now, such factors varied far more on the Indian subcontinent than in all of Europe. Even so, it was almost exclusively from Punjab that South Asian immigrants came. To understand why this was so one must look briefly at Punjab and its peoples, especially the Sikhs.

THE SOURCE

Bounded by the Himalayas to the northeast, the rising mountains to the west of the Indus River, and the Sutlej River in the south, Punjab has a certain degree of geographical unity that distinguishes it from the rest of the Indian subcontinent. It is a huge, flat land broken by five rivers that give the area its name: *Panch* (five) *Ab* (waters). It is a land of radical changes in climate, which oscillates from the blazing months of summer to the frosts of winter. These are interspersed by the monsoons, upon which so much in this basically agricultural area depends. It is also an area with its own distinct cultures and languages.

The same geography has cursed Punjab with a turbulent history. Punjab is on the traditional invasion route from the Middle East to India. The Aryans conquered the area some 3,500 years ago. The Persians and the Greeks followed a thousand years later. After them came the Bactrians, Sythians, Huns, a variety of Afghan tribes, and eventually the Moguls. The Moguls were to rule over Punjab from the early 1500's until the late 1700's. By the 1700's Punjab was the home of many ethnic and religious groups.

During two centuries of Mogul domination the Punjab changed dramatically. Ruthless taxation, war, and incessant brigandage put a premium on resourcefulness, individuality, and physical prowess; they also increased the strength and self-reliance of the peasantry. This was particularly true of the Jats, who were one of the major cultivator castes of the region. Under the Moguls the Jats consolidated considerable social and political autonomy at the village level. This independence even extended to caste matters, and Hindu Jats often refused to acknowledge the higher status of Brahmins and Kshatriyas.[25] These farmer-warriors

9

typically formed all-Jat villages, where they developed their own institutions and a strong sense of self and group identity.

Mogul rule also gave an overlay of Islamic religion and culture to a basically Hindu society. This produced great intellectual and religious ferment, out of which arose an altogether new religion – Sikhism.[26] Sikhism came into being at the same time as the Protestant Reformation in Europe, and has many parallels with it. The founder of Sikhism, Guru Nanak (1469-1539), was influenced by the Hindu Bhakti (devotional) tradition and the Muslim Sufis, both of whom preached religious tolerance, asceticism, and mysticism. Nanak was an uncompromising monotheist. Like the Sufis he had no use for idols, exotic rituals, or elaborate social practices; these all interfered with one's understanding of God and the world. Like the Bhaktis he emphasized the need for spiritual teachers. He took a strong stand against all forms of religious retreat from the world. His was to be the religion of working people. In a radical break with tradition he rejected the validity of caste and installed in the religion means to break down caste barriers.[27] This democratic approach extended to the use of vernacular Punjabi for all of the religion's sacred texts. His approach had great appeal among the peasant classes and within his lifetime Guru Nanak gained many followers.

As Sikhism was preached by the next nine Gurus its relationship to the ruling Islamic state worsened, and oppression grew with each generation. After the fifth Guru (Arjun, 1563-1606) was tortured and killed by the Muslim authorities, Sikhs grew increasingly militant.[28] Hargobind (1595-1644) was Arjun's son and successor. With him, the use of power and arms in defence of the faith became an integral part of the religion.[29] Hargobind initiated the first of many military expeditions against the Moguls, which steadily increased in intensity. The ninth Guru, Tegh Bahadur (1621-1675), was executed by the Mogul emperor, which set the stage for the final evolution of the Sikh *Khalsa* (brotherhood of the pure) under his son, Guru Gobind Singh (1666-1708). It was Gobind Singh who established the five *Kakkas* (K's), which since that day have become symbols of the Sikh religion. Men were to keep their hair and beards uncut (*Kes*). In addition, they were to carry a comb (*Kanga*), a steel bracelet (*Kara*), and a dagger (*Kirpan*). They were also to wear a form of short pants (*Kach*). Gobind Singh also reinforced Nanak's assertion that caste made no difference by making all of his male followers take the last name "Singh" (lion). Women took the name "Kaur" (princess). Gobind Singh's creed stressed democracy within the *Khalsa* and prideful defence of its existence. These ideas had great appeal, especially among the Jats.

Gobind Singh's death in 1707 signalled the beginning of 100 years of continuous war. Afghanis invaded Punjab nine times between 1747 and 1769. This effectively destroyed Mogul rule there. By 1809 most of Punjab had been consolidated under one Sikh ruler, Ranjit Singh. The primary threat was thereafter from the British, who had occupied the area south of the Sutlej River in 1809. The Sikh state expanded continually until Ranjit Singh's death in 1839, and a confrontation was inevitable. In 1845 the British invaded Punjab and their victory was complete. After the failure of a revolt in 1848-49 Punjab was formally annexed. It was the last major part of the Indian subcontinent to fall under British domination. The British so effectively consolidated their rule over this wartorn land that most Sikhs did not join in the great sepoy revolt of 1857. The British appreciated the fighting prowess of the Sikhs and they soon became a mainstay of the British Indian army.

Once Punjab was politically and militarily subordinated the British developed irrigation systems that added millions of acres of arable land to Punjab and greatly increased its wealth. Through preferential access to new lands opened by irrigation and through their growing participation in government service, the status of the Jat Sikhs increased steadily.

It was mainly from these people that early South Asian immigration to Canada was drawn, and one of its most striking characteristics is its homogeneity. Virtually everyone who came before World War II was from Punjab. Ninety to 95 per cent were Sikh, even though Sikhs composed a minority of the Punjabi population. Moreover, these individuals tended to come primarily from a few districts of the east central Punjab – Hoshiarpur, Jullundur, and secondarily Ludhiana, Ferozepore, and Amritsar. They were from an area not much more than 200 miles across.

Several things account for this immigration flow. First, the unending turbulence of the area up to 1857 generated among Sikhs a high degree of independence, flexibility, and resolve. These qualities thereafter were at a premium as the British systematically transformed the economy of the area. In this respect Sikhs were "pre-adapted" for immigration. They were relatively unbound by caste and tradition, and many Sikh Jat families had become quite well off.

Second, the central Punjab already had an immigration tradition. People from Jullundur and Hoshiarpur had migrated in the thousands to the new agricultural areas of Punjab opened by irrigation. They kept ties with their home villages alive and there was a constant movement of people from one place to another. Men also moved throughout the Indian subcontinent and overseas in the British Indian army and as policemen.

Third, in the central Punjab there were strong economic incentives to branch out from agriculture. Hoshiarpur and Jullundur produced bountiful harvests, but agricultural success did have its limits. Land prices rose by a factor of ten to twenty between 1870 and 1920, making further agricultural consolidation impossible. Rural debt increased.[30] Many families in the region already had savings from military service or work overseas, and their successes provided yet another incentive for short-term emigration.

Finally, a series of socio-political events unsettled Punjab between 1900 and 1910. The Land Alienation Act of 1900 was designed to reduce the power of moneylenders over mortgaged land. A secondary effect was

11

to increase insecurity about land tenure. These fears rose again in 1906 when the government put forward a bill that implied that colonists in newly irrigated areas of the Punjab were not actually the owners of the land.

These concerns over land tenure corresponded with a growing sense of estrangement from the British among some elements of the population.[31] Sikh and Hindu reformist movements such as the Singh Sabha movement and the Arya Samaj stimulated people's awareness of and pride in their roots and were frequently vehicles for anti-British political action. This was particularly true after the partition of Bengal in 1905, an act that inflamed nationalist sentiments. In the same year a movement was begun to reject goods made outside of India. Rising nationalism was given further impetus by the Japanese military victory over the Russians in 1905 – the first decisive defeat of a European power by an Asian nation. In 1907 the British cracked down on political dissent in Punjab, which led to much local dissatisfaction.

THE JOURNEY

The decision to emigrate to Canada was usually made on the basis of very concrete considerations. This becomes evident when one retraces the paths of individuals from their homes in India to British Columbia.[32] The social, economic, and psychological risks involved in immigration were quite low, even in comparison with many immigrant groups from Europe, so the decision to go was not monumental. Immigrants predominantly were the younger or more economically marginal members of well-off farming families. Many were farmers' sons who had not yet established families. Many anticipated that their share of familial lands would be very small unless somehow augmented. Others had spent a good deal of their lives in the army and were familiar with the risks and rewards of migration.

Travelling steerage class, one could go from Punjab to Vancouver in those days for about $65. This was not an insignificant amount, even by Canadian standards, in a time when working people in Canada typically earned between one and two dollars a day. In Indian terms, it was a large sum indeed – 650 rupees. Early South Asian immigrants were able to make use of friends and relatives to lower the risks of immigration, either drawing on their own personal savings accumulated through army service or tapping their family networks. Many of those who came after 1904 borrowed the money from friends and relatives already working in Canada. Potential economic difficulties were further reduced because immigrants could count on their relatives to manage their land and support their immediate families while they were gone. If things did not work out in Canada virtually everyone had a secure place to which he could return.

Kin and village friends also provided psychological support during the trip. Men considered going to Canada only when they had some concrete evidence of the possibilities here – usually a letter from a relative, friend, or co-villager who was already established in Canada. Although immigrants had little accurate knowledge about life in Canada when they made the decision to leave, they rarely knew that this was so. Dependent for information on letters from immigrants who had gone before, their images of life in Canada were very unclear. The key thing they "knew" was that economic prospects were good; such letters usually glossed over disappointments and were silent on poor social and cultural conditions. Thus, they were optimistic and were convinced that they were doing the right thing. How could one go wrong earning the equivalent of ten rupees a day?

For most, immigration was a sharing, collective experience. Typically, men from the same village would travel together in groups of four to fifteen. They would go by train from Punjab to Calcutta, then stay in Calcutta for a number of weeks while they waited for a ship to take them to Hong Kong. At the height of the flow several hundred immigrants would be on each ship. People could generally travel this leg of the trip for less than $25.

The subsequent long voyage from Hong Kong to British Columbia was an experience that often bound fellow travellers for life. Conditions in steerage were primitive. South Asian immigrants were physically segregated from other passengers and spent much of the time below decks in cramped, crowded quarters. In deference to their different dietary customs, the shipping lines let them cook their own food over open hearths set up on deck. For instance, on what afterwards became the "900 boat" in 1907, the S.S. Monteagle, there were nine such hearths.[33] People cooked in shifts: fifty at each hearth in the morning and fifty in the evening. Washing and toilet facilities were few and there were no recreational facilities at all. Violent Pacific storms would make a shambles of shipboard routine and leave scores groaning in their bunks. Here are the personal accounts of two early immigrants:

I was born and raised in the village of Thauli, close to Phagwara. Our family was involved in blacksmith work and by local standards was not badly off. We learned about Canada from the relatives of people in the village. In 1907 eleven of us set out together for Canada. I was nineteen. Most of us were pretty young, but one fellow was at least fifty.

It took us over two months to get to Canada. The most dramatic part of the trip was the long voyage from Hong Kong to Vancouver aboard the "900 boat." With so many people travelling together there was a great anticipation of what we were to experience in Canada; no one you met on board had actually been there, so all kinds of rumours circulated. Some said that we would be rich in no time. Others said that we might freeze. Generally, though, people

13

were pretty realistic. They were willing to work hard, and thought of Canada as being a place where opportunities were available to make good use of hard work. Few of us had such opportunities in India.
My first job was for an English farmer in Langley. I didn't know any English except the day of the week and "I want work." When I tried my single English sentence on the farmer he responded in Hindi! He had been the manager of a tea estate in India, and he took me on.—N. Singh Thauli

My brother, Kapur Singh, was one of the first Sikhs to go to Canada. He soon wrote back to our village saying that work was available at Rs. 7 a day – a princely sum in those days. Sixteen of us assembled to go off and try our luck. I was just eighteen. Some were reserve army men, but most were farmers' sons. After a quick train trip to Calcutta and the short voyage to Hong Kong we had to wait quite a while for the next ship to Canada. We were on the "113 boat" that arrived in Vancouver in October, 1906. We were very worried about being rejected because of disease or some other reason – I think I aged two years – but not one of us was.—Tara Singh Siddoo

The trials and tribulations, as noted above, were not over when one arrived at a British Columbia port. There, all efforts so far would be put to the final test: would one be let in at all? From the first, South Asian immigrants were considered undesirable and immigration officials used their wide discretionary powers to deport prospective immigrants on any pretext. For some the only Canadian experiences they would have would be at dockside in Vancouver or Victoria.

Still, there were some positive aspects of life on the immigrant ships. Friendships and alliances were formed, and these proved to be invaluable in the trying times ahead. Whatever scanty information the men had about Canadian life was widely shared. Individuals were forced out of a village reference group and into an ethnic one. The realization grew that immigration was a leveller: differences in status, customs, and belief that seemed significant in India became less so under the common constraints of the voyage.

The hardships of the voyage were a portent of what was to come. Once in Canada, South Asians faced the full brunt of anti-Asian hostility that had been building in British Columbia for over thirty years.

NOTES

1. Here, race refers to social categories defined by people on the basis *perceived* biological differences. Hence, when words like "white," "non-white," and "race" are used, they are not meant to imply actual biological categories but rather categories defined by the people in question.

2. John Nelson, *The Canadian Provinces* (Toronto, 1924), pp. 171-2.

3. *Archivo General de La Nacion,* Mexico City, Indios: XVI, fol. 29.

4. South Asians are not mentioned in the 1901 census, nor in the immigration statistics until 1904. Neither are they mentioned in the local press before 1904.

5. Queen Victoria's Diamond Jubilee has often been cited as the event that triggered South Asian immigration. There is no support for this, and it seems clear that these two events were confused with each other at an early date. A few early references suggest 1902-03 as the date of the first immigration. Saint Nihal Singh and J. Barclay Williams, "Canada's New Immigrant: The Hindu," *Canadian Magazine,* 28 (1907), p. 387; Fred Lockley, "The Hindu Invasion," *Pacific Monthly* (1907), pp. 584-95.

6. London *Times*, July 23, 1902, p. 11.

7. Most newspaper references give one officer and twenty-two men. However, an extended article in the *Vancouver Weekly News Advertiser* (June 18, 1902, p. 1) cites the smaller figure.

8. J.C. Hopkins, *The Life of Edward VII* (London, 1910), pp. 372-3.

9. *Victoria Daily Times*, June 3, 1902, p. 5.

10. *Vancouver Weekly News Advertiser*, June 18, 1902, p. 1.

11. *Vancouver Daily Province*, June 3, 1902, p. 1.

12. *Vancouver Weekly News Advertiser*, June 10, 1902, p. 1.

13. London *Times*, August 13, 1902, p. 4.

14. *Vancouver Daily Colonist*, September 7, 1902, p. 3.

15. *Victoria Daily Times*, September 8, 1902, p. 3.

16. W.G. Parmelee, Deputy Minister of Trade and Commerce, to J.A. Smart, Deputy Minister of the Interior, October 15, 1904, Public Archives of Canada (PAC), Immigration Branch Records (henceforth, RG 76), #536999, part 1. Unfortunately, an attempt to discover who these people were has failed.

17. *Ibid.*

18. Thomas F. McGuigan to R.W. Scott, September 15, 1904, PAC, RG 76, #536999, part 1.

19. R.W. Scott to Thomas McGuigan, September 23, 1904, PAC, RG 76, #536999, part 1.

20. W.G. Parmelee to J.A. Smart, October 19, 1904, PAC, RG 76, #536999, part 1.

21. Robert Kerr, CPR Passenger Traffic Manager (Montreal), to J.A. Smart, November 16, 1904, PAC, RG 76, #536999, part 1.

22. Dr. A.S. Munro to W.D. Scott, August 16, 1906, PAC, RG 76, #536999, part 1.

23. For instance, Thomas Shaughnessy, writing to Minister of the Interior Frank Oliver on November 14, 1906, stoutly denied that the CPR was soliciting immigrants from India (PAC, RG 76, #536999, part 1). Nevertheless, evidence collected in government investigations does not bear him out.

24. *Vancouver Province*, July 20, 1906, p. 7; W.L.M. King, *Report* of the Royal Commission appointed to inquire into the Method by which Oriental Labourers have been induced to come to Canada (Ottawa, 1908). Nothing is known of Dr. Davichand's past.

25. In the orthodox Hindu hierarchy of castes, Jats would be considered lower than Brahmins but nearly equivalent to Kshatriyas.

26. There are a number of good sources on Sikh religion and history. See Kushwant Singh, *A History of the Sikhs*, vol. 1 (Princeton, N.J., 1966); I. Singh, *The Philosophy of Guru Nanak* (New Delhi, 1963); W.O. Cole and Piara S. Sambhi, *The Sikhs: Their Religious Beliefs and Practices* (London, 1978); Teja Singh, *The Religion of the Sikh Gurus* (Amritsar, 1963); Harbans Singh, *The Heritage of the Sikhs* (New York, 1964).

27. This has been carried on in the Sikh tradition of *Langar*. In each Sikh temple free meals are provided to anyone who comes. This practice of people eating together symbolizes the equality of all people before God.

28. Arjun completed the collection of the religious writings of the Sikhs, the Guru Granth Sahib. The text is accorded the honorific title of Guru, because Sikhs recognize it as the pre-eminent, living source of religious guidance.

29. It is from Hargobind that Sikhs derive their primary symbol – that of two swords. These two swords signify religious power (*piri*) and temporal power (*miri*).

30. Kushwant Singh, *A History of the Sikhs*, vol. 2, (Princeton, N.J. 1966), p. 151; M.L. Darlings, *The Punjab in Prosperity and Debt* (London, 1928), p. 49. Jullundur and Hoshiarpur had the highest agricultural debt in the Punjab.

31. For details, see Laxman Prasad Mathur, *Indian Revolutionary Movements in the United States, 1922-* (Delhi, 1970); S.C. Mittal, *Freedom Movement in Punjab (1905-29)* (Delhi, 1977).

32. Much of the following information on the trip to Canada was derived from interviews with the few pioneers of the 1903-08 era still living in 1979.

33. Immigrants frequently knew the boats only by the number of South Asian passengers on it. Thus, there was the "900 boat," the "700 boat," etc.

TWO

Pioneers

South Asians were a small minority against whom were soon to be arrayed the substantial resources of the majority: the law, government, labour unions, media, and public sentiment all stood against them. Their own resources were comparatively scanty. Few were educated or skilled. Many did not know English and lacked experience with North American life. Most were young, and all had been detached from the world in which they had been born and raised. The battle for the right to full participation in Canadian society was unequal and South Asians eventually lost it. Even so, the defeat was neither automatic nor total.

The first few South Asians who came to Canada between 1903 and 1906 set the direction of the community for a long time. They also set it on fairly firm foundations. For most, their principal objective was to accumulate savings that could be used as a stake back home. These pioneers were therefore willing to work hard and to suffer many inconveniences. Securing a high-paying job was the first priority.

These pioneers entered without notice; British Columbian concern was at that time focused on the Japanese and Chinese. Consequently, they entered Canada with no special legal restrictions. There were no specific immigration regulations dealing with them, nor were they singled out by the British Columbia legal code. They generally enjoyed all of the rights and privileges of British subjects in Canada. Neither was there any agitation against their presence.

They enjoyed several other advantages not shared by South Asians who came afterwards. Times were good, and a scarcity of cheap labour had resulted from reduced Chinese and Japanese immigration. Moreover, many of these very first immigrants had served in the British Indian army and knew a little English and a lot about European ways. In contrast, those who would arrive thereafter came chiefly from agricultural backgrounds.

Most were able to find work quickly, at least in the summer months of 1904 and 1905. Some found work in Port Moody sawmills. Others were

17

employed on road and railway construction and in land clearance. Wages were from $1 to $1.25 a day, about 25 per cent less than the rates received by whites.[1] Soon, they dispersed across the province, going wherever work was available.

Getting the other necessities of life did not prove to be so easy. This was particularly true of housing, especially for those living in the Vancouver area. Vancouver's population was increasing rapidly and housing was in high demand. Landlords could pick and choose their tenants and consequently refused to rent to South Asians. This problem was compounded each winter, when many of those working outside of Vancouver were laid off and returned to the city. This led to severe overcrowding in marginal housing. Sometimes over twenty people were forced to live in the same house. By the time of the mass influx of 1907-08 the number might occasionally be as high as fifty.

Until then there was no concerted opposition to South Asians. After all, there were fewer than 300 in B.C. in March, 1906, and they were in demand as workers. Their wages had risen to $1.50 to $2 a day.[2] From about that time immigration increased exponentially as people began to come directly from India. More people (325) arrived in the first half of 1906 than had come previously. In November alone over 700 South Asians arrived.

This increase brought South Asian immigration into the public eye. While such immigration was comparatively small, it had enormous symbolic value in a white population already panicked by the "spectre of non-white immigration." Labour was very sensitive to this issue and reacted sharply. In August, 1906, the Trades and Labour Councils in Vancouver and Victoria both sent resolutions to the government condemning South Asian immigration. They wished:

> . . . to place on record an emphatic protest against the proposed introduction into this Province of Hindoo laborers, and call on the workingmen of British Columbia to assist by every means in their power, in preventing this further attempt to flood the country with cheap Asiatic labor.[3]

These and other petitions prompted the Department of the Interior to send W.D. Scott to survey the situation in Vancouver.

Things moved steadily toward a crisis in the fall of 1906. Two hundred seventy South Asians arrived September 1 on a single ship, which prompted a sharp objection from the Vancouver city government.[4] Local federal immigration officials were no more sympathetic and deported a number on medical grounds. Superintendent of Immigration Scott was hard-pressed to defend the government's lack of restrictions on South Asian immigration. This also brought South Asian immigration into national and world politics. Local MPs approached Prime Minister Laurier to stop the flow. Mayor Buscomb of Vancouver contacted a number of

British government officials. While there was some media support for South Asians, particularly in central Canada, this was the exception to the rule. From then until the outbreak of World War I, coverage of South Asians in papers was to be the most negative accorded to any British Columbia ethnic or racial group.[5]

Things grew steadily worse as the resource sector of the British Columbia economy shut down for the winter of 1906-07. Improperly clothed and housed, one party of South Asians quit work in the Cariboo and walked back to Vancouver.[6] Many others laid off across the province also returned to Vancouver or Victoria, compounding the pressure already put on local services by 1,000 new immigrants who had come between July 1 and September 30.

Government attitudes toward South Asians began to harden. When 125 arrived October 15 on the *Empress of Japan* they were allowed to land by federal officials only to be stopped by the Vancouver city police.[7] The city government tried unsuccessfully to force the CPR to return them to Hong Kong. Local hysteria mounted when it was realized that as British subjects South Asians would be eligible to vote. It was reported that 850 would soon arrive on a single ship. The federal government applied pressure to the Indian colonial government and the CPR to restrict the flow of immigrants.[8] Lurid stories in the local press warned of the danger to "white women" posed by South Asians. Then, on November 16 the *Tartar* arrived carrying over 850 new immigrants. Both the Vancouver and Victoria immigration officers telegraphed Ottawa claiming that no housing would be available for them. In Vancouver over 200 spent their first Canadian night outside. As a consequence, Scott threatened the CPR with the prospect of returning indigent South Asians to Hong Kong at CPR expense; the CPR denied any responsibility.[9]

At the same time, hostility to those who were already in B.C. increased dramatically. They were denied accommodation even though able to pay for it, and the massive overcrowding that resulted led to many evictions. Feelings against them were so strong that South Asians had difficulty buying food and firewood.[10] The city government searched for means to evict all South Asians from Vancouver.

During this period there were some courageous attempts to help South Asians deal better with their plight. Without authorization, the local immigration officer, A.S. Munro, rented the abandoned Greenwood Cannery in Eburne as temporary housing for the immigrants until they found work. Munro expected that over 600 would soon be employed in railway work and that $50 a month was little enough for the government to pay to house them in the meantime. The Minister of the Interior saw things rather differently. He reprimanded Munro and ordered him to deport any South Asians unable to support themselves.[11]

Things looked bad, but it is remarkable how quickly the South Asians rebounded. Faced with hard economic times and white hostility, they were forced to look to their own community for support – support that was always forthcoming. Literate, English-speaking individuals like Nihal Singh immediately became intermediaries between the community and the local population, the media, and government. Nihal Singh only arrived in early November, 1906, yet by mid-month he was helping new immigrants get settled, all the while defending his community in the local press. By mid-December he had travelled to Ottawa to talk directly with the Minister of the Interior.[12] Others quickly developed support systems to help compatriots who were less well off than they. Food and housing were offered whenever available and word of job possibilities moved quickly through the community.

> Oh, in those days we knew so little about Canada! And people were generally so unfriendly; we couldn't at first understand why this was so. Even then, we survived by banding together and helping each other out. Those who had found a place to stay always had a bit more room for someone else. Men who we hadn't even known before who knew English would often help us communicate with "the British" – as most of us saw Canadians then. Times were hard, but we survived.—Anonymous[13]

The results of this community solidarity were impressive. By December of 1906 no South Asian in the Victoria area was unemployed or on relief. Railway construction, brickyard labour, and land clearance were typical jobs. In fact, those working at the Union Mines in Nanaimo felt economically confident enough to strike for higher wages. While things were not quite so good on the mainland, a comprehensive report showed that by the end of 1906 only one person was being held for deportation as an indigent.[14] Furthermore, to that point no South Asian had been convicted of a crime in Vancouver. In nearby Millside a substantial community of South Asian sawmill workers had sprung up, and Sikhs talked of organizing their own militia unit. With so many immigrants arriving in so short a time these communities were by no means stable, but by the end of 1906 they were able to help individuals achieve the basic necessities of life.

The year 1907 was marked by two unequal processes: the development of strong, defensive community institutions, and the inexorable rise of limitations on South Asian rights and privileges. Immigration from India was low during the first half of 1907 and community organization grew much stronger. Things continued to improve economically and very few remained unemployed. At the same time housing difficulties abated as enterprising individuals, such as Harnam Singh, set up several rooming houses for their compatriots.[15] Rents were very low – 15¢ a day or $3 a month.

The first South Asian formal organizations in Canada were founded in 1907. The Vancouver Khalsa Diwan Society was created early in the year to deal with the development of Sikh religious institutions.[16] It quickly involved itself in matters of general community welfare and became the focal point for subsequent South Asian battles against discrimination. Although it was a Sikh institution, the Khalsa Diwan Society spoke for all South Asian Canadians regardless of religion.

Somewhat later in the year the Hindustani Association was formed in Vancouver. It was chiefly the work of Taraknath Das, an educated, radical Bengali nationalist who had come to Vancouver via San Francisco to try to gain community support for the Indian Independence movement. The Hindustani Association was initially devoted to bettering the lot of Indians in Canada but quickly turned into an organization devoted to the overthrow of British rule in India. Das was to become one of the most articulate community spokesmen of the period before World War I.

At the same time, moves to restrict South Asians continued apace. The first legal restrictions against South Asians were put into effect in March, 1907, when British Columbia Premier Bowser introduced a bill to disenfranchise all "natives of India not of Anglo-Saxon parents"; this bill was passed by a unanimous vote of the legislature on March 27.[17] In April, South Asians were denied the vote in Vancouver by a change in the Municipality Incorporation Act.[18] The effects of this move were profound. It denied them the federal vote, because in British Columbia the criterion for voting federally was being entered on the provincial voters' list. For the next forty years, South Asian Canadians would remain excluded from the political process in British Columbia. They were simultaneously excluded from a host of other things that were dependent on being a provincial voter: they could not vote for or become school trustees or trustees of improvement districts; neither could they be elected to provincial public office nor serve on juries. Although exclusion from the voters' list did not legally restrict them from public service this became a universal practice. Public works contracts specified that they not be employed. The same restriction applied to the sale of Crown timber, and the professions of law and pharmacy were informally closed to them.

The ideological consequences of disenfranchisement were also significant. For half a century the British in India had cultivated the fiction that Indians were equal members of the Empire; as the thesis went, Indians were British subjects, with the same rights, privileges, and responsibilities as Canadians and New Zealanders. Sikhs in particular had long played an important and privileged role in British India, and so in 1907 most Sikhs had some reason to believe this fiction. Indeed, many who had served the British in the army, in its police forces, or as government officials were intensely loyal to their colonial masters. By the denial of the vote local South Asians were being pointedly told that this loyalty was misplaced. The short-term disabilities imposed by disenfranchisement were not objectively great, but these disabilities forced many to reconsider their relationship to the British, especially with respect to colonial rule in India.

The level of hostility against South Asians followed the same upward trajectory in 1907 that it had in 1906. During the first half of the year, anti-South Asian sentiment was fairly low. Thereafter, things got steadily worse as economic conditions in the province deteriorated. Though South Asians were as much affected by the economic downturn as any group, they were soon being made the scapegoat for increasing white unemployment.[19] While hostility against Chinese and Japanese also increased, South Asians were a particular target because of their novelty, the recent sharp increase in their numbers, and their rapid entry into traditionally "white" jobs in the province's lumber mills.

The conflict exploded first in nearby Bellingham, Washington. On September 5 over 500 white lumber workers attacked South Asians working there in the mills.[20] They were evicted from their lodgings by the mob and many of their belongings were destroyed. For their own protection hundreds of South Asians were forced to spend the night in the local jail or city hall. Most left for Vancouver, despite offers of "white wages" by their previous employers. Similar but smaller-scale attacks on South Asians in Washington continued for months.

The racial unrest was as bad in British Columbia as it was in Washington. In August, the Asiatic Exclusion League was formed in Vancouver, with the support of both the Liberal and Conservative local associations.[21] On September 7, 1907, a meeting of the League chaired by the mayor of Vancouver touched off the most serious race riot in Canadian history.[22] Chinese property was extensively damaged. A concerted attempt to wreck the Japanese area of the town was thwarted only by the strong resistance of the Japanese, who met the mobs in the streets. Although anti-South Asian activities in Washington and reports of the *S.S. Monteagle*'s imminent arrival with 900 South Asian immigrants were leading causes of the outbreak, South Asians did not suffer at the hands of the mob. This was primarily because most of them lived well away from where the riot began.

Nevertheless, subsequent events were effectively to terminate South Asian immigration. Four days later, the *Monteagle* arrived in Vancouver, having brought the predicted 900 South Asian passengers from Hong Kong to Canada. This influx overtaxed the resources of both the South Asian community and the local governments. Some of those who disembarked in Victoria spent their first night in a dockyard cattle pen; they later were allowed to sleep in the city jail. In Vancouver some camped in Stanley Park while others slept in the streets.

In response to furious telegrams from Vancouver Mayor Bethune, Laurier dispatched the Superintendent of Immigration to investigate the situation.[23] Laurier had already decided to terminate immigration. Writing to Governor General Lord Grey about Asian immigration and the Vancouver riot, he considered that, in comparison to the Japanese, "The situation with regard to the Hindoos is far more serious, and to speak frankly I see no solution for it, except quietly checking the exodus from India."[24]

The report on South Asian immigration was unfavourable and the only remaining question was the method by which South Asian immigration would be banned.[25] The government had already resorted to deportation as a tool to limit immigration, but this had proved too costly and too open to court review.[26]

Stopping immigration proved to be technically difficult. South Asians came from a British colony, and the federal government did not have to worry about affronting a foreign power with discriminatory legislation. It was also true that local South Asians were politically powerless and could not impede any such power on the part of the government. There was, however, one major obstacle: the possibility of generating resentment against British rule in India. The British India government had been worried for some time that a direct Canadian ban on immigration would be seized upon by Indian "seditionists" and revolutionaries, who were on the rise in 1907. Proposals such as that by the Minister of the Interior to impose a $500 head tax on South Asian immigration were consequently unacceptable to the British.[27] South Asian immigration had to be terminated without specifically mentioning South Asians.

The first step in effecting such a ban was to send W.L. Mackenzie King, then Deputy Minister of Labour, to investigate how South Asians were coming to Canada.[28] Mackenzie King's report was essentially a legitimation of the forthcoming immigration ban. It dwelt heavily on the instances where individuals had gone into debt to pay for the passage and neglected to point out that these were exceptions; it stressed the problem of unemployment when all but the most recent arrivals were working; it raised the spectre of new immigrants starving in the streets when the Hindustani Association had just given immigration officials a $3,800 cash bond against any South Asian being indigent.[29]

Eventually, the government acted. On January 8, 1908, an Order-in-Council was approved that required any immigrant arriving at a Canadian port to come on a continuous journey from his or her country of origin.[30] In actuality it was aimed at two types of immigrant only – South Asians and Japanese, who were entering Canada via Hawaii. Although the exact meaning of the term "continuous journey" changed over the years, it eventually referred to the ability of an individual to purchase a ticket for through-passage from his or her home port all the way to Canada.[31] There were no ticketing arrangements between India and Canada; no shipping line plied between the two and those that sailed the first leg from Calcutta to Hong Kong did not have ticketing arrangements with those that sailed the second leg. A continuous journey from India to Canada simply could not be made.

This ban hit the local community hard. The ban was total, and no one was exempted. It even included the wives and children of those who were already in Canada. If a man wished to remain in Canada it would be without his family. Moreover, it shattered any illusions that South Asians' status as British subjects meant anything. Even Chinese and Japanese aliens could immigrate, while they could not.

The ban also denied them the recognition they felt their considerable successes merited. Ironically, the same month that their countrymen were banned from Canada, Vancouver Sikhs dedicated the first permanent Sikh Temple in North America.[32] In less than two years these supposedly indigent, ill-adapted immigrants had subscribed $6,000 toward the construction of this building – the equivalent of twenty man-years of income at prevailing wage rates. Moreover, hundreds of whites were among the crowd of over 1,000 who attended the dedication. Managers of two nearby False Creek sawmills, the Alberta Lumber Company and the Rat Portage Lumber Company, had provided the lumber for its construction at cost in order to keep their South Asian workers from moving elsewhere. Clearly, even in Vancouver not all whites were anti-South Asian. This temple on West 2nd Avenue instantaneously became the organizational centre for the spirited attack on the continuous passage restrictions that was to last without letup for the next fifteen years.

The initial skirmishes in this battle were not long in coming. On the bureaucratic front, Mackenzie King was sent to England to quiet British and British Indian fears that such a ban would provoke an international incident.[33] The British Columbia legislature remained unconvinced that this ban would be sufficient and passed its own restrictive legislation – an act barring immigrants who could not pass a test in a European language. It was declared *ultra vires* in March after a court challenge funded by local South Asians.

The first test of the continuous passage regulation was made by six South Asians from Fiji, who arrived in early February, 1908. They had sailed directly from Fiji, but immigration officials interpreted the regulation to refer to one's country of *ultimate* origin (in their case, India) and they were held for deportation.

A more substantial challenge presented itself in early March when twenty South Asians arrived on the *Empress of Japan*. Word of the continuous passage regulation had already worked back to India, where resourceful individuals played their first countermove: if connections are not available between India and Canada, arrange for them to be created. With a little help from the CPR they arranged for a Calcutta broker to operate as an agent for the CPR. This broker then sold immigrant passage on a non-CPR ship to Hong Kong along with a voucher for travel on the next CPR ship from Hong Kong to Canada.[34] Immigration officials could do nothing but land individuals who were ticketed this way.

Just about that time, the *Monteagle* arrived in Vancouver from Hong Kong with 186 South Asian passengers. Instantly, the bureaucratic re-

24

sponse hardened. Twelve were rejected for disease; twenty-three more were held because they lacked the $25 required of all unsupported immigrants to show that they would not become indigents. Seventy-eight others were to be deported even though they had left India before the continuous journey order went into effect. Another seventy had made the requisite continuous journey and had CPR statements to that effect; nevertheless, the Superintendent of Immigration ordered that they should be deported with the others.[35] Mass protest meetings were held in the South Asian community and a petition on the matter was sent to John Morley, Secretary of State for India. Morley was subsequently questioned about South Asian immigration in the British House of Commons.[36] The CPR challenged the deportation order in court, and on March 24, 1908, the court ruled that the continuous journey provision was technically invalid and ordered all individuals held for deportation to be released.[37] The Order-in-Council was quickly rewritten.[38]

During this time Mackenzie King was quietly negotiating with representatives of the British government. King found the British sympathetic to Canada's wish to stop South Asian immigration, subject to the qualification that the method of doing so did not create problems in India. The continuous journey provision had already been found acceptable.[39] This emboldened the Canadian government to go further, especially considering the problems that were being experienced with court challenges to the continuous journey provision.

The Canadian government moved immediately to restrict immigration further. It pressured the CPR not to accept South Asians as passengers from Hong Kong to Canada. The CPR conceded, largely because the costs of deportation were borne by the shipping line that brought the individual to Canada. The government also forced the CPR to stop issuing through tickets. Soon, scores of individuals were stuck in Hong Kong in the most desperate straits.

The immigration issue by now had begun to generate what the British authorities had feared – nationalist, anti-British sentiment in the local community. In April, Taraknath Das published the initial edition of *Free Hindusthan* in Vancouver.[40] *Free Hindusthan* was the first South Asian publication of any kind in Canada and was one of the first in North America. The violently anti-British English-language monthly provoked a quick reaction when it first began to appear in India. Nothing like it was allowed to be published there and the Indian government pressed for its suppression. Moreover, Das's activities had attracted the attention of T.R.E. McInnes, who had been delegated by the Superintendent of Immigration to keep an eye on the local community.[41] Local "sedition" also engaged the interest of William Hopkinson, who would become infamous in the community over the subsequent years. Hopkinson was an Anglo-Indian police inspector from Calcutta then on a health leave in Vancouver.[42] In April, Hopkinson volunteered information that an English school that Das and two Sikhs had begun in Millside was in real-

25

ity a centre for Indian sedition.[43] It was quickly shut down by local authorities. By June, *Free Hindusthan* was banned from the Canadian mails and had moved to Seattle.[44] Concern about South Asian sedition spread.[45] This intensified governmental efforts to stop immigration once and for all.

Consequently, in April the government had amended the Immigration Act toward this objective. Provision for continuous journey restrictions was thereafter written into the Act. The government then required that all Asian immigrants from countries without "special arrangements" would be required to possess $200 on arrival in Canada.[46] In effect, this was meant for South Asians. Like the continuous passage restriction, this requirement was to stand for the next forty years.

The government did not stop here. Instead, it attempted to remove those South Asians already in Canada. South Asians were already leaving for the United States, where conditions were better; perhaps one out of three South Asians who landed in Canada had already done so. In July, 1908, the federal government developed a scheme to get the South Asian community to emigrate voluntarily to British Honduras.[47] Labour was in high demand there and it was felt that this might attract those in the local community who were then out of work. London agreed, and proposed that a delegation of two South Asian leaders and an immigration official be sent to British Honduras to investigate conditions. The community was willing to consider the proposal and elected Nagar Singh and Sham Singh to go. They were accompanied by J.B. Harkin and William Hopkinson.

The conditions they found in British Honduras were far inferior to those in Vancouver. For instance, wages were a maximum of 50¢ a day for farm labour and involved an indenture contract. As an enticement, the British Honduras government offered free land grants to farmers and railway work to those wishing wage labour. By the time this fact-finding committee returned to Vancouver economic conditions had changed dramatically. Most individuals were working and even the governor of British Honduras (who had gone to Canada to talk to the local community) admitted that "all indigent Hindoos in Vancouver had been provided for by the Hindoo community."[48] There was therefore little incentive to leave. Nagar Singh and Sham Singh soon reported unfavourably about conditions in British Honduras.[49]

In the meantime the community had received another powerful leader in the imposing figure of Teja Singh. Like Taraknath Das, Teja Singh was literate, well educated, forceful, and completely bilingual. Teja Singh had a master's degree from Punjab University and had subsequently taught at Khalsa College, Amritsar. He had come from the United States as a visitor and lecturer specifically to help out the local community, bringing with him his wife and two children; they may have been the first South Asian family to come to Canada.[50] In contrast to Das, he was a Sikh and this allowed him to rally community opinion against the move to British Honduras. Teja Singh was the first community leader who was able to contradict effectively the media stereotype of South Asians as ignorant, rural peasants.[51] He was also the first to have enough astuteness and sophistication to force the politicians and bureaucrats to consider South Asian concerns seriously. With the negative report on British Honduras, improved economic prospects in British Columbia, and the rise of strong leadership, the proposal to emigrate died a quick death.

Even so, the end of 1908 marked the low point for South Asians in Canada. By then, they had been politically neutralized, at least as a voting force. Immigration had been effectively terminated. Economically, the racial line had been set: South Asians were to be unskilled blue-collar workers if they were to work at all. They were frequently the last hired and the first fired. Extending their exclusionary policy from the Chinese and Japanese to South Asians, no union would have them.

Socially, things were little better. The ban on immigration made normal family life impossible; not a single wife or young child had come to Canada before the ban was imposed. The "community" was not yet a community at all, at least in any normal sense. Social relations between South Asians and other Canadians were almost non-existent outside of work. Canadian ethnocentrism magnified South Asian cultural differences and permuted them into an extremely negative racial stereotype. In this, the press played an important role, for few British Columbians had direct contact with South Asians. So also did prevailing imperial prejudices against Indians. This stereotype generally characterized South Asians as racially different, biologically inferior, dirty, lazy, immoral, untruthful, litigious, and violent.[52] Although some commentary countered this image by mentioning the Sikhs' military record and their growing reputation as hard workers, it had little impact.

Despite these powerful constraints the end of 1908 also marked the first stirrings of community organization and a collective community identity. The constraints were starting to turn a weak, disorganized collection of individuals into something rather more. Over the next ten years South Asians battled continuously against racial subordination. In the process they developed a set of community institutions that were remarkable given the circumstances. It is to this saga that we now turn.

NOTES

1. Dr. A.S. Munro to W.D. Scott, August 16, 1906, PAC, RG 76, #536999, part 1.
2. *Ibid.*
3. *Vancouver Province*, August 3, 1906, p. 1; Resolution of the Victoria Trades and Labour Council, August 6, 1906, PAC, RG 76, #536999, part 1.

4. F. Buscomb to the Honourable Minister of the Interior, September 4, 1906, PAC, RG 76, #536999, part 1.
5. Doreen Indra, "The Portrayal of South Asians in the Vancouver Press: 1905-1976," *Ethnic and Racial Studies*, 2, 2 (1979), pp. 164-87; Indra, "Ethnicity, Social Stratification, and Opinion Formation: An Analysis of Ethnic Portrayal in the Vancouver Newspaper Press, 1905-1976" (Ph.D thesis, Simon Fraser University, 1979).
6. *Vancouver Province*, October 6, 1906, p. 1; *Victoria Daily Colonist*, October 6, 1906, p. 1.
7. *Vancouver Province*, October 15, 1906, p. 1. Each carried over $25 and could not therefore be deported as indigent. A.S. Munro to W.D. Scott, October 15, 1906, PAC, RG 76, #536999, part 1.
8. *Ibid*. T. Shaughnessy to F. Oliver, November 14, 1906, PAC, RG 76, #536999, part 1.
9. W.D. Scott to T. Shaughnessy, November 20, 1906, PAC, RG 76, #536999, part 1; T. Shaughnessy to F. Oliver, *ibid*.
10. George Halse *et al.* to W. Laurier, November 24, 1906, *ibid*.
11. A.S. Munro to W.D. Scott, November 26, 1906, *ibid.*; Frank Oliver to A.S. Munro, November 27, 1906, *ibid*.
12. Saint Nihal Singh to Frank Oliver, December 12, 1906, *ibid*.
13. We have chosen to make this and most other personal accounts in the book anonymous. They are drawn from hundreds of interviews conducted by the authors between 1976 and 1983.
14. E. Blake Robertson to W.D. Scott, December 7, 1907, PAC, RG 76, #536999, part 1.
15. Colonel Falk Warren to the Undersecretary of State, Indian House, January 2, 1907, *ibid.*; B.S. Dodd, "Social Change in Two Overseas Sikh Communities" (B.A. honours essay, University of British Columbia, 1972), p. 16.
16. Kushwant Singh and Satindra Singh, *Ghadar 1915: India's First Armed Revolution* (New Delhi, 1966), p. 14. Dodd, "Social Change," p. 16, lists Teja Singh as the first president, Tara Singh as the treasurer, and Sundar Singh as being on the executive. However, Teja Singh did not arrive in Vancouver until the subsequent year.
17. *Vancouver Province*, March 20, 1907, p. 1: *ibid.*, March 27, 1907, p. 1.
18. *Ibid.*, April 18, 1907, p. 1.
19. It was estimated that by the worst months of winter one out of three South Asians was unemployed. See J.B. Harkin, *The East Indians of British Columbia. A Report regarding the Proposal to provide Work in British Honduras for the Indigent Unemployed among Them* (Ottawa, 1909), p. 6.
20. William Peter Ward, "White Canada Forever: British Columbia's Response to Orientals, 1858-1914" (Ph.D. thesis, Queen's University, 1973), p. 200; Robert E. Wynne, "American Labour Leaders and the Vancouver Anti-Oriental Riot," *Pacific Northwest Quarterly*, 42, 4

(1966), p. 173; W.D. Dodd, "The Hindu in the Northwest," *World Today*, 13 (1907), p. 1158.

21. Mary E. Hallett, "A Governor General's View on Oriental Immigration to B.C., 1904-1911," *B.C. Studies*, 14 (1972), p. 58.

22. Howard H. Sugimoto, "Japanese Immigration, the Vancouver Riots, and Canadian Diplomacy" (M.A. thesis, University of Washington, 1966).

23. W. Laurier to A. Bethune, September 15, 1907, RG 76, #536999, part 2. The government saw the situation as serious enough to also send T.R.E. McInnes under an assumed name to interview South Asians on what initiated immigration (report, October 2, 1907, PAC, RG 7, G 21, v. 199). He pointed to the CPR's agents in Hong Kong.

24. W. Laurier to Lord Grey, September 16, 1907, PAC, Grey Papers, MG 27, #B 2, v. 21.

25. Report by W.D. Scott, October 23, 1907, PAC, RG 76, #536999, part 2. Scott found that of the approximately 4,000 who had arrived in Canada, 1,274 had left for the United States and another 1,649 had applied to do the same.

26. For example, of the 500 who arrived on October 10 on the *Tartar*, 200 were deported – 100 for lacking the required $25 and 100 for various diseases (*Vancouver Province*, October 10, 1907, p. 1).

27. Order-in-Council (PC) 2059-60 of September 12, 1907, PAC, RG 2, 1; F. Oliver to the Governor General in Council, October 29, 1907, PAC, RG 76, #536999, part 2.

28. PC 1663 of November 14, 1907, PAC, RG 2, 1; King, *Report* of the Royal Commission.

29. A.S. Munro to W.D. Scott, November 8, 1907, PAC, RG 76, #72-921, parts 1-2.

30. PC 27 of January 8, 1908, PAC, RG 2, 1.

31. It did *not* specify that one had to be continuously on board a single ship from one's country of origin to Canada, as is often assumed.

32. *Vancouver Province*, January 20, 1908, p. 7. Balwant Singh officiated at the event, with Taraknath Das translating for the large white crowd.

33. W.L.M. King, *Report* by W.L. Mackenzie King on his Mission to England (Ottawa, 1908); Confidential Memorandum accompanying *Report of W.L. Mackenzie King on his Mission to England*, May 2, 1908, PAC, RG 7, G 21, v. 332.

34. A.S. Munro to F. Oliver, March 2, 1908, PAC, RG 76, #536999, part 2.

35. W.D. Scott to A.S. Munro, March 16, 1908, *ibid*.

36. *Ottawa Citizen*, March 24, 1908, p. 1; *Vancouver Province*, March 25, 1908, p. 1.

37. The technical error was that the provision illegally delegated the responsibility of the Governor General in Council to the Minister of the Interior.

38. PC 662 of March 2, 1908.

39. Confidential Memorandum, May 2, 1908, PAC, RG 7, G 21, v. 332; Government of India to Lord Grey, January 22, 1908, *ibid.*, v. 199.

40. Copies of most issues of *Free Hindusthan* are available in PAC, RG 7, G 21, v. 200-01.

41. T.R.E McInnes to F. Oliver, March 23, 1908, PAC, RG 76, #536999, part 2.

42. Hopkinson's father was a non-commissioned officer in the British India army, who was reputed to have been killed by Afghan raiders when Hopkinson was young. He was raised in India by his Brahmin mother. He was fiercely anti-"seditionist" and spoke fluent Hindi.

43. W. Hopkinson to F. Oliver, September 6, 1908, PAC, Laurier Papers, MG 26, V, v. 532.

44. W. McLeod, Lieutenant, SD 10 to D 10, MD 11, Vancouver, September 10, 1908. By this time Das was sending the paper worldwide, including to South Africa and to S. Krishnavarna in London. Das was also in communication with Leo Tolstoy, whom he asked to support the cause of Indian freedom. Tolstoy characteristically declined, arguing that religion, not the ideas contained in Das's *Free Hindusthan*, was the key to Indian freedom. Gandhi received a typed copy of the reply. See James Hunt, *Gandhi in London* (New Delhi, 1978), pp. 153-4.

45. Confidential Memo of Mackenzie King to the effect that Certain Hindoos are Using Vancouver for Sedition, n.d., PAC, RG 7, G 21, v. 209. Later in the year the Dominion Secret Service got wind of a bomb factory in Millside (R. Brittain to Assistant Director of Intelligence, Militia Headquarters, November 18, 1908, PAC, RG 7, G 21, v. 200). King was then sent to confer with the British on revolutionary activity (Lord Grey to Lord Crew, December 9, 1908, *ibid.*). Subsequently, the local community was continuously under surveillance (Lord Grey to W. Laurier, December 3, 1908, *ibid.*).

46. 7-8 Edward VII. Bill #135 to Amend the Immigration Act; PC 932 of May 27, 1908, invoked the continuous passage restriction in the light of the amended Act. PC 1255 of June 3, 1908, enacted the $200 requirement.

47. Harkin, *The East Indians of British Columbia*, p. 8; Lord Crew to Lord Grey, September 19, 1908, PAC, RG 7, G 21, v. 300.

48. Governor Swayne to the Governor General, December 14, 1908, *ibid.*

49. Community animosity to the move was further heightened by Nagar Singh's charge that Hopkinson had offered him $3,000 to report favourably on British Honduras. Harkin, *The East Indians of British Columbia*, pp. 27-33.

50. W. Hopkinson to W. Cory, September 25, 1909, PAC, RG 7, G 21, v. 200.

51. For instance, see the full-page *Vancouver Province* article, "Mystery and Power of Teja Singh," December 12, 1908, section 2, p. 1. For his efforts the Canadian government quickly sought grounds for his deporta-

tion (Lord Grey to Lord Crew, December 7, 1908, PAC, RG 7, G 21, v. 200).

52. For an early example of this stereotyping, see Lockley, "The Hindu Invasion." See Indra, "The Portrayal of South Asians," for comparisons with other ethnic media stereotypes.

THREE

Resolve

After an initial period of disorientation and hardship, the lives of South Asians in Canada quickly stabilized. There was virtually no new immigration, hence, no new community members. South Asians continued to be excluded from mainstream British Columbia society; although integrated into the economy as a subordinate labour force, in all other respects routine discrimination resulted in nearly total isolation. Few social agencies or concerned citizens were interested in their plight. Even the local clergy opposed their presence.[1] Despite their imposed isolation, however, South Asians quickly put together the semblance of normal life and developed many means to combat subordination. New and effective forms of household organization, economic adaptation, community institutions, mutual aid, and leadership quickly arose regardless of the profound economic and informational constraints. The South Asians were able to use their substantial cultural resources to better their situation.

First and foremost, they had their religion and the social institutions and ideologies that went with it. By 1910 most of the comparatively few South Asian Muslims and Hindus in Canada had left; some had returned home, while others had gone to the United States. Those who stayed had already contributed money and labour to building the Vancouver Sikh temple, for they saw it as a secular rallying point for everyone from "Hindustan." The community became more religiously and culturally homogeneous and Sikh institutions became central to community life.

Sikhism arose in a defensive, minority group situation. As such, it evolved a number of ways to develop community solidarity and resist oppression. For example, Sikhism emphasizes collective worship in local temples (*gurdwaras*). This need for a place of worship was quickly fulfilled by the rise of *gurdwaras* everywhere in British Columbia, even where there were only a handful of Sikhs. At first they were in temporary, rented quarters, but soon these were replaced by permanent structures. By 1920, temples existed in Vancouver, New Westminster, Victoria, Nanaimo, Golden, Abbotsford, Fraser Mills, and Paldi. Sikh religious

32

organization quickly provided people with a sense of place, order, continuity, and community pride. Religious institutions also brought people together and provided an organizational focus for collective action on many issues. As in India, the temples were used as meeting places to discuss community problems. For example, virtually every aspect of the ongoing battle against the immigration ban was planned, supported, and orchestrated through temple management organizations. Many members of the democratically elected temple executive committees either became or already were important secular leaders. On issues of community concern temple organizations spoke for all South Asians, not just Sikhs.

Moreover, Sikh pioneers came to Canada with a strong group identity born out of 500 years of struggle. As a result, despite hardship, discrimination, and social isolation, they rarely doubted their self-worth or the correctness of their position. They had also developed a tendency to unite together under threat and go on the defensive; one sees this continuously over the next decade. In addition, the South Asian community was fortunate to develop a strong leadership structure composed of both grassroots leaders and sophisticated, literate, middle-class individuals who came to Canada to assist the community or develop revolutionary feeling within it.

A HOME AND A JOB

Community structure coalesced at every level. The most important building blocks were the development of a somewhat normal home life and the establishment of a measure of economic security. By all indications, from 1905 through 1908 neither of these objectives had been achieved. Discrimination produced households that were frequently so grossly overcrowded and ill-organized that they were little more than places to sleep and eat. There was an enormous turnover of housemates. On the job front South Asians were equally insecure. Unemployment was high and people took whatever work was available.

The demographic stability brought on by the immigration ban of 1907 led to a quick change for the better. Households became much more orderly as people sorted out their new socioeconomic context and their personal goals. Most of these South Asian men had no familiarity with running a household; cooking, most househould chores, and shopping in India had been done by their wives, mothers, sisters, and daughters. Even so, the men proved to be quite resourceful. Usually, they formed themselves into living groups of four to a dozen individuals. This helped them save money while providing a measure of psychological security. Standard practice in each household was for members to pool their money for rent, fuel, and food. In larger groups the cooking chores might be delegated to an individual who could not find other work.[2] In all other economic respects each household member was completely independent:

33

Looking back, it's amazing how little we knew about household life. But we learned quickly enough! Some men had previously lived in army or worker barracks, and so helped set the pattern. I think we would have wound up living about the same even without them. After all, there were no wives, no families. No one thought of living alone.

After a while, it worked out pretty well. We ate well, saved a lot of money, and generally got along with each other. If men lost their jobs, well, what really did it cost to carry them along? If it got so that people couldn't stand living with each other there was always someplace else to stay.

Unencumbered by the expense of supporting a family or of paying for separate accommodations, men were able to save a substantial portion of their wages. For instance, in 1909 room and board in Vancouver in such households cost about $2 a week, whereas an individual might then be earning $9 for a week's work.[3] This low rate of expenditure allowed them to ride out economic hard times and to support the sick and unemployed. From 1909 on, South Asians rarely applied for any sort of public relief. A thousand South Asians were out of work during the winter of 1909, but even hostile government observers were forced to admit that they were all well provided for.[4]

Their economic sophistication also increased in other respects. Racial restrictions limited what jobs were available. Even so, South Asians soon developed a reputation among employers for hard work and this made it easier for them to get better-paying, more secure jobs. Many moved out of land clearing and other purely manual work into the better-paying lumber and shingle mills. Others in the employ of the railroads upgraded their jobs from land clearance to track and yard work. For a short while a number worked seasonally in the British Columbia fish canneries. Still others moved into farm labour. As an example of this early occupational diversity, in 1909 in the Lower Fraser Valley alone, thirty-five South Asians were working on farms in Mission and Matsqui, fifteen worked at construction in Abbotsford, while 160 worked at mills in Abbotsford, Huntington, and Harrison Mills.[5] Another forty were workers at a brick company in Clayburn. Several hundred more were employed in the saw-mills at Fraser Mills[6] until they were replaced by French-Canadian workers.

It isn't surprising that so many of us wound up working in the mills. Some of us worked there from the very beginning, and the bosses knew that we worked hard and could take that kind of dangerous work. Unfortunately, a lot of the time when Sikhs were taken on it was at the expense of the Chinese and Japanese; they thought that they could get more out of us for the same money.

The advantages of mill work were most importantly the pay. Nothing else that we could do or were allowed to do paid as much.

Besides, in good times the mills ran all year round, not like many construction jobs. Often we were able to work together, too, which was a good thing, since so few of us knew much English.

South Asians likewise increased their economic possibilities by fanning out across the province in search of high-paying work. By 1910 at least 100 were working in Revelstoke, chiefly in the mills, and another 200 were engaged in similar work along the Upper Fraser River.[7] A few had wandered as far afield as Nelson and Golden. In addition, several hundred South Asians were in Victoria and a similar number worked in mills and on construction around Nanaimo.

In contrast to their rapid establishment at wage labour, before World War I their successes in business were quite limited. Unlike the Japanese and Chinese, South Asians were not numerous enough to support many of their own businesses. Small retail stores were begun in Vancouver, Millside, Nanaimo, and Victoria, which catered primarily to other South Asians. By 1914 there arose some interest in farming and dairying around Abbotsford and Mission, first as tenants and then as owners. This latter option was highly restricted by the total absence of families to operate such farms. There were fewer than fifty South Asian farms in existence at any one time in British Columbia prior to the 1960's.[8]

The most significant early business successes among South Asians were in real estate and in the ownership of lumber mills. From the beginning, South Asians expressed a keen interest in buying small lots and houses in and around Vancouver. By 1910, this practice was endemic, and several South Asians were independently employed as real estate agents.[9] In late 1908 the interest in real estate led to the creation of the Guru Nanak Mining and Trust Company in Vancouver.[10] Teja Singh was its first manager and offices were established in the Sikh temple building on 2nd Avenue. In accord with Teja Singh's vision of an independent, self-supporting community, the company was to raise enough money through share subscriptions to buy and develop large tracts of agricultural land where community members could settle. Several attempts to buy land in 1909 and 1910 failed due chiefly to poor organization and an inability to hold a consensus, by which time many frustrated shareholders withdrew their support. A similar fate befell the rival Canada-India Supply and Trust Company, which was organized in 1910 by leading political radicals – Uday Ram Joshi, Taraknath Das, Radhikrishnan, Balmukand Shidhar, and others.[11]

South Asian participation in real estate ventures came early and faded quickly, but their involvement in the ownership and management of lumber mills began late and grew steadily until the Great Depression destroyed the lumber market in 1931. With so many South Asians working in the mills, it was inevitable someone would eventually try to run one. However, the opportunity did not arise until the outbreak of World War I, which temporarily reduced the market for British Columbia lumber in the Prairies and the selling prices of local mills. Seven mills in the Fraser Valley were bought, each by a small group of South Asian entrepreneurs. For a few, these mills were to serve as stepping stones on the way to the purchase and development of large logging and mill complexes on Vancouver Island in the 1920's.

By the 1910's most South Asians enjoyed a degree of economic security despite the racial restrictions under which they laboured. From the first, it was unthinkable that one South Asian would deny another food and housing. As friendships and alliances strengthened, personal loans and partnerships became commonplace, and these allowed South Asians to lower the risks of financial dealings and unemployment. Once South Asian organizations got on a sound footing they mirrored these informal practices in their extensive support of the interests of individual community members.

THE RISE OF POLITICAL PROTEST

South Asians were hardly content with their subordinate political status in Canada. At first, their sojourner attitude severely limited their political initiative. Their inability to vote was of no consequence, inasmuch as few planned to stay long enough for the privilege to be relevant. Job discrimination could be tolerated, as long as it did not interfere with the rapid accumulation of savings. The impact of prejudice was mitigated by retreating into the South Asian community. Nevertheless, as the years passed and commitment to life in Canada grew, so did concern about racist restrictions.

Dwarfing all other limitations in significance was the ban on South Asian immigration. It negated any intent to settle permanently in Canada by forbidding the wives and children of those who were here from joining their husbands and fathers. Most immigrants were married and husbands were separated from their wives by a journey of several months. The ban on immigration consequently interfered with the normal functioning of families, with all the attendant economic and social difficulties that this implied. No other discriminatory practice provoked such great resentment or did so much to revise South Asian political attitudes as did this ban. The fight against it was to be the central theme in their battle for full Canadian rights from 1908 until well after World War II.

It was also a cause that nationalist revolutionaries would adroitly use to gain community support for their views. As mentioned, a handful of Indian nationalists and revolutionaries had arrived in Canada in 1906 and 1907, well before the rise of organized dissent on any local issue. They became a driving force against the immigration ban even while their growing movement for Indian independence provided the British and Canadian governments with a rationale for keeping the ban in place.

At that time, the British rigorously controlled dissent in colonial India through spies, the police, and the systematic restriction of political rights. All printed material was subject to censorship and most nationalist organizations were outlawed. So thorough was British intelligence that no political movement in India could develop very far without being infiltrated by the intelligence police. Consequently, a number of nationalists left India to begin their attack from without. Most notable among these was S. Krishnavarma, whose London home for budding nationalists (India House) and anti-British journal (*Indian Sociologist*) were great embarrassments to the British. Other centres of nationalist discontent quickly developed in Paris, Berlin, New York, and Berkeley, California. Although few in number, Indian revolutionaries by 1905 circled the globe, moving from one South Asian community to another.

The British were determined not to let the nationalist "infection" spread to Canada. The immigration ban itself was part of this strategy, but it went much further. Faced with relatively large South Asian communities in British Columbia and on the Pacific Coast of the United States, authorities planned to limit the growth of "seditious" activities in both countries. The first step in this campaign was to develop an extensive spy system to keep tabs on South Asian activities. In direct response to such worries, William C. Hopkinson was hired in January, 1909, by the Canadian immigration service.[12] Although his overt job was to work as a "hindoo interpreter" for the immigration service, from the start his covert responsibility was to send to Ottawa regular reports on South Asian political activity; he had already been volunteering such information for a year. In late 1910 he secretly was placed on the Northwest Mounted Police payroll.[13]

Thus, as early as 1908 there were to be two inextricably intertwined political movements among South Asians in Canada – the specific drive to remove the continuous passage regulation and the more generalized attempt to convert community members to the cause of Indian independence. In the beginning, concern over immigration was clearly more important to most than were affairs in India. While Sikh suspicions about the British were not uncommon, few if any immigrants were overt revolutionaries. Indeed, a number had vigorously supported British rule in India and elsewhere as British Indian troops. Even radical nationalists such as Taraknath Das appreciated that any support they were to get would stem chiefly from their espousal of local grievances, principally the immigration question.

THE FIRST SKIRMISHES IN THE IMMIGRATION BATTLE

British and Canadian suspicions about the loyalty of local leaders were frequently counter-productive, as loyal individuals consequently were driven into coalition with nationalists. This process began in 1909 with Teja Singh. Although he had no strong revolutionary connections, so worried were immigration officials about the rise of local Indian political movements that he was instantly suspected of preaching sedition and sending funds to revolutionaries in India.[14]

Because shipping companies would not sell them tickets to Canada, South Asians after 1908 could not easily mount a direct challenge to the immigration ban. Consequently, other strategies had to be employed. In November, 1909, Teja Singh and Hari Singh were sent to England at community expense to raise support for their cause in liberal British circles.[15] There, Teja Singh spoke to a number of sympathetic audiences and had a brief interview with Gandhi, all to no effect. The recent assassination of Sir William Curzon in London by an Indian revolutionary more or less assured this.

At about the same time others tried a different tack. In late October, a small party set off for India to get their wives and children. The party included Raja Singh and Balwant Singh, who were then the president and priest of the Vancouver temple. At that point, only Teja Singh and Dr. Sundar Singh had their wives with them, and the loss of family was being acutely felt.[16] When these men returned in 1911 they were to become the centre of a major immigration battle.

In the meantime, though, things heated up considerably. In Vancouver, Guru Dutt Kumar began publication of the Punjabi-language newspaper *Swadesh Sevak*. It was the first regular North American publication in the Sikh language and began as a moderately nationalist paper.[17] By late 1910 its tone had become much more critical and the threat of mail censorship forced it to move to Seattle. The Indian government responded to this publication by censoring all mail from Canada and the U.S. Before he left Vancouver, Kumar began Swadesh Sevak House on 2nd Avenue, where he carried on English-language night classes for South Asian workers. He was also active in establishing the Hindustani Association, the first expressly political South Asian organization in Canada.

In February, 1910, the wife of Millside store owner, labour contractor, and political activist Uday Ram arrived in Vancouver and was admitted. On January 12, 1911, Mrs. Ram was to give birth to the first South Asian born in Canada.[18] Her entry provoked a sharp rebuke of local immigration officials by the Minister of the Interior, but this was not known in the community.[19] The rumour spread that the government was moderating its immigration ban. In April, Bhag Singh, then president of both the Vancouver Khalsa Diwan Society and the Guru Nanak Mining and Trust Company, was sent to India to put pressure on the Indian government. Teja Singh and the visiting H.A. Talchekar of the Bombay Workingman's Association were sent to England with similar objectives. As with previous attempts at personal representations, these came to nothing.

A somewhat more effective strategy was that of sending petitions to government officials, if for no other reason than that they had to be formally dealt with. This helped to keep the issue of immigration alive. Petitions also sensitized the Indian government to the negative propaganda potential of the immigration ban. For example, a petition from Hussain Rahim, G.D. Kumar, and Bhag Singh from early 1910 to the Secretary of State for the Colonies was routinely sent to the Canadian Privy Council. The Privy Council was forced to claim, falsely, that there was in fact no immigration ban – only a requirement involving ticketing.[20]

The Canadian government responded to these protests by stiffening its stance. A provision of the new Immigration Act gave the government the right to restrict British Indian immigration by name; the section was not deleted despite an objection by the Secretary of State for the Colonies. Both the continuous journey and the $200 requirements remained law.[21] The government also stepped up attempts to deport individuals who took up leadership positions. A committed revolutionary, Hussain Rahim, who had arrived in Vancouver in 1910 claiming to be in transit to Boston, was soon held for deportation and the ensuing half-year court battle became a rallying point for community action. Despite evidence that Rahim possessed information on making explosives and letters from known revolutionaries, he was eventually released on a writ of *habeas corpus*.[22] Another unsuccessful attempt was made to deport another activist, Dr. Sundar Singh; he, too, received solid support from the community.

In addition, the government introduced another strategy: refusal to readmit those who had gone to visit their families in India. A few such cases materialized in 1909, but they increased in number so dramatically in the subsequent years that the government was petitioned to grant certificates of residence to those wishing to visit India. The local immigration officers steadfastly refused to grant such certificates, with the effect that South Asians feared that if they left Canada there would be no point in trying to return. Uday Ram and Sundar Singh attempted to circumvent the exclusionary policies of the government by arranging through passage from Calcutta to Vancouver, but the plan died when the Vancouver travel agent grew fearful of the local Anti-Asiatic League.[23]

By 1911, the community was economically healthy but was in serious numerical decline. Of the approximately 6,000 pioneers, only 2,342 were enumerated in the Canadian census of that year.[24] Of these, 490 were resident in Vancouver and eighty-five were in Victoria. Most of the rest were distributed along the Fraser Valley and up the east coast of Vancouver Island. Fewer than fifty were outside of British Columbia. Disenchanted with the hostile reception they had received in Canada, most of those who had left had gone to the United States, where both economic and political conditions were better for them; the rest had returned home.

Despite diminished numbers, South Asians were able to increase their attack on the immigration restrictions. On April 16, 1911, they initiated a series of public rallies designed to attract press attention to their plight. A

39

petition was sent to Lord Crewe, then Secretary of State for India, protesting the immigration ban. Other petitions to the Governor General and the Minister of the Interior soon followed. On other fronts, H. Rahim and G.D. Kumar banded together with Dr. D. Spencer of Vancouver to form the first South Asian-white organization in Canada, the Hindu Temperance Association, shortly renamed the Friends of the Hindu. Rahim and Atma Ram created the United India League at about the same time.

What initiated this protest was the realization that those who had left to bring their wives and children back to Canada were not going to have an easy time returning. Bhag Singh and Balwant Singh had been refused tickets for a continuous passage in Calcutta and had to buy tickets to Hong Kong; even a court suit proved unsuccessful. When these South Asians arrived in Hong Kong they found that the steamship companies would not sell any of them tickets to Canada, even those who were legal Canadian residents. Like many other returning men, they were stranded in Hong Kong. Unlike the rest, they had their families with them.

Ill feeling against the government increased when Hira Singh returned to Vancouver in mid-year with his wife and child. He was admitted, but his wife and child were held for deportation. After a vigorous protest they were let in as an act of grace on August 1, 1911.[25] In the meantime Bhag Singh, Balwant Singh, and their party of eighteen had met with another series of misfortunes. Unable to sail to Canada, they had bought passage to San Francisco, only to be refused entry despite the efforts of Taraknath Das and others.[26] They were required to return to Hong Kong.

As a result, the protest movement increased substantially. Kartar Singh began publication of the *Aryan*, an English-language monthly designed primarily to explain the plight of South Asians to other Canadians; it was regularly published from August, 1911, to November, 1912, and was widely distributed.

On September 24 a mass meeting was held at the Vancouver temple to raise the money to send a delegation to Ottawa. In late November, Sundar Singh, Teja Singh, Raja Singh, and Reverend L.W. Hall met with Robert Rogers, the new Conservative Minister of the Interior in Ottawa. Although the Minister was unwilling to consider removing the continuous passage regulation, he did appear to be amenable to allowing in the wives and children of legal residents.[27] The local leadership once again approached local shipping agents on the possibility of selling continuous passages, and the latter pressed the government to have the regulations changed. An early petition to the Governor General had been "leaked" to the eastern Canadian press, which generated considerable editorial comment attacking the governmental restrictions on wives and children. In addition, yet another petition had resulted in a stiff protest from the government of India to the Canadian government.[28]

Near the end of 1911, Sundar Singh began an intensive campaign in eastern Canada and got a number of church groups to petition the government on the question of family reunification. In another meeting with the Vancouver delegation, Rogers finally agreed to allow wives and children in, contingent upon the results of a personal investigation by an Ottawa official, F.C. Blair. The announcement of his trip produced such a strong negative reaction in British Columbia that the government reconsidered the advisability of changing the law; Blair's report was never made public. The feeling in British Columbia was that changing the regulation in any way would be the first step toward unrestricted South Asian immigration. This was also Blair's view, which was shared by the Ministerial Association of Vancouver.[29]

On January 21, 1912, Bhag Singh and Balwant Singh returned to Vancouver aboard the *Monteagle* and their wives and children were immediately held for deportation.[30] The threat posed by this deportation case galvanized the community, as did the return of Bhag Singh and Balwant Singh. Both of them were grassroots leaders who had risen to positions of respect in the community. Both had earlier served with distinction in the British Indian army, but the hardships they encountered on the long trip back from India had won them over to the nationalist cause.[31]

Even before they had arrived a letter was sent to Rogers reminding him of his earlier promise, followed shortly by a petition from the Vancouver Khalsa Diwan Society. The community went directly to the courts to challenge the law and the families were quickly freed on bail. The government countered by seeking grounds to extradite Teja Singh. The case stagnated in the courts until a false rumour arose that 300 South Asians would soon arrive on a chartered ship to test the law.[32] This prompted the government to issue a deportation order on April 22, 1912, just after the courts had closed for the day and just before a ship was leaving for Hong Kong. Only by the community's lawyer going to the judge's house was the deportation temporarily stayed. Thereafter, a writ of *habeas corpus* was secured from the British Columbia Supreme Court, which forced the release of the women and children on $2,000 bail.

This deportation decision received a great deal of adverse criticism in the press outside of British Columbia and from a wide variety of public figures. For this reason (compounded by the possibility that the court case would be won by South Asians) H.H. Stevens proposed to the Deputy Minister of the Interior that the families be let in without creating a precedent. This was a quick turnabout for the violently anti-Asian British Columbia MP, who only a few months before had been entirely opposed to the possibility. The Deputy Minister subsequently allowed the families of Bhag Singh and Balwant Singh into Canada on May 23, 1912.

By itself, this incident might seem of little consequence. Two women and three children were allowed to enter Canada, but the continuous passage law remained unchanged. In actuality, it had some significant repercussions. It focused the attention of Canadians and people in India on the situation of South Asians in Canada. It provided the rationale for further petitions to government officials, including some in India. Thereafter, the government began to make it easier for South Asian visitors to enter the country. It also provoked several complaints by bureaucrats in India about discrimination against South Asians.

Within the community it increased people's confidence that they could work together, gave the leadership credibility, and emphasized the necessity of fighting every immigration case that came along. The local immigration officials knew this, and on their own initiative began to loosen their strict interpretation of the regulations.[33] They also began to allow a few wives and children of "loyal" resident South Asians into the country when the application was made through a white intermediary. Nevertheless, by the end of 1913 there were no more than six South Asian wives and twenty children in Canada.[34] This process was slow and informal and often did not address the hardship involved. For example, Hakam Singh, his wife, and four children remained in Hong Kong for almost two years before they were let in as an act of grace on July 16, 1913.[35]

Predictably, the fight also augmented Indian nationalist feelings in the community. All through 1912 the revolutionary leadership expanded its following; it also increased its interests in Canadian and American political movements of the left. For example, Taraknath Das developed strong links with American anarchists and the Industrial Workers of the World and became a prominent socialist much in demand as a speaker in the San Francisco area. He had begun organizing nationalist study groups among Indian students at the University of California at Berkeley as early as 1910. By the end of 1912 he and Lala Har Dayal (or Hardayal) had created an incipient revolutionary party in California. Das was considered so dangerous by Canadian government authorities that Hopkinson successfully tried to stop his naturalization as a United States citizen. In January, 1913, Hopkinson felt the issue so pressing that he personally went to California to gather information.[36]

Political sophistication increased in Canada as well. Up to 1912, local revolutionaries had gathered support chiefly through the immigration issue and by presenting concrete examples of the inequities of British rule in India. Thereafter, they began to incorporate more political theory in their attacks, drawn largely from the Socialist Party and the IWW in British Columbia. As early as 1912 most of the leadership were said to be Socialist Party members, including H. Rahim, G.D. Kumar, Bhag Singh, Balwant Singh, Raja Singh, and Sundar Singh. A considerable amount of IWW literature was translated into Punjabi. Interest grew in independence movements outside of India, including those in Ireland and China.

In their own small ways, individuals and groups also began to show political discontent with their situation. For example, the Vancouver

Khalsa Diwan Society pointedly refused a request by the mayor of Vancouver to turn out for a visit of the Duke of Connaught, arguing that they could not give support to a political system that denied them full participation in Canadian society.[37] Hussain Rahim protested the franchise restriction by placing himself on the Vancouver voters' list and voting.[38] He was immediately arrested on a charge of perjury and his name was removed from the list. South Asians also continued their publishing tradition. In Victoria, Sundar Singh and Kartar Singh began *Sansar* (1912-14), another Punjabi-language monthly devoted to Sikh affairs. *Bande Mataram* (1911-13), a nationalist monthly published in Paris, was widely available despite an attempt to ban it from the Canadian mails.

THE GATHERING STORM

By the beginning of 1913 frustration and bitterness against the government were rife, and not only in Vancouver. Locally supported and controlled Sikh temples had been built in Abbotsford (1911), New Westminster (1912), and Victoria (1912) and their membership quickly added support to the growing unrest. Throughout 1913 South Asians stepped up the immigration battle, at the same time covertly developing what would soon become an important political movement for Indian independence.

Toward both these ends the Vancouver Khalsa Diwan Society and the United India League decided to send still another delegation to England and India to protest conditions in Canada. Balwant Singh, Narian Singh, and Nand Singh Sirha left for England on March 17, 1913. By this time Hopkinson was the main source of Canadian and British information on Indian sedition in Canada, so he was sent to England to prepare British officials for the delegation's arrival.[39] A short time later Teja Singh and his family returned permanently to India, from where he was to continue to be a prime mover in the drive toward independence.

By the time the delegation arrived in London the British government had decided on a strategy to deal with them. The Secretary of State refused to grant the delegation an interview on the grounds that they did not represent the government of Canada; the British claimed Canadian restrictions were a Canadian matter – this despite the fact that British interests in limiting the growth of Indian communities in Western countries were served by them. An informal interview was granted by Sir John Anderson, Undersecretary of State for the Colonies, who argued that the matter was entirely outside of British jurisdiction. The delegation then went to India to approach the Viceroy and the Indian National Congress.[40] They also sounded out the nationalist movement in Punjab and presented it with information about their plight in Canada.

All the while, the immigration battle continued. Those who had returned to their villages in India kept interest in coming to Canada alive, so that local commissioners in the Punjab were constantly receiving applications to leave. As with chain migration everywhere, the stories of the few who had struck it rich were listened to rather than those of the many who had not. Who could doubt that if one man could save Rs. 15,000 in eight years, the average person might be able to make a few thousand? People continued to travel from India to Hong Kong, only to find that they could go no further for want of tickets.

In Canada the government position on immigration hardened when courts in the United States ruled that a resident Indian yogi was a "free white person" and thus was eligible on racial grounds for citizenship. [41] Such a South Asian, as a United States citizen, would be able to fulfil the continuous passage regulation simply by travelling from the United States to Canada. This court ruling polarized the west coast press:

> There's No Law to Bar 100,000,000
> 200 Arrive in Seattle
> They Breed Like Rats, Live in Squalor and
> Die by the Millions of Plague and Starvation[42]

In mid-1913 the CPR shipping line in Hong Kong began to sell tickets to South Asians who could show some documentary evidence of being Canadian residents. As protection against possible deportations, the CPR required these people to buy return tickets, even if they were not going to use them. Because of their inability to provide sufficient documentation of their residency, many of these individuals were held for deportation upon arrival in British Columbia. For their roles in these deportations, Hopkinson and a few South Asians who worked for him became hated men in the community. In order to limit these deportation cases the government developed an informal system of issuing registering-out certificates to legal South Asian residents when they left the country. Eventually, no one would be let back into the country without one.

Enterprising would-be immigrants promptly tried other ways to get around the law. Some attempted to enter the country via east coast ports, coming from Europe or Cuba. A few others secured continuous passage tickets issued by the Nippon Yusen Kaisha shipping line, which had recently established connecting service from Calcutta and Bombay to Victoria. Having fulfilled the requirements, seven of them were let in. There were general fears that the continuous passage restriction would become irrelevant. [43] In response, the government pressured the shipping companies not to sell tickets to South Asians in Hong Kong, even if they were Canadian residents who paid a return fare.

In the fall, things began to look bleak for any change in the law. In October, Bhagwan Singh "Gyani," a respected revolutionary leader, was arrested for fraudulently entering the country as a returning immigrant. Despite the fact that at the deportation inquiry not a single community member would testify that he was in the country illegally, he was ordered deported. [44] Another thirty-nine who had recently arrived in Victoria representing themselves as returning immigrants were also detained subject to deportation.

The threatened deportations produced an immediate response. Eight hundred people met in Vancouver's Dominion Hall to protest the government action. Lawyers paid for by community subscription attempted to get these detained individuals released on *habeas corpus* and tried to represent them at their deportation boards of inquiry. In late November, Bhagwan Singh was deported, even though local immigration officials knew that a writ of *habeas corpus* had been secured from the British Columbia courts stopping the deportation proceedings.[45] The community was enraged, and soon a Punjabi-language essay titled *Tyranny, Tyranny*, attacking the deportation of Bhagwan Singh, was circulating along the Pacific Coast.

Just as things looked the bleakest, fate once more offered some hope. In November, 1913, Chief Justice Hunter of the British Columbia Supreme Court struck down both the continuous passage regulation and the provision that each immigrant have with him or her $200 upon landing.[46] Although Justice Hunter's objections to the Orders-in-Council were based on legal technicalities, thirty-nine people held for deportation were released. Twenty others who had arrived two days before on the *Chicago Maru* were also allowed in. Fourteen more who had landed in Victoria aboard the *Seattle Maru* were released on *habeas corpus* by Justice Gregory of the British Columbia Supreme Court.[47] The community was convinced that the onerous immigration restrictions had been destroyed. As a Vancouver immigration officer put it, "the Hindus are openly boasting that they have always beaten the Government [in] the courts."[48]

As so often happened, South Asian hopes were to be dashed again. On December 8, 1913, the government enacted an Order-in-Council (PC 2642) stopping the immigration of all "artisan or general unskilled labour classes" through British Columbia ports of entry. The overt rationale for the ban was a labour surplus in British Columbia, but the chief reason was the fear that South Asians had circumvented the continuous journey restriction. The ban was to continue in effect through World War I. On January 7, 1914, reworded versions of the continuous passage and $200 Orders-in-Council were re-enacted (as PC 23 and 24, respectively). Despite nearly continuous representations by the British government to allow South Asian wives and children some consideration, the Canadian government steadfastly refused. The official rationale was that all other immigrants were subject to the continuous passage provision.[49]

By 1914, Japanese immigration had been severely reduced by treaty, as had Chinese immigration by the $500 head tax. South Asian immigration was stopped altogether. In both absolute and relative terms, the Asian population of British Columbia was quite small and was almost entirely contained by racially specific laws and informal practices. Even so, people had become so sensitized to race in the province that Asians continued to be viewed as a threat. Worries about South Asians undermining "white labour" persisted, and of the many labour organizations in British Columbia, only the radical IWW expressly supported South Asian workers. The belief was general that South Asians lived at such a low socioeconomic level that they would undercut white labour. Increasing nationalist and revolutionary activities in the community had not yet become an issue outside government circles, perhaps because their existence was not yet widely known, but lurid popular accounts of poverty, disease, and starvation in India were pervasive and these influenced local stereotypes of South Asians. Consider this rather mild example from J.S. Woodsworth:

> The Hindu is a rather picturesque figure. When he arrives his dress consists of an undergarment, a pair of scanty pantaloons, and probably an old military coat; but he gradually adopts the Canadian costume, retaining his turban. The effect is decidedly grotesque. So far the Hindus have been employed only in the lowest kinds of manual labor. They are very slow, and do not seem capable of hard, continuous exertion. Their diet is light, and physically, they are not adapted to the rigorous climate of Canada.
>
> Owing to his peculiarities the Hindu cannot work with men of other nations; indeed, only with Hindus of his own caste. Their standards of living and manner of life and thought are far different than ours. However estimable they may be in India, they are sadly out of place in Canada. [50]

South Asians were also seen as immoral, deviant, and, hence, unfit to be Canadians. Much was made of (Indian) child marriage practices, both as evidence of immorality and as the supposed cause of lack of stamina and responsibility. South Asians were believed to be a product of "Too many generations of vice; too many generations of birth from immature mothers; no dower of strength from birth." [51] There was also perverse Edwardian concern about the moral effects of intermarriage:

> What is feared is the effect of that union on the lewd Hindu, the effect on the safety of the average white woman and white girl; and there is no one on the Coast, who had lived next to Asiatics, who does not know what that means in terms of fact that cannot be set down here. [52]

In this regard, whites chose the more negative, competitive of the two British colonial stereotypes of Indians then common: the "cruel scheming Oriental" as opposed to the "tractable, mild Hindu." [53]

In addition, the conviction remained that South Asians would never assimilate to Canadian customs and would forever pose a numerical threat. As the Ministerial Association of Vancouver declared:

> They form a people apart, and are proud of their separation. To

allow them to settle in that way in Canada would mean the transplanting of a little section of India into the heart of Canada, which would retain its distinct individuality for all time. The leaders desire to break down the regulations that at present stem this tide of immigration, and when they are broken down, the inundation will begin. To this, British Columbians cannot consent. The policy of a white Canada is absolutely necessary, and must be maintained now or never.[54]

These mutually reinforcing beliefs about South Asians pervaded every level of British Columbia society and manifested themselves in political action. As late as 1914 it was impossible to find a provincial or federal member from British Columbia who did not publicly support the full range of existing anti-South Asian legislation. Consequently, as far as the immigration question was concerned, the concerted action of the community from 1907 to the end of 1913 had brought very meagre results. While most South Asians were convinced that the battle had been won, this was far from true. In actuality, the stage had been set for a massive confrontation between South Asians and the Canadian government. The lines were drawn, and the situation was past the possibility of negotiation and compromise. One of the most shameful tragedies in Canadian race relations was soon to be acted out by the shores of British Columbia.

NOTES

1. William Peter Ward, "The Oriental Immigrant and Canada's Protestant Clergy," *B.C. Studies*, 22 (1974), pp. 9-19; G.C. Pidgeon and E.D. McLaren, "East Indian Immigration," *Westminster Hall Magazine*, 7, 8 (1912), pp. 23-28; Elizabeth Ross Grace, "East Indian Immigration," *Westminster Hall Magazine*, 3, 3 (1908), pp. 10-12. There were two exceptions. Kenneth Grant unsuccessfully attempted a ministry among South Asians in Vancouver, as did W.L. Macrae in Victoria. See Kenneth James Grant, "Among the Hindus of British Columbia," *Missionary Messenger* (1915), pp. 106-09; Grant, *My Missionary Memories* (Halifax, 1923).

2. See Tien Fang Cheng, *Oriental Immigration in Canada* (Shanghai, 1931), and Rajani Kant Das, *Hindustanee Workers on the Pacific Coast* (Berlin, 1923), for more details of early household life. This form of household organization seems to have first developed when South Asians were housed in worker barracks by the mills and the railroads.

3. J. MacGill to W. Cory, February 12, 1909, PAC, RG 76, #536999, part 3.

4. W. Hopkinson to W. Cory, December 20, 1909, PAC, RG 7, G 21, v. 200.

5. W. Hopkinson's diary for November 26 to December 3, 1909, *ibid*. Perhaps 15 per cent were involved in farm labour at this time. W.

Hopkinson to F. Oliver, September 6, 1908, Laurier Papers, MG 26, G, v. 532.

6. *Vancouver Province*, August 5, 1909, p. 1. Button claims that as early as 1908, 176 South Asians were employed at Fraser Mills. See R.A. Button, "Sikh Settlement in the Lower Mainland of British Columbia" (B.A. essay, University of British Columbia, 1964), p. 40.

7. W. Hopkinson's diary for December 4 to December 16, 1909, PAC, RG 7, G 21, v. 200.

8. Button, "Sikh Settlement," p. 44.

9. W. Hopkinson, Report, February, 1910, PAC, RG 7, G 21, v. 200; Nand Singh Sirha, "Indians in Canada," *Modern Review*, 14 (1913), p. 146.

10. *Vancouver Province,* December 7, 1908, p. 1.

11. Prospectus of the Canada-India Supply and Trust Company, Ltd., PAC, RG 7, G 21, v. 200. Radhikrishnan (variously spelt Radha Kishan) was Uday Ram's business partner. Although born in the Northwest Provinces of India, he had spent most of his life in Fiji (Information as to the Hindu Agitators in Vancouver, probable author Governor Swayne, c.a. 1909, *ibid.*).

12. Hopkinson today remains an enigmatic figure in South Asian Canadian history. See Hugh Johnson, *The Voyage of the Komagata Maru: The Sikh Challenge to Canada's Colour Bar* (Delhi, 1979), for biographical details. The suggestion to hire Hopkinson was made first by Governor Swayne (see Hindu Agitators, PAC, RG 7, G 21, v. 200) and then by the Governor General to the immigration authorities (Governor General to W. Cory, January 13, 1909, *ibid.*).

13. W. Cory to J. McGill, February 5, 1909, PAC, RG 76, #808722, v. 561, part 1; W. Hopkinson to W. Scott, December 21, 1910, *ibid.*

14. J. McGill to W. Cory, January 21, 1909, PAC, RG 76, #536999, part 3. He was said to be aided by "Balmokund," who may have been an active revolutionary in Bengal. See R.C. Majumdar, *History of the Freedom Movement in India,* vol. 1 (Calcutta, 1963), p. 306. Balmokund was hanged in 1913 for a bombing incident in Lahore (Mittal, *Freedom Movement in Punjab*, p. 14).

15. On the trip, see W. Hopkinson to W. Cory, November 16, 1909, PAC, RG 7, G 21, v. 200; Hunt, *Gandhi in London*, p. 133; A.C. Bose, *Indian Revolutionaries Abroad, 1905-1922* (Patna, 1971), p. 25. Hopkinson reported a groundless rumour that Teja Singh was carrying $20,000 with him for revolutionary purposes.

16. Dr. Sundar Singh landed in Halifax on March 12, 1909, claiming to be a visitor travelling through Canada. Born in Lahore, he had a doctor's degree from Punjab University and an M.D. from Glasgow.

17. The journal's title is a reference to the home industry movement in India – a plan to boycott imported goods. Most editions are in PAC, RG 7, G 21, v. 200-1. Two short-lived papers also made their appearance in 1910, Hira Singh's *Pardeshi Khalsa* and the *American-India Samachar*. Kartar Singh's *Khalsa Herald* followed in 1911.

18. W. Hopkinson claimed that Mrs. Ram had fulfilled the requirements of entry, which was impossible (W. Hopkinson to W. Cory, February 19, 1910, PAC, RG 7, G 21, v. 208). Nathu Ram, a passenger on the same boat who had tried to book in Calcutta, was held for deportation. This gives further support to the widely held belief that Hopkinson could be bought. On Mrs. Ram's child, see *Vancouver Province*, January 13, 1911, p. 1.

19. F. Oliver to W. Scott, February 23, 1910, PAC, RG 7, #536999, part 3.

20. Immigration of British Indians: Report, PAC, RG 2, 1, August 1910, #1489.

21. In accord with the new Act the continuous journey provision was rewritten as PC 920 of May 9, 1910. The requirement to have possession of $200 became PC 926 of the same date.

22. W. Hopkinson to W. Cory, February 17, 1911, RG 76, #536999, part 3.

23. W. Hopkinson to W. Cory, November 19 and 28, 1910, PAC, RG 7, G 21, v. 201. The plan was to have CPR tickets for the Hong Kong-to-Canada leg honoured by agents in Calcutta for the India-to-Hong Kong leg.

24. *Census of Canada*, 1911, vol. 1, p. 367.

25. W. Hopkinson to W. Cory, August 4, 1911, PAC, RG 76, #536999, part 4.

26. W. Hopkinson (San Francisco) to W. Cory, October 13, 1911, PAC, RG 7, G 21, v. 20. Hopkinson routinely spied on Indians in the United States and had established a network of informers in San Francisco.

27. *Vancouver Province*, November 29, 1911, p. 1.

28. Government of India, Department of Industry, to Lord Crewe, September 14, 1911, PAC, RG 76, #536999, part 4.

29. Private Memorandum re: Hindu Immigration, January 26, 1912, City of Vancouver Archives, H.H. Stevens Papers, 69-1. For an analysis of the clergy's position on Asian immigration, see Ward, "The Oriental Immigrant."

30. Bhag Singh's wife was Harnam Kaur, who arrived with a year-old daughter. Balwant Singh's wife, Kartar Kaur, arrived with two children, Udom and Narazan.

31. Bhag Singh had been in the 10th Indian Calvary and was afterwards a policeman in Hankow. Balwant Singh had been in the 36th Sikhs. Both came to Canada in 1906.

32. Hopkinson suggested that this rumoured challenge to the immigration ban could be dealt with by deporting the whole shipload because of non-existent diseases. The government agreed to the plan. W. Hopkinson to W. Cory, April 16, 1912, PAC, RG 76, #536999, part 5.

33. For example, M. Reid allowed eight returning men entry at Vancouver, even though they did not have documentary evidence of their residence status. M. Reid to W. Scott, June 3, 1912, *ibid.*

34. Isabella Ross Broad, *An Appeal for Fair Play for the Sikhs in Canada* (Victoria, 1913), p. 13.

35. Once more, H.H. Stevens intervened, writing to Minister of the Interior W.J. Roche (W.J. Roche to H.H. Stevens, July 9, 1913, H.H. Stevens Papers, HH-3).
36. W. Hopkinson to W. Cory, March 26, 1912, PAC, RG 7, G 21, v. 202; J.S. Smith, Office of Examination, Department of Commerce and Labor, Seattle, to W. Hopkinson, June 7, 1912, *ibid.*; Emily Brown, *Har Dayal: Hindu Revolutionary and Rationalist* (Tucson, 1975). Thereafter, the mail of California revolutionaries was routinely opened by American authorities. Har Dayal was at that time the secretary of the IWW association in San Francisco (W. Hopkinson to W. Cory, April 1, 1912, PAC, RG 7, G 21, v. 202).
37. Bhag Singh to the Mayor of Vancouver, September 8, 1912, PAC, RG 7, G 21, v. 202.
38. *Vancouver Province*, March 29, 1912, p. 1. Rahim was a Socialist Party scrutineer in Ward 4.
39. By that time, Hopkinson's reports were being routinely sent to the British India government (L. Harcourt to the Governor General, March 8, 1913, PAC, RG 7, G 21, v. 202). So also were lists of addresses in India to which local South Asians mailed letters and packages. Hopkinson was put on the India government's salary as of July 22, 1913 (J. Holderness, India Office, to the Undersecretary of State, Colonial Office, *ibid.*, v. 203).
40. Sirha, "Indians in Canada."
41. *Vancouver Province*, March 15, 1913, p. 1.
42. *Seattle Star*, June 26, 1913, p. 1.
43. *Vancouver Province*, August 28, 1913, p. 1. The government wrote to the British Privy Council to see if the Indian government could restrain shipping companies from offering a continuous passage (PC 2218 of August 25, 1913).
44. Bose, *Indian Revolutionaries Abroad*, pp. 262-3; Minutes of the Board of Inquiry re: Bhagwan Singh, October 21, 1913, H.H. Stevens Papers, HH-5.
45. K. Singh and S. Singh, *Ghadar 1915*, p. 11.
46. G. Milne to W. Scott, November 24, 1913, PAC, RG 76, #536999, part 8.
47. *Vancouver Province*, November 9, 1913, p. 1.
48. M. Reid to W. Scott, December 15, 1913, PAC, RG 76, R.O., part 1.
49. PC 2445 of September 27, 1913; PC 304 of February 23, 1914. Some other nationalities, such as Arabs, were indeed restricted by the continuous journey provision when it suited the needs of the government.
50. J.S. Woodsworth, *Strangers within our Gates* (Toronto, 1909), pp. 188-9.
51. Agnes C. Laut, *Am I My Brother's Keeper? A Study of British Columbia's Labour and Oriental Problems* (Toronto, 1913), p. 39.
52. *Ibid.*
53. C. Bolt, *Victorian Attitudes to Race* (Oxford, 1973), p. 178.
54. Pidgeon and McLaren, "East Indian Immigration," p. 27.

FOUR

Revolution

GHADAR

It was perhaps inevitable that difficulties faced by South Asians in British Columbia would move them to more and more revolutionary action. The traditional Sikh response to domination had always been to fight back rather than give in, and those in Canada needed only an ideological and organizational focus to activate that response. The vehicle was to be the Hindustan Ghadar Party, which, though it originated in the United States, was active in Canada from the time of its creation.

South Asian communities on the Pacific Coast of the United States had in many ways developed similarly to those in Canada. They had begun about the same time, were predominantly Sikh, and had faced many forms of racial discrimination. But in contrast, there arose in and around San Francisco a small group of Indian intellectuals who became the nucleus for growing anti-British sentiment. Taraknath Das had been active intermittently there since 1907. Early in 1911 he was joined by Lala Har Dayal, an intellectual and firebrand who had just resigned a British scholarship to Oxford in protest over colonial rule in India.[1] These two soon built up a following, first among Indian university students and then within the Sikh communities that had established themselves in California, Oregon, and Washington.

In mid-1913 a meeting was held in Oregon to form an umbrella association uniting South Asians in Canada and the United States – the Hindu Association of the Pacific Coast. Sohan Singh Bhakna and Lala Har Dayal were elected president and secretary, respectively. By November the Ghadar (Mutiny) Party was formally organized to promote national independence in India. South Asian workers in Canada and the United States immediately pledged $2,000 to set up a nationalist publishing centre in San Francisco. Under Har Dayal's leadership the first run of 4,000 copies of the Punjabi-language newspaper *Ghadar* was printed there and mailed to every South Asian community in North America as well as to

51

India, Europe, and the Far East. Two more issues of the violently revolutionary paper were published within the month.

The Ghadar Party was considered to be so dangerous by the British that they set out covertly to destroy it, even though it operated quite legally in the United States. Hopkinson moved his family to San Francisco for an extended stay to establish a spy system and infiltrate the organization. While there, he kept tabs on the activities of the leadership, reported on how *Ghadar* and other revolutionary materials were being smuggled into India, recruited informers, and prevailed upon the American postal officials to record the Ghadar Party's overseas contacts. By June, 1915, he convinced Prime Minister Borden to ban *Ghadar* from the Canadian mails.[2] Ghadar responded with an ever-increasing printing schedule and with attempts to keep its activities more secret.

The British authorities had some reason to fear the Ghadar Party. It had committed support among rank-and-file Sikhs, who had been politically awakened by their harsh treatment in North America. Moreover, Ghadar was explicitly revolutionary. It did not entertain the hope of moderating British rule in India and attacked it mercilessly. Its objective was straightforward – violent revolution, somewhat in the image of the American War of Independence. Virtually all previous Indian nationalist movements were either reformist or religiously based; Ghadar was neither, and though its membership was chiefly Sikh, it was not a Sikh religious organization. Rather, Ghadar's leadership was heavily influenced by IWW, anarchist, and popular socialist thought, especially in its analysis of British rule in India. Ghadar saw the economic role of the British in India as pure exploitation. *Ghadar* and other Ghadarite publications were filled with articles contrasting Indian poverty with the wealth extracted from India by the British. This "drain" theory of British rule was a powerful propaganda weapon among disenchanted Sikhs.

In British Columbia the rise of the Ghadar Party gave additional coherence to political ideas that had been maturing for some time. Only two months after the first issue of *Ghadar* rolled off the press, Sohan Lal Pathak was reading revolutionary poetry from it at a mass meeting in the Vancouver temple.[3] At the same meeting Kashi Ram read his own poem advocating that Hopkinson and his clique of informers be done away with. Hussain Rahim soon announced the establishment of the English-language *Hindustanee* to counter anti-South Asian propaganda; 1,000 copies of the first issue were sent covertly to India. Plans were made to publish issues of *Ghadar* in Vancouver and copies of the paper printed in California were soon being sent to India via British Columbia.

Political feelings in the community were further inflamed when it became known that the delegation sent to India on their behalf had failed. Balwant Singh, Narian Singh, and Nand Singh Sirha had met with the Viceroy on December 20, 1913, and he only agreed to press for a removal of the continuous passage restriction as it applied to wives and children.[4]

Suspected of revolutionary activity, Nand Singh Sirha was not allowed to return to Canada and later joined the Ghadar movement in California.

At the same time, the Ghadar Party was developing an active strategy for revolution in India. As the red-ink Ghadar poster "The Bugle of the Army of Mutiny" of February, 1914, announced: "We must return to India and start a revolution. Get on a boat and go to your country and prepare some men to fight for the mutiny." *Ghadar* frequently put it more polemically in its "Want Ads":

Wanted:	Enthusiastic and heroic soldiers for organizing Ghadar in Hindustan
Remuneration:	Death
Reward:	Martyrdom
Pension:	Freedom
Field of Work:	Hindustan.[5]

As early as February, 1914, Ghadar's leadership believed that a European war was inevitable and that such a war would require Britain to move the bulk of its large Indian army into service outside of India. This would give Ghadar members the chance to sow revolution among British Indian troops still left in India and to raise a mass movement among the people. The rise of this strategy alarmed the British, who increased pressure on their United States government counterparts to restrict Ghadar. On February 2, 1914, American immigration authorities applied for a deportation warrant for Har Dayal as an anarchist; the evidence was from Hopkinson. He was arrested on March 26, got bail, and promptly fled to Switzerland. Even though $800 had been sent from British Columbia for his court defence, the risks of being deported to a British possession were too great. Ghadar quickly reformed under new leadership.

THE *KOMAGATA MARU* INCIDENT

The escalation of political consciousness was closely linked to an escalation in the immigration battle. Objectively, virtually all hope of successfully challenging the immigration regulations had disappeared. The continuous journey and $200 provisions had been rewritten so that they were constitutional. The bar to artisans and labourers also continued in force as a backup. Nevertheless, there was a certain optimism in the community about their ability to beat the regulations in court; after all, eighty-eight South Asians were let into the country in 1913, while only nineteen secured entry in the previous two years. It was well known that the restriction on immigrant artisans and labourers was due to lapse March 31.

The optimism was shared by men in the Far East who wanted to come to Canada; 150 prospective immigrants were residing temporarily in and around the Hong Kong Sikh temple alone. However, no one of South

Asian origin could then buy a ticket to Canada from Hong Kong, let alone gain entry. There still was no way to travel from India on a continuous passage.

Into this vacuum stepped an enterprising Sikh, Gurdit Singh Sarhali. Gurdit Singh had done well as a labour contractor for railway and rubber plantation work in Malaya at the turn of the century.[6] Thereafter, he had returned to India and only arrived in Hong Kong in January, 1914. He was then fifty-five years old. He quickly became aware of the plight of those wishing to travel to North America and devised an ambitious plan to deal with it. He would circumvent the intent of the Canadian immigration ban by following it to the letter. Gurdit Singh decided to charter a ship in Calcutta, pay for its rental through ticket sales and cargo, and then sail for Canada. He believed that the $200 that each South Asian immigrant was to have could be easily raised in the Vancouver community upon arrival and was willing to gamble that the ban on artisans and labourers would not be renewed. Once the first trip was carried out successfully he would return to India and repeat the process. On February 13, 1914, he issued advertisements notifying the Hong Kong community of his plan.

There was at once interest in and objections to this scheme on the part of potential immigrants. True, they desperately wanted passage to Canada. At the same time, they were in Hong Kong, not Calcutta, and did not wish to incur the expense of travelling to Calcutta, only to return promptly to Hong Kong on their way to Canada. They pointed out that hundreds of other South Asians also were scattered across the other main ports in the Far East in similar situations.

Gurdit Singh was easily persuaded to change his plans, for he had nowhere near the capital to charter a ship of his own. He would deal with the immigration ban when the ship arrived in Canada. In early March of 1914 he began selling tickets in Hong Kong and shortly afterwards used the proceeds to charter the *Komagata Maru* for a half year for $66,000 (Hong Kong). The Japanese shipping company that owned the aging freighter would provide a crew, and Gurdit Singh, the coal, water, food, and other necessities.

The Hong Kong colonial government had been monitoring developments and tried to thwart the voyage. Hong Kong law proved insufficient to the task, and on April 6 the *Komagata Maru* set sail for Shanghai with 165 passengers on board. There, 111 more joined the expedition, each paying $100 (Hong Kong). Moji, Japan, was the next stop on the route of the *Komagata Maru*, by then renamed the *Guru Nanak Jahaz*. After some difficulty in raising enough money to buy sufficient coal, the ship embarked once more, adding eighty-six more passengers while in port. Its last stop was Yokohama, where the final fourteen boarded. The government later charged that while in Yokohama the ship was visited by Bhagwan Singh and Maulvi Muhammad Barakatullah, who had become important members of the Ghadar Party.

The imminent arrival of the *Komagata Maru* first became news on April 16, and it immediately produced a storm of protest in British Columbia. H.H. Stevens asked for and received a government guarantee that the ban on artisans and labourers would be renewed. In Vancouver, immigration officials asserted that they would not be let in. The South Asian community steeled itself for yet another immigration battle.[7]

The *Komagata Maru* arrived at the Victoria quarantine station May 21 with 376 passengers on board, including two women and three children. Two days later the ship steamed into Vancouver and was anchored in the middle of Burrard Inlet. An armed guard was placed aboard several launches by immigration officials to keep those on the ship isolated from people on shore. When an official party went aboard, the lines were immediately drawn. Only the twenty-two returnees on board would be allowed to land; the rest would be held on board until deportation orders for them were secured. They would then be sent back to the Far East. In the meantime, no one from shore would be allowed on board.

Despite the isolation in which they were placed, those on the *Komagata Maru* were able to smuggle a letter to Mit Singh Pandori, a leader in the Vancouver community. A temple committee to deal with the expected legal battle had already been formed, and a lawyer was hired to represent the ship's passengers. The committee also offered to provide bail while the case worked its way through the courts.

The government also had its strategy ready. To make the deportation proceedings more certain, the government used an old trick: finding non-existent disease in prospective immigrants. Ninety passengers were declared to have trachoma and thus to be ineligible as immigrants. In Ottawa there was concern over what was becoming an international incident. At cabinet level it was decided to press for a single test case to cover the deportation proceedings of all the passengers. The hope was that one case rather than 354 would offer less negative publicity. There was no thought of landing them. Gurdit Singh was adamantly opposed to this position of a single test case, and a stalemate developed.

The next phase of the affair was ceded to the press, which kept the *Komagata Maru* on the front pages.[8] A poem titled "Gurdit Singh" by "Rudyard Tippling" graced the pages of the *Saturday Sunset* on May 30, to which the *Province* replied with a series of scurrilous cartoons portraying hordes of blackface "Hindoos" perched in a dinghy-like boat.

The South Asian community was not idle. A temple support committee for the *Komagata Maru* was established, headed by Bhag Singh, Balwant Singh, Mit Singh, and Hussain Rahim; they were all Ghadar supporters and their election was indicative of the depth of revolutionary feeling in the community. On June 1, the temple committee organized a protest meeting in Vancouver's Dominion Hall. Six hundred South Asians attended – about one out of three then resident in Canada. At that meeting over $100,000 was pledged in support of those on the beleaguered ship. One individual alone pledged $2,000 and another offered

55

property worth $6,000. By June 10 the committee had collected over $20,000 in cash, which was applied to the balance still owed by Gurdit Singh for the charter of the ship.

In the meantime, conditions were rapidly deteriorating on board. Some individuals had been on the ship for two months already, and the hardship of confinement was becoming compounded by the accumulating garbage that immigration officials refused to remove and by rapidly depleting supplies of food and water. By June 10 many had become sick and one passenger had died. Once they were accorded the right to send messages, petitions began to flow from the *Komagata Maru* alleging starvation. The immigration officers did nothing. Only on June 20 was the committee's lawyer able to force the immigration officials into court. By then, the ship had been sitting in Vancouver harbour for a month.

From that date the conflict steadily increased in severity as both sides became more intransigent. For their part, the community joined with the radical Socialist Party of Canada to stage an even larger rally than the one at the beginning of the month.[9] This was immediately countered by an anti-South Asian rally chaired by Mayor T.S. Baxter of Vancouver. An estimated 2,000 people listened approvingly as Baxter and H.H. Stevens attacked Asian immigration and the "incorrectness" of the courts in interfering in deportation proceedings. Stevens later publicly proposed a plan to shanghai those on the ship, serve them with deportation papers, and force them onto a CPR ship bound for the Far East before the courts could react. Ottawa declined to support him.

On board, conditions grew worse. By June 25 there was virtually no drinking water on board and food supplies were very low.[10] In reaction to this, members of the temple committee, led by Bhag Singh, Balwant Singh, and Hussain Rahim, attempted to board the ship. They were turned away. Factions soon appeared on the *Komagata Maru* and by June 20 a committee of five had developed enough support among disaffected passengers to claim some of Gurdit Singh's decision-making power. Together, they agreed to the government's original proposition to select a single individual for a court test to stand for all on board. Munshi Singh, a young Sikh farmer, was picked.

In agreeing to this arrangement those on board unknowingly lost an enormous resource – delay. By law, each potential immigrant had the right to his or her own hearing before an immigration Board of Inquiry and thereafter had access to the courts. Three hundred fifty such cases would have taken many months and would have given ample opportunity for defence lawyers to pick apart the immigration regulations once again. As it was, Munshi Singh's case went before a Board of Inquiry on June 28 and he was ruled inadmissible. The next day the case was unsuccessfully appealed to a panel of five judges in Victoria and on July 5 the legal battle was over. The *Komagata Maru*'s passengers had lost their last legal option.

It did not, however, exhaust their extra-legal options. Both on board and on shore the sentiment quickly developed that at least the incident could be used to make an anti-British revolutionary statement. By the time of the adverse court decision, Gurdit Singh and the committee of five completely controlled the ship, for neither the Japanese crew nor the immigration officials were willing to risk confronting 350 very angry men. The leaders on board refused to allow the ship to leave port, at least until the food and water situation was rectified. At the same time, Gurdit Singh heightened his propaganda campaign, writing to the Governor General that the forcible return of his compatriots would lead to serious disaffection in India; as an alternative, he proposed that they be allowed to homestead somewhere in the Prairies.[11] There was no reply.

On shore, the continuing plight of the *Komagata Maru* daily strengthened the hand of the Ghadar Party. In early July, Harnam Singh Sahari and Hukam Singh unsuccessfully attempted to buy twenty-five handguns in Victoria with the intent of smuggling them onto the ship.[12] They failed also to secure guns in the state of Washington. This plan was part of a larger one to engineer a mass escape of those on the *Komagata Maru*. The latter had already threatened to rush the lifeboats if something was not quickly done about the food situation. Realizing that they had no options, the government agreed to provide the *Komagata Maru* with food and water for the return voyage. The conditions, though, were severe. Only after the ship had steamed to the three-mile limit would the supplies be transferred to her. Gurdit Singh refused, suspecting that it was a ruse to get the ship out of Canadian jurisdiction. The conflict inched up still another level.

South Asians on shore had not been idle through these negotiations. On July 13 a vain two-boat attempt was made to bring some of those on board ashore. As far away as San Francisco the Ghadar Party issued the *Second Echo of the Ghadar*, lambasting the Canadian government. More attempts were made to secure guns from Washington. Then, on July 17, the *Komagata Maru*'s passengers were served with deportation orders. At the same time, the ship was provisioned with water in order to get up steam in her boilers and the Japanese captain was ordered out of the harbour. The captain refused to be responsible for the consequences that such an action would have on board. On his own initiative the local head of immigration, Malcolm Reid, decided to storm the ship, subdue its passengers, and sail it out to international waters. The stage was set for what has since been called the Battle of Burrard Inlet.

The next day the sea-going tug *Sea Lion* approached the *Komagata Maru* with 125 police and thirty-five ex-military men on board. All were armed. The expectation was that once those on the *Komagata Maru* saw their firepower the takeover would be quickly accomplished. They were wrong to be so optimistic. When they arrived at the ship's side they found that the *Sea Lion*'s deck was over ten feet lower than the ship's and that its passengers were not going to give up without a fight. An attempt to board was met with a hail of projectiles from the deck of the

Komagata Maru. There was total panic on the *Sea Lion*, as people fled for non-existent cover. So effective was the South Asian barrage that those on the *Sea Lion* soon were on the defensive. Hooked to the ship by a grappling line, the *Sea Lion* could not even beat a retreat. For fifteen minutes the one-sided battle raged until the tug could get away.

The South Asian victory was temporary. The Battle of Burrard Inlet provided H.H. Stevens with the ammunition he needed to enact a more formidable scheme to remove the *Komagata Maru*. Writing to Prime Minister Borden the next day, he proposed that the government authorize the use of the cruiser *H.M.C.S. Rainbow*, which was then in drydock in Victoria. Borden had "no confidence in the Rainbow" proposition, but agreed to make the attempt.[13] To keep the lid on the situation, Borden sent Martin Burrell, his Minister of Agriculture, to Vancouver to oversee the event. By July 20 the anticipated arrival of the *Rainbow* dominated the news in Vancouver, which began to take on a circus-like atmosphere.

The *Rainbow* made its appearance the next day and a contingency plan was quickly evolved. It was hoped that the intimidating presence of half of the Canadian Navy would coerce Gurdit Singh and the others to leave. As an incentive, the promised supplies of food and medicine, $4,000 worth in all, were put aboard on July 22. The temple committee was allowed on board to ease negotiations. The ship was supposed to leave the next day. If it did not, the plan was to overpower those on board and if necessary send them off in irons aboard another ship. The presence of the *Rainbow* proved a sufficient threat and the *Komagata Maru* set sail for the Far East on Thursday morning, July 23, 1914, after two months at anchor in Vancouver. Thousands of Vancouver residents cheered its departure.

THE AFTERMATH OF THE *KOMAGATA MARU*

In British Columbia, events surrounding the *Komagata Maru* were soon to eliminate many of the dozen or so leaders who had done so much to maintain community solidarity over ten years of struggle. This process began while the ship was still in port. As mentioned, there had been an unsuccessful attempt to smuggle arms into Canada from Washington. On July 17, Bhag Singh, Balwant Singh, Harnam Singh, and Mewa Singh crossed the border for this purpose, little imagining that each was soon to die for his revolutionary convictions. Once across, they met Taraknath Das in Sumas, Washington, who had come up from San Francisco to lend his support. They then proceeded to buy four handguns and several hundred rounds of ammunition at a local store. Mewa Singh then separated from the rest, only to be caught on the British Columbia side of the border with a concealed pistol and 400 rounds of ammunition. The others were arrested in Sumas by the American authorities.

The immigration officials reacted quickly. While none of those caught in the United States had broken the law, Harnam Singh had previously been deported from Canada. He was held and eventually deported to the Far East. Mewa Singh's position was more serious since he had been caught with a concealed weapon in Canada. Hopkinson used this to try to get Mewa to implicate Bhag Singh and Balwant Singh in a plot to smuggle arms to the *Komagata Maru*. Thus, Mewa Singh was kept isolated in jail until Hopkinson extracted from him what he claimed to be a secret confession.[14] In the document, Mewa Singh supposedly outlined their foray into Washington, claiming to be along by accident. He was said to have stated that "as far as I am aware and from what I could understand it was the intention of these people to try to convey those weapons to the Komagata Maru."[15] As he claimed, if such a confession were to become public, his life would be in danger; it never did, for subsequent reasons that had little to do with Hopkinson's compassion. Mewa Singh was finally released upon payment of a $50 fine. Ironically, the fine was paid by the Vancouver Khalsa Diwan Society, whose leadership Hopkinson may well have just forced him to implicate.

Shortly after the departure of the *Komagata Maru* and the outbreak of World War I, the return of Ghadar revolutionaries to India became a mass phenomenon. The war fitted in exactly with Ghadar revolutionary plans, for the British indeed began removing troops from India. The first to leave were British units, but Indian troops soon followed as the war consumed a generation of British men in short order.

The flow of returnees began through San Francisco but quickly started up in Vancouver. In early August forty men applied to the immigration office in Vancouver for the registering-out certificates that were necessary for return to Canada. The head of the local immigration office discovered that they were revolutionaries whose way was being paid by the Khalsa Diwan Society. Despite the fact that they were Canadian citizens, he suggested that they not be granted registering-out certificates; the Superintendent of Immigration concurred, but suggested that they be allowed to buy tickets.[16] That way, they could not return to Canada, thereby solving part of British Columbia's "Hindoo problem."

Prospective returnees had initial difficulty in securing tickets on Japanese ships due to the German submarine threat and were forced to turn to the hated CPR, which they associated with the Canadian government. By August 19, 160 were attempting to secure tickets from reluctant CPR agents in Vancouver. Mit Singh and Sohan Lal negotiated with the CPR officialdom in Montreal and got the tickets released. The first brigade of forty left for India on August 22, twenty-six from Vancouver and fourteen from Victoria. As with those who would follow thereafter, these forty were searched for arms and their names taken as a precondition of sailing. By mid-October, 110 had left British Columbia. This movement of returnees from British Columbia and California inspired many émigrés living in the Far East and Southeast Asia to go with them.[17]

The British India government countered with the Ingress to India Ordinance of September 5, 1914. This regulation allowed the government a free hand in dealing with returnees during the war. By March, 1915, the government knew of 3,200 Punjabi émigrés who had arrived in India, of whom 200 were jailed for the duration and 700 were confined to their villages. Ships arriving with returnees, such as the *Tosa Maru* that docked in Calcutta on October 28, faced a wall of army and police officers. In this case, 173 returnees were met by two companies of Royal Fusiliers, 200 armed police, and 500 native police. All of them were jailed and about 100 were kept in prison.[18] Ghadar supporters quickly shifted to travelling in smaller groups to less obvious ports, such as Colombo in Ceylon.

The *Komagata Maru* incident itself was by no means closed when the ship steamed away from Vancouver. On the same day the *Komagata Maru* left port the governor of Hong Kong requested that the ship's passengers not be allowed to land there, citing fears that they would be "too seditious" to be easily dealt with. When they arrived in Yokohama and then in Kobe, they learned that they were not to be allowed to land in Singapore, either; rather, they would be sent to India, where most of them no longer resided. In Yokohama they were met by Sohan Singh Bhakna, a Ghadar leader who had been sent there to provide them with arms and literature. On September 29 the *Komagata Maru* arrived at Budge Budge, fourteen miles south of Calcutta. Under the powers of the Ingress to India Ordinance it was planned to send everyone to Punjab, where it would be decided who would be detained and who would not. The 321 still on board were not told that this was their fate until all preparations were made. Once ashore, only the seventeen Moslem passengers initially agreed to board the train. The great majority of Sikhs wished to take the copy of the sacred Guru Granth Sahib, which had accompanied them on their travels, to the temple in Calcutta. While doing so they were met by a reinforcement detachment of armed police and a standoff ensued while troops were called in. In the early evening an attempt to extract Gurdit Singh from the crowd surrounding the Guru Granth Sahib provoked a serious riot. When it had ended twenty-six people were dead – twenty Sikhs, two European officers, two Indian police, and two local residents. Thirty-five people were seriously injured.[19] Twenty-eight Sikhs escaped, among them Gurdit Singh, who remained at large until 1921, when he turned himself in to the authorities.

The Budge Budge conflict was one of the most serious to occur in India in several years. Even by the account of the Committee of Inquiry set up to examine the affair, the great majority were killed or wounded either by the police or by the army troops; the latter contingent fired 177 shots alone. When news of the event made its way to Punjab and Canada, it produced a strong anti-British reaction. As the Lieutenant Governor of Punjab put it:

The incident showed the defiant and highly explosive temper of the returning Sikhs. It was distorted by unscrupulous agitators in the Punjab and the Ghadar agents abroad into a gratuitous attack by an oppressive Government on unoffending Sikhs. In this form it was presented to the thousands of Sikhs now on their way back from America and the Far East, and thus it gave a powerful stimulus to Ghadar propaganda already at work among them.[20]

While the *Komagata Maru* and the first wave of returning revolutionaries were making their way back to India, a series of spectacular events rocked the South Asian community in British Columbia. The *Komagata Maru* incident was the final straw in the rising hatred against the small group of informers in the employ of Hopkinson. By then they had incurred the wrath of both the revolutionaries and deeply religious Sikhs who felt that their spying activities violated the spirit of the *Khalsa*. On August 17, 1914, Harnam Singh vanished, only to be found murdered at the end of the month.[21] He had been an underling of Bela Singh, one of Hopkinson's key informants. Shortly thereafter Arjan Singh, another Sikh in the employ of the government, was "accidentally" shot dead by Ram Singh.[22] Ram Singh was an elderly, religious man who had not been highly visible before this. He was later acquitted when tried for Arjan Singh's death.

Long before this trial, Bela Singh had reacted violently against the death of two compatriots. On September 5 the body of Arjan Singh was cremated. This was followed by an evening memorial service in the Vancouver temple in which about fifty people participated. Shortly thereafter, Bela Singh arrived and sat down behind Bhag Singh, who was leading the service. Twenty minutes later he began shooting, first at Bhag Singh and then at others. When he finished Bhag Singh and Battan Singh were mortally wounded. Seven others were also shot, including Sohan Lal, Jawallah Singh, Labh Singh, Dalip Singh, and Uttum Singh.[23] Bela Singh was arrested.

These acts enraged the community still further. Beyond the loss of those murdered and wounded, the event had occurred in the temple, which was considered so sacred that even non-Sikhs normally entered it with their shoes off and heads covered. A hundred Sikhs crowded into Bela Singh's inquest, where he was bound over for trial. The situation was exacerbated when Hopkinson spies Gunja Ram and Baboo Singh uncovered a Ghadar bomb-manufacturing operation in Victoria. Gurdit Singh Porhiar and Dalip Singh were arrested and the house of the deported Harnam Singh was searched. The former two were tried on September 24 and got four and two years in jail, respectively. During the trial Mit Singh and Hari Singh, the priest of the Victoria temple, were implicated but not tried.

As the October 21 date for Bela Singh's trial approached there was great concern among South Asians that he would be acquitted, despite his obvious guilt; no informer had yet been successfully prosecuted, although informers had been brought to court many times. This feeling increased when Hopkinson publicly stated that he would give evidence to substantiate Bela Singh's claim of self-defence. Rumours arose that Hopkinson would state that while disguised as a Sikh he had heard Bhag Singh plan to kill Bela Singh. [24]

Plans were made to ensure that Hopkinson would not triumph again. Hopkinson was to be assassinated. It would be a martyr's lot, for escape was unlikely. Either by lot or by volunteering, Mewa Singh was delegated to carry out the deed. [25] On the morning of Bela's trial, Mewa intercepted Hopkinson in the corridors of the Vancouver court house and shot him dead without saying a word. He then quietly surrendered.

Reaction to Hopkinson's death was quickly forthcoming. H.H. Stevens wrote to Prime Minister Borden suggesting the forcible mass deportation of all South Asians in Canada. [26] Mewa Singh was indicted on October 23 and his trial was set for October 30, with Hussain Rahim, Sohan Lal, Balwant Singh, and Kartar Singh charged as co-conspirators. Hopkinson was a local hero and was given a huge public funeral: a band, 200 police and firemen, and a crowd of 2,000-3,000 attended.

In such a climate, Mewa Singh's trial was a mere formality. He offered no defence, save for one of overriding morality. He had been outraged at Bela Singh's desecration of the temple and the fact that Bhag Singh's family were left alone. He claimed that he shot Hopkinson because the latter had brought the community so much grief. After a two-hour trial the jury deliberated only five minutes. Mewa Singh was convicted and sentenced to be hanged on January 11, 1915.

The white British Columbia population, outraged at Hopkinson's death, was not to be satisfied with retribution against Mewa Singh alone. Sohan Lal, who had been arrested for conspiracy, was tried and acquitted; the others were then released. Before that, he and H. Rahim had been indicted on a charge of attempted murder against Baboo Singh, an accomplice of Bela Singh. This charge also failed to produce a conviction because Baboo Singh gave perjured testimony against them. Public outrage even carried over to Bela Singh's subsequent trial for murder. Despite the overt and public nature of his crime, he was acquitted and set free, just as Mewa Singh had feared.

In the meantime, the imminent execution of Mewa Singh galvanized the local community to revolutionary action. Throughout his wait for death, Mewa Singh was visited by Mit Singh Pandori, who relayed his thoughts to the community and then to California. On the morning when Mewa Singh was hanged hundreds of South Asians assembled in the rain outside the New Westminster penitentiary to receive his body. From there it was ceremoniously taken to Fraser Mills for cremation.

Mewa Singh became a martyr in the classic Sikh mold. He struck out against a threat to his people and religion and was thereafter willing to pay the price for his actions. Within days of his death his last statement was circulated to every South Asian community on the Pacific Coast. In it, he claimed that:

> My religion does not teach me to bear enmity with anybody, no matter what class, creed or order he belongs to, nor had I any enmity with Hopkinson. I heard that he was oppressing my people very much. I made friendship with him through his best Hindu friend to find out the truth of what I heard. On finding out the fact, I – being a staunch Sikh – could no longer bear to see the wrong done both to my innocent countrymen and the Dominion of Canada. This is what led me to take Hopkinson's life and sacrifice my own life in order to lay bare the oppression exercised upon my innocent people through his influence in the eyes of the whole world. And I, performing the duty of a true Sikh and remembering the name of God, will proceed towards the scaffold with the same amount of pleasure as the hungry babe does towards its mother. I shall gladly put the rope around my neck thinking it to be a rosary of God's name. I am quite sure that God will take me into His blissful arms because I have not done this deed for my personal interest but to the benefit of both my people and the Canadian government.[27]

In Stockton, California, the last section of the Guru Granth Sahib was read in memorium, as was his wish. Every year thereafter a memorial service was held for Mewa Singh at the temple in Fraser Mills. The practice continues to this day at several British Columbia temples.

The deaths of Bhag Singh and Mewa Singh were but the beginning of a sequence of Ghadar-related events that would systematically dismantle the local leadership structure of South Asians in Canada. Teja Singh, Harnam Singh, and Bhagwan Singh had already left. G.D. Kumar had gone to Manila to promote Ghadar there. In late December of 1914 Balwant Singh and his family left Vancouver, supposedly bound for India. In actuality, he had been sent to Bangkok by the Ghadar Party. The plan was to use independent Siam as a base for smuggling arms into India. Not long afterwards, Sohan Lal left Vancouver on a similar mission to Burma, where he joined up with the previously deported Harnam Singh Sahri and Santokh Singh, a principal Ghadar organizer. As with many of Ghadar's initial overseas plans, these met with disaster. In Siam, Balwant Singh and four others were arrested and handed over to the British. In Burma, Sohan Lal and Harnam Singh were captured spreading Ghadarite propaganda among the Indian troops stationed there.[28]

Sohan Lal was kept in jail for a year and then hanged in February, 1916. Balwant Singh was tried and executed in the wake of the revolt of the 5th Light Infantry in Singapore. Harnam Singh was held until 1916, when he was tried in the Mandalay Conspiracy Case. So tenuous was the evidence that the court prosecutors asked the Canadian government to send someone to Burma to give evidence against him. Even so, Harnam

Singh was one of the seven Ghadarites hanged as a result of the trial. Other leaders left the community to support Ghadar elsewhere. In 1916, Taraknath Das was sent to Japan and Berlin, where he attempted to consolidate Ghadar's organization among South Asians there. Even Bela Singh was eventually removed from the scene; after several attempts on his life failed, he was jailed for a year for an assault on Lachman Singh. Thereafter, Bela Singh left for India, his passage paid for by the government.[29] Of the original leadership only Mit Singh Pandori, Hussain Rahim, and Sundar Singh remained in Canada by 1917.

Thereafter, a degree of stability began to develop among South Asians in Canada. The bitterness and factionalism that had arisen over revolutionary activity and government spying lessened after Hopkinson, his assistants, and so many revolutionaries were removed from the scene. Canada's entry into the war distracted the government from the issue of South Asian immigration and eventually led to full South Asian employment. The war also made it virtually impossible to challenge the immigration ban directly, inasmuch as a great deal of available shipping in the Pacific was reorganized to serve the war effort.

THE DEMISE OF GHADAR

In the meantime Ghadar was quickly losing momentum, the result of their disastrous revolutionary attempts overseas, internal organizational problems, and effective measures taken by the British to disrupt their operations in the United States. Despite the care with which the Indian government screened returnees, many Ghadarites made their way into India. They soon found that conditions were far from ripe for a revolution. They were few in number, without strong community support, poorly financed, and weakly organized. In contrast, the British had an efficient police and spy apparatus, control over the press, co-operation of the leadership of Punjab, and a certain sense of loyalty among the many Punjabis who had been in their employ. With the outbreak of hostilities in Europe virtually all the other Indian nationalist movements supported the British war effort.

Returnees were quickly reduced to raiding government offices, robbing rich government sympathizers, and attempting to talk the Indian regiments into revolt. None of these activities was successful, for the British secret police (Criminal Investigations Department) systematically infiltrated Ghadar. By mid-1915 the Ghadar revolution in India had been crushed. Two hundred ninety-one Ghadarites were sent to trial in a series of what became known as the Lahore Conspiracy cases. Of these, forty-two were sentenced to death, 114 were transported for life, ninety-three were imprisoned, and forty-two were acquitted.[30]

In California the British did what they could to disrupt Ghadar Party operations. They knew from the start that Ghadar had received considerable German financial aid, with which they had mounted several failed attempts to smuggle arms to India. Until the United States entered World War I it tolerated Ghadar, for there was strong American support for independence movements around the world. With the American declaration of war against Germany the United States government quickly arrested 124 Ghadarites, American sympathizers, and German consular officials for conspiracy to violate the neutrality of the United States.[31] After one of the longest and most expensive trials in American history, all but one defendant were found guilty. Taraknath Das, Bhagwan Singh, and Santok Singh were jailed.

The San Francisco conspiracy case severely disorganized Ghadar's activities in Canada and the Canadian authorities were able easily to contain the party's activities for the duration of the war.[32] Few Ghadar émigrés were let back into the country despite their Canadian citizenship. British offers to quiet the resulting discontent by sending "loyal" Sikh religious leaders to British Columbia proved unnecessary.

THE IMMIGRATION BATTLE RESUMED

In the meantime, the political climate surrounding the immigration issue had changed dramatically. With their army in India seriously reduced and with thousands of Indian soldiers fighting overseas, the British came to believe that limited South Asian immigration should be allowed into Canada to diffuse discontent in India. The Canadian government remained unwilling, but some change was inevitable. The first indications of it came from an unlikely source – W. Scott, the Superintendent of Immigration. Writing to the Canadian Undersecretary of State for External Affairs on January 7, 1916, he first suggested that the wives and dependent children of South Asian Canadian men be allowed in.[33]

Scott's suggestion had little impact, but it augmented similar suggestions from India and the local community. In late 1915, Sundar Singh once more went to the East to rally support from the Canadian Conference of Friends and the Ontario Women's Christian Temperance Union. In late 1916 he formed the Canada India Committee in Toronto, which published several pamphlets on the treatment of South Asians in Canada.[34] Kartar Singh Hundle augmented these by the short-lived Toronto newspaper *Canada and India*.

Scott continued to press for a change in the regulations. For example, on February 1, 1916, he supported a petition of Kapoor Singh Siddoo to get his family admitted, using the case as a pretext to review the policy of exclusion.[35] He also told local officials in British Columbia to cease harassing legitimate South Asian Canadian residents at border crossings and tried to stop the CPR from denying South Asians passage to Canada. Beginning in 1917 Scott began to give his assent to a series of petitions from Reverend W.L. Macrae of Victoria for the admission of the families of "loyal" South Asians.[36]

Still, the most substantial factor in changing the regulations was external pressure, as exemplified in the Imperial War Conferences of 1917 and 1918. At the conference in 1917, Robert Borden argued that Canadian public opinion was against such a change but that he would take it under advisement.[37] In November, the Minister of the Interior first suggested a fully bilateral immigration policy between Canada and India allowing the immigration of families and the free flow of tourists in either direction.[38] No action was taken by the government until the Imperial War Conference of 1918. At that conference, Sir S.P. Sinha, representing India, sponsored a resolution including the provision that the wives and children of South Asian Canadians be allowed into Canada. Canada accepted the resolution, which was carried on July 24, 1918.

This was not the victory for South Asian Canadians that it appeared to be, for the Canadian government delayed the implementation of the resolution as long as possible. No families would be allowed into the country for the duration of the war, and the government did not enact the required Order-in-Council until Borden was once more faced by a determined Indian delegation in Paris, in March, 1919. He then telegraphed home a request for an appropriate Order to be framed.[39] On March 26, 1919, PC 641 was passed by the Privy Council, eleven years after the ban was first put in place.

Scott was told not to give the new regulation any publicity and the means of legally bringing one's family to Canada were still not resolved; at first, no registering-out certificates were issued to husbands who wanted to leave Canada to get their wives. Thereafter, Canada asserted that it would accept wives and children as legitimate only if they were acknowledged as such by officials in India. According to the plan outlined in an Order-in-Council (PC 2498) of December 24, 1919, an immigrant in Canada was to apply for his family. The papers were then to be sent to the appropriate district officer in India, who would interview the family. The papers would then be sent back to Canada. If approved, word would then be sent for the family to start out. Only eleven dependants were allowed in between 1914 and 1922 and a practical procedure to register wives and children was not put into place until June 12, 1924.

Consequently, the end of the war did not produce peace in race relations in British Columbia. Community members continued to press the government on the family issue until its final resolution. In addition, they supported another immigration cause: the inability of South Asian Canadian citizens to return to Canada. This fight would continue well into the 1920's.

POSTSCRIPT OF AN ERA

As South Asian Canadians moved into their third decade in this country they surveyed a land in which for them much had changed while much remained the same. Time and tribulation had winnowed their numbers but had produced a community with a strong commitment to life in Canada. Those who remained were sojourners no longer. Their goals, resources, and, indeed, many of their life experiences were inextricably tied up with Canada. In the midst of hostility, rejection, and discrimination they had found a place of their own, carving household, job, and community out of very hard stone. By 1920 they were to begin to lay the final part of this foundation – family life.

At the same time, it was not a peaceful twenty years, nor one of which Canada can be proud; the early history of South Asians was character-ized more by heroics and suffering than by happiness. South Asians bore the full brunt of racial ideologies, social isolation, economic subordina-tion, and political disenfranchisement. In these matters, the year 1920 saw South Asians in much the same situation as in 1908, save that they were now Canadian citizens – citizens with few rights in a country that still did not want or respect them. If they were "Canadians in the mak-ing," they had become so only through their own efforts.

It could be argued that the racial situation the South Asians shared with the Chinese and Japanese was a British Columbia aberration, un-characteristic of Canada at the time. This is only partially true. South Asian Canadians did live primarily in the province and the practical liabilities they incurred there did not exist in the rest of the country. The same could not be said of ideas of race and racial exclusion. British Co-lumbia racial stereotypes differed little except in intensity from those in the rest of Canada, the United States, and Britain. Neither the Canadian nor the British government used its influence to lessen the liabilities in-curred by South Asians in British Columbia. Canada steadfastly held to its South Asian immigration ban and would extend it in 1923 to the Chinese; the Dominion Elections Act of 1920 retained the provision that no one barred on account of race from voting provincially could vote federally; during World War I, South Asians were not accepted for military service.[40] Liberal sentiment in the East was never strong enough to force a single significant change in federal policy toward South Asians.

For those twenty years, Canada's approach to South Asians was that they were Indians in Canada rather than Indo-Canadians, and for the most part the implementation of this idea in discriminatory word and deed guaranteed its validity. Rejected by others, South Asians turned toward their own for security, assistance, and self-definition. Bridges to other Canadians were consequently weak. After two decades in Canada most South Asian Canadians had few non-South Asian friends, knew only a little English, and had little familiarity with most Canadian in-stitutions. By 1920, South Asians were no longer feared, but they re-mained confined to a sharply bounded racial enclave. It would take another twenty years for them to escape from it.

NOTES

1. For a biography of Har Dayal, see Brown, *Har Dayal.*
2. R. Borden to the Governor General, June 22, 1914, PAC, RG 7, G 21, v. 205.
3. Unsigned declaration, December 27, 1913, *ibid.*, v. 204.
4. Secretary of State for the Colonies to the Governor General, March 4, 1914, PAC, RG 76, #536999, part 9.
5. *Ghadar*, November 15, 1913, as translated in K. Singh and S. Singh, *Ghadar 1915*, p. 20.
6. Governor of Hong Kong to L. Harcourt, April 8, 1914, PAC, RG 7, G 21, v. 211. Ted Ferguson, *A White Man's Country: An Exercise in Canadian Prejudice* (Toronto, 1975), and Johnson, *The Voyage of the Komagata Maru*, deal extensively with the *Komagata Maru* incident. See also Baba Gurdit Singh, *Voyage of the Komagata Maru or: India's Slavery Abroad* (Calcutta, n.d.); *Komagata Maru* Commission of Inquiry (1914).
7. For example, a placard stolen on May 26 from the Vancouver temple by informers working for the immigration officials exhorted the community to pull together to support those on the *Komagata Maru* (PAC, RG 7, G 21, v. 211). Inasmuch as letters flowed continuously between the temples in Hong Kong and Vancouver, the Vancouver community knew about the *Komagata Maru* well before the local immigration officials did.
8. In particular, see *Vancouver Province*, June 2, 1914, p. 1.
9. Minutes of a meeting June 21, 1914, at Dominion Hall (H.H. Stevens Papers, HH-16). At this point in time most of the local leadership were also members of the Socialist Party of Canada.
10. *Komagata Maru* passengers to the Governor General, June 25, 1914, PAC, RG 7, G 21, v. 211.
11. Gurdit Singh to the Governor General, July 8, 1914, PAC, RG 7, G 21, v. 211.
12. Note on the Hindu Revolutionary Movement in Canada, March 21, 1919, PAC, RG 76, #536999, part 11.
13. H.H. Stevens to R. Borden, July 18, 1914, PAC, RG 7, G 21, v. 211; R. Borden to J.D. Hazen, July 19, 1914, *ibid.*
14. Statement of Mewa Singh, n.d., *ibid.*, v. 205. The accuracy and validity of this statement is problematical because it was secured by Hopkinson, written in English, and unsigned.
15. *Ibid.*
16. M. Reid to W. Scott, August 18, 1914; W. Scott to M. Reid, August 18, 1914; W. Scott to M. Reid, August 19, 1914, PAC, RG 76, #536999, R.O., part 1.
17. For example, the *Korea* left San Francisco on August 29 with sixty-two returnees on board. By the time it left Hong Kong the number had swelled to over 300. Mathur, *Indian Revolutionary Movements*, p. 75.

18. Allahabad *Pioneer Mail*, November 6, 1914; Sir Michael O'Dwyer, *India as I Knew It, 1885-1925* (London, 1926), pp. 194-5.
19. Report of the *Komagata Maru* Commission of Inquiry (1914).
20. O'Dwyer, *India as I Knew It*, p. 194.
21. This is not the same Harnam Singh caught smuggling arms from Washington.
22. *Vancouver Province*, September 1, 1914, p. 1; *ibid.*, October 21, 1914, p. 10. He was, however, on the Vancouver temple committee and could not possibly have been sympathetic to Ram Singh and his faction.
23. See Bhag Singh's and Bahan Singh's deathbed testimony in W. Hopkinson to W. Cory, September 18, 1914, PAC, RG 7, G 21, v. 205.
24. This story was made much of by immigration officials after the fact. See Ferguson, *A White Man's Country*, pp. 157-60. Those pioneers still living claim that Hopkinson's spoken Punjabi was so poor that he could not possibly get away with such a ruse; even in disguise he would be instantly recognized in such a small community.
25. Pioneers consistently claim that lots were drawn, and this cannot be discounted. On the other hand, Mewa Singh was not active in leadership circles and it is hard to see how he would have been included except at his own request. Whether or not his supposed prior confession was authentic, it was certain to become public at the trial and thus Mewa had a strong motive. He had $385 on his person when he was arrested (*Vancouver Province*, October 22, 1914, p. 1).
26. H.H. Stevens to R. Borden, October 21, 1914, PAC, RG 76, #536999, part 9.
27. K. Singh and S. Singh, *Ghadar 1915*, pp. 30-1.
28. See Sohan Singh Josh, *Hindustan Gadar Party: A Short History*, 2 vols. (New Delhi, 1977-78), for the most detailed account available of Ghadar activities in Southeast Asia.
29. L.A. Jollife to W. Cory, June 6, 1916, PAC, RG 7, G 21, v. 207. Bela Singh paid dearly for his role as a police informer. Even in the late 1920's a distant relative of Bela's visiting him in his home village noted that Bela was terribly afraid of something. He slept in several different places each night and always carried a pistol. His fear was well founded. In 1934 Bela Singh was assassinated by two Sikh revolutionaries.
30. K. Singh and S. Singh, *Ghadar 1915*, pp. 40-7. Of those sentenced to death, most were imprisoned for life. Nevertheless, about seventy-five people were executed in India and Southeast Asia as a result of Ghadar activities.
31. Josh, *Hindustan Gadar Party*; Joan M. Jensen, "The 'Hindu Conspiracy': A Reassessment," *Pacific Historical Review*, 48, 1 (1980), pp. 65-84; Giles T. Brown, "The Hindu Conspiracy and the Neutrality of the United States" (M.A. thesis, University of California, 1941); G.T. Brown, "The Hindu Conspiracy, 1914-1917," *Pacific Historical Review*, 17 (1948), pp. 299-300; D.K. Dignan, "Hindu Conspiracy in Anglo-

Indian Relations," *Pacific Historical Review*, 40 (1971), pp. 57-77; Alan Raucher, "American Anti-Imperialism and the Pro-Indian Movement, 1900-1932," *Pacific Historical Review*, 42 (1974), pp. 8-110. The trial records are on microfilm. See Franz Bopp, defendant, in the Bibliography.

32. For example, none of those applying in July, 1919, for readmission who had left in October, 1914, on the *Tenyo Maru* were allowed into Canada (M. Reid to W. Cory, August 4, 1919, PAC, RG 76, R.O., part 2).

33. W. Scott to Sir Joseph Pope, January 7, 1916, *ibid.*, #536999, part 9.

34. See the following publications of the Canada India Committee: *A Call for Canadian Justice* (Toronto, 1915); *The Hindu Case* (Toronto, 1915); *India's Appeal to Canada or: An Account of Hindu Immigration to the Dominion* (Toronto, 1916).

35. W. Scott to W. Cory, February 1, 1916, PAC, RG 76, #536999, part 9. Kapoor Singh Siddoo was to become one of the foremost South Asian Canadian entrepreneurs of the 1920's and 1930's.

36. The families of Bishan Singh, Hackman Singh, Sohan Singh, and Amar Singh were let in this way.

37. Imperial War Conference, 1917, Minutes, pp. 117-20.

38. Minister of the Interior to W. Cory, November 12, 1917, PAC, RG 76, #536999, part 10.

39. Robert Borden, March 16, 1919, *ibid.*, part 11.

40. Chapter 46, 10-11, George V, July 6, 1920 (the Dominion Elections Act); PC 1459 of June 12, 1918, barred South Asians from enlisting in the Canadian armed forces.

PART TWO

The Quiet Years, 1919-1947

FIVE

Consolidation

The decade after World War I brought increasing stability and security to South Asians in Canada. Ghadar Party emigration prior to and during the war had drained the community of activists, and vocal protests about anti-South Asian discrimination subsided. No substantial attack on either the immigration ban or discriminatory British Columbia legislation was to develop again until the late 1930's. Consequently, the only new blood the community received was through the 300 or so wives and children who arrived from India during the decade. In essence, the decade was one of growth and development limited by paternalistic racial subordination. To the extent that they did not challenge discriminatory custom and law, they enjoyed a considerable degree of independence and self-determination. South Asian Canadians used their carefully delimited freedom to consolidate their familial, economic, and community organization. Energy used for political protest in the previous decade was directed toward turning Canada the host into Canada the home.

IMMIGRATION

Canadian immigration regulations and their interpretation continued to affect the structure of the community profoundly throughout the 1920's. As such, immigration remained an important issue, though in a much more muted form than before. The first of a series of immigration difficulties involved South Asian Canadians who wished to return to Canada from India. From the earliest days of South Asian settlement in Canada there had been a steady flow of immigrants back and forth between India and Canada, which had been much augmented by Ghadar Party activities during the war years. Many found it impossible to return to Canada during the war due to the unavailability of shipping. Thereafter, they found that the CPR and other shipping lines plying between Hong Kong and Canada refused passage to all South Asians whether they had Canadian residency or not. The Vancouver Khalsa Diwan Society claimed that the CPR would not sell tickets to naturalized South Asian Canadians even when they offered to post a cash bond to protect the company from bearing the cost of their possible deportation.[1]

In 1920 the Canadian government decided that any South Asian Canadian outside the country who did not hold a registering-out certificate had lost domicile and would not be allowed to sail to Canada.[2] This was done despite the registering-out requirement being an *ad hoc* procedure that originally had no support in law or in the immigration regulations. In addition, the government banned the return of any suspected revolutionaries. No proof of revolutionary activity was required. Shortly before, an Order-in-Council had been passed to withhold passport privileges from "undesirables" wishing to go to India.[3] Returning immigrants continued to arrive in Hong Kong throughout the early 1920's only to find their way to Canada barred. From 1921 on, the government stiffened entry further by setting three years as the maximum time a South Asian Canadian could be out of the country without losing domicile, registering-out certificate or not. The majority of men who had returned to their families in India prior to 1920 were never allowed back into Canada and were lost forever to the community.

Government policy was similarly restrictive about the entry of non-immigrant South Asians. Government assurances were given as early as 1920 that South Asian students were thereafter free to enter Canada for university study, but this was discouraged in practice; in 1924, Vancouver immigration officials were informally requiring that a $1,000 cash bond be posted by any prospective South Asian who wished to enter Canada for the purpose of study. There were then no more than ten South Asian university students in the whole country. In addition, well-educated South Asian visitors were occasionally banned from entering Canada as late as 1929.

The ingenuity of government immigration policy was briefly taxed by the question of whether Anglo-Indians were to be considered British or South Asians for the purposes of immigration. The group in question was composed of the children of British fathers and Indian mothers and their descendants. In 1924 it was decided that an Anglo-Indian with a British father could immigrate, while a person with a British mother and an Indian father could not. A similar sexist strategy was used to resolve the difficulty posed by prospective British immigrants with South Asian spouses.[4]

The most important issue by far continued to be the immigration of South Asian wives and children. Although allowed by the Order-in-Council of 1919, relatively few were able to overcome the practical hurdles involved. An adequate system of registering families in India was not worked out until 1924-25, and many men were so concerned that they would not be let back into Canada that they were reluctant to go to India to get their families. During the five-year period between fiscal 1914-15 and 1920-21 only one South Asian family member was allowed into Canada. As one of the first post-war immigrants remembers,

> When my father returned with me after World War I it was very difficult to get to Canada because of the immigration regulations. Even after being approved to come in India we spent four months in Hong Kong trying to get tickets on a ship to Canada. Many others had been stuck there for a long time. When I arrived, I was surprised at the "community" because it was almost all men. In 1921 I knew of only three Sikh women in Vancouver. For a while, I think I was the only Sikh in grade school in Vancouver.

Thereafter, the number slowly increased.

TABLE 2

South Asian Immigration, 1920-21 to 1929-30

Fiscal Year	Adult Males*	Adult Females	Children	Total
1920-21	7	2	1	10
1921-22	5	4	4	13
1922-23	12	5	4	21
1923-24	25	11	4	40
1924-25	21	14	11	46
1925-26	6	18	39	63
1926-27	6	19	37	62
1927-28	2	25	29	56
1928-29	4	25	24	53
1929-30	2	21	35	58
TOTAL	90	144	188	422

* Of adult men allowed to immigrate, some were the children of legal immigrants who were admitted because they were unable to come while still legal dependants; a few of the others entered under the special exceptions of PC 182 of January 31, 1923, which otherwise banned all Asians from entering Canada. The latter had to fulfil the requirement of PC 715 of April 12, 1922, that they have $250 on arrival.
SOURCE: Stanislaw Andracki, "The Immigration of Orientals into Canada with Special Reference to Chinese" (Ph.D thesis, McGill University, 1958).

This feeble immigrant flow in no way compensated for the enormous losses to emigration between 1911 and 1921; in 1911 there were 2,342 South Asians in Canada and 2,292 in British Columbia, while in 1921 there were only 1,016 in the country and 951 in the province. Virtually all of them were Sikhs. The population would not reach the 2,000 figure again until the late 1940's.

Moreover, the continuous journey restriction was making the age and sex distribution of the community more and more unbalanced. By 1925 about 90 per cent of the population was made up of men who were forty or older; because most adult children could not immigrate there were only a handful of young men in the community. There were no more than forty women, all of whom were married to immigrant men. On average, one man lived with his family for every thirty men who did not. Even by 1930 there were fewer than 200 South Asian families in all of Canada.

Because of its effects on family and community life, the continuous passage restriction remained a bitter reminder of Canadian injustice all through the 1920's. Even though anti-South Asian racism in British Columbia declined substantially throughout the decade, Canadian government opinion about banning Asian immigration hardened. In 1923 the government finally subjected the Chinese to an exclusionary Act even more restrictive than that affecting South Asians. The Japanese were beginning to be squeezed out of the salmon-fishing industry that they had done so much to develop, and the federal government successfully got the Japanese to limit still further the number of their nationals leaving Japan for Canada. No changes in the immigration regulations concerning South Asians could be expected in such a climate.

CHANGES IN HOUSEHOLD AND COMMUNITY LIFE

The arrival of immigrant families had a great impact on South Asian community life. Still, one should not forget that for most South Asian Canadians in the 1920's family life remained an unrealizable ideal. The multi-male households developed in the 1910's remained the normative type.

They did not, however, remain static in form or personnel. Time brought an increasing sophistication to these all-male households, at least where economic and social conditions allowed it. In urban contexts these households became closer knit and more stable. Friendship, common origin, and common experience made it possible for them to fulfil many of the functions of families.

As more Sikhs became permanently involved in the woods industries, this shifted a high proportion of men into lumber and other rural work camps. There, men without their families generally preferred to live together in worker barracks provided by the company. As always, those who were unemployed, sick, or too old to work were routinely supported by the community.

These households were like kin groups in other ways as well. Constant association with other household members and isolation from other Canadians were a powerful force for cultural retention – so much so that South Asian Canadians were losing track of some changes occurring in India; they remained Indian men of the turn of the century, not of the

1920's. Nevertheless, these households effectively provided individuals with a sense of place and security. They were sociocultural fortresses, out of which individuals forayed into a hostile world they did not fully understand.

These households were extremely efficient economically. Even though individual Sikhs were willing to devote a substantial amount of their income to good food, their total costs for food and housing together in the 1920's averaged between ninety cents and a dollar a day.[5] This was considerably less than single Chinese or Japanese paid for room and board. Because some men still harboured the thought that they might even yet return to their families in India, they were extremely frugal. Sikh clothing costs in the mid-1920's were estimated at no more than $60 a year. South Asian households spent the bare minimum on furnishings – they had only the bare essentials of beds, tables, and a few chairs. Recreational costs were minimal, save for those who drank heavily. The only other expenses of consequence were contributions to charitable and political causes and to the maintenance of local Sikh temples. By 1925, South Asians were able to spend less of their hard-earned money on everyday necessities than any other group in British Columbia with the exception of native people.

Only a few social and psychological problems arose from this Spartan life and the hostile environment in which they lived. Loneliness remained a great problem. Heavy drinking became common by the 1920's and some individuals were consumed by it. Most heavy drinking was carried on in a quiet, private fashion and arrests for it were almost unheard of. Community conflict and factionalism remained prevalent.

Life in the growing number of families was soon quite different from that in multi-male households. Sikhs in India at that time would likely have lived in extended households made up of elderly parents, married sons and their families, unmarried daughters, and perhaps one or two other relatives. The Canadian immigration regulations made these household arrangements impossible. The only candidates for immigration were a man's wife and under-age children. Of necessity, early South Asian Canadian families were variations on the nuclear family. Many resulted from single men returning to India in the early 1920's to get married. Almost equal numbers were composed of couples who had married prior to the husband embarking for Canada between 1904 and 1908; as the result of their long separation most of these either had no children or had children who were fifteen or older. Occasionally, men brought over their adolescent sons but not the rest of their families. Some illegally brought in their nephews or their friends' sons, claiming them as their own.

These new households brought many challenges. For example, what were to be appropriate roles for husband and wife, parent and child in Canada? Husband-wife relations tended to conform most closely to Indian models. In fact, South Asian Canadian wives inherited many of the

75

difficulties of women in India with few compensating benefits. Husbands worked at wage labour in the cash economy while wives worked at home. Wives continued to defer to their husbands on important issues. They had even fewer opportunities to explore their new homeland than their husbands and most learned little English and acquired few Canadian acquaintances. At the same time, they lost the rich social community they had in India – the hundreds of friends, relatives, in-laws, and acquaintances with whom they would have associated on a day-by-day basis. Their families became their world and their isolation was often profound:

> My mother had it hard when I was growing up. We had a small rented farm in the Okanagan Valley, where there were then very few Sikhs. I made friends with Canadians at school. Since I knew English fluently I often talked with neighbours, as did my father. Mother wasn't so lucky. She never learned English well enough to communicate easily, so never really had any good Canadian friends. There were so few other Sikh families around that she had little contact with them either. For her, the family was everything.

In many respects, relations between parents and children developed along lines followed by other immigrant groups and faced a similar challenge: as the leading edge of community destiny, were their children to be oriented toward Canadian society and culture or toward their own traditional values and practices? As with so many immigrant parents, Sikh parents wanted it both ways. They were aware of the value of education and occupational training and were not closed-minded about Canadian cultural practices. Consequently, they sent their children to public school, and in the late 1920's the whole community was proud that a few Sikhs were attending the University of British Columbia.[6] They allowed their children to wear European clothes and permitted their sons to dispense with wearing turbans and their hair uncut. Nevertheless, they hoped that these accommodations to Canadian life would have little effect on their children's identities and values; they wished their children to conform to their world, yet they allowed them access to another one. By the late 1920's children lived in a dual universe, moving between their parents' world and that of their Canadian peers. Increasingly, the second generation became middlemen between two cultures. Those children of marriageable age had all been born and raised in India, so the question of intermarriage between Sikh children and white Canadians was not yet an important concern. Throughout the 1920's and 1930's Canadian Sikhs looked to India for their spouses.

Even after twenty years in Canada few South Asians had many Canadian friends. Neither did they often participate in Canadian social institutions or organizations. One cause for this is obvious: other Canadians actively isolated themselves from South Asians. However, this social isolation was also partially a function of Sikh attitudes about themselves and others. Sikh identity remained very strong and it led people to orient themselves to the community. As with any group with such a strong identity, the result was a certain degree of ethnic chauvinism on the part of the Sikhs – suspicion of others and a devaluation of what they did. This chauvinistic tendency was amplified by their continued rejection by other Canadians. This is well illustrated by the far higher rates of assimilation and acculturation of Sikhs in California. Involved chiefly in farming, they were not so frequently isolated by their neighbours, many of whom were of Mexican origin. There were many marriages between Mexicans and Sikhs in California by the end of the 1920's.[7]

During this time of continuing social isolation, ties to India remained strong. Letters flowed back and forth, keeping people informed of marriages, deaths, births, family problems, and successes. After Canadian immigration officials became more sure that the immigration ban would not be seriously challenged it became far easier to visit India with some hope that one would be able to return to Canada. Thus, by the late 1920's there was a continual movement of men to India and back; women rarely travelled alone. Men returned to see their families, to get married, or just to visit their places of birth. Here are two examples:

> My father returned to India twice before World War I. When war broke out he could not get back to Canada. He and the rest of us came to British Columbia in the early 1920's and stayed until the depression. Out of work, my father decided that we should return to India, where he owned some land. We stayed there for several years, then returned in 1933. The rest of the family came back in 1935.

> Father was already married in 1906 when he came to Canada. He did not return to see my mother until 1925. He had a son then, who later died. He went back to Canada in 1927. In 1930, my mother and cousin arrived; my father got his nephew into the country by claiming that he was actually his son.

ECONOMIC GROWTH AND CHANGE

The 1920's saw many changes in the economic situation of South Asians in Canada. First, there arose a small entrepreneurial class, chiefly in the various woods industries. Second, there was a dramatic occupational concentration in the lumber mills, with a resultant increase in South Asian living standards. Third, there was a geographical fluidity, as people moved to where good jobs were available. Finally, there was a slight broadening of the occupational base into farming.

By the outbreak of World War I many South Asians were already working in the woods industries. Because the actual logging operation was a chosen domain of whites, most South Asians wound up in the lumber and shingle mills, where they were at first restricted to manual labour. It was inevitable that attempts would be made to break out of these limitations. As early as 1908 a few men were selling scrap wood as home heating fuel in Victoria. This wood would have otherwise been burned at the mills and could be had for a nominal fee. All that was required was a cart or truck and minimal facility with English. This entrepreneurial niche was quickly developed by South Asians, who soon became a familiar sight on Vancouver and Victoria streets. By 1927 there were twenty-one South Asian fuel dealers in the Lower Mainland and about sixty in the province. One of them, Sohan Brothers of Burnaby, owned thirty fuel trucks. Sikhs maintained a strong presence in the fuel business right up to the late 1950's, when the availability of cheaper alternative fuels led to its demise. Most fuel dealerships were very small, typically involving a single truck and one or two men. Because of its low capital costs it was an easy business to get into and perhaps 10 per cent of working men were involved in it by 1930, primarily as owner-operators.

The other major South Asian move followed naturally from their heavy involvement as lumber workers. In 1914-16 there began the lease, purchase, and operation of mills and logging camps. Seven small mills were bought or leased by South Asians in the Fraser Valley, chiefly near Abbotsford and Chiliwack. Each was controlled by several people in partnership – about forty people in all.[8] Owners worked alongside others, sharing in the profits rather than receiving a wage.

By the end of the war some of the mills purchased did not have enough local wood available to continue production. Other mill managers lost their leases. Between 1916 and 1923 most of these mills were sold, the owners moving to Vancouver Island where timber was more accessible. Soon the East India Lumber Company at Ladysmith and the Mayo Lumber Company near Duncan were in full operation. Other mills sprang up in Coombs and Barnet and were soon complemented by a half-dozen logging camps.[9] By 1930, the South Asian-run Kapoor Lumber Company at Barnet employed about 350 men, one-third of whom were South Asian.[10] Mayo Mills was equally successful, employing seventy-three whites, 181 Chinese, ninety-seven South Asians, and forty-one Japanese in the same year. The other mills owned by South Asians were very small, typically employing only ten to twenty workers.

The rise of these mills and logging camps significantly aided the development of South Asian communities on Vancouver Island. Communities there were founded as early as in Vancouver but had always been smaller, closer knit, and perhaps a bit less involved in the major social issues of the day. Many of the early immigrants who went there settled in Victoria, while others mostly went to the Nanaimo area. Railway work was important, especially because well-paying alternatives at first were largely lacking. The economic possibilities were substantially better on the mainland, so that fewer than 250 South Asians lived on Vancouver Island in 1920. With the rise of the lumber industry there in the 1920's this Vancouver Island community soon equalled that around Vancouver in wealth and influence. By 1930 the economic elite, such as

Kapoor Singh Siddoo and Mayo Singh, were by far the most visible community leaders, partially replacing the revolutionary leadership lost during the war.

These leaders were instrumental in closing the gap between South Asians and the host society. In addition to their extensive involvement in community affairs, they had an increasing impact on non-South Asians. Mayo Singh became well known for his philanthropy, especially toward handicapped children and the hospital in Victoria; it is said that whenever a South Asian child was born there he paid the entire hospital's expenses for the day. Both of Kapoor Singh's daughters became medical doctors, who later founded hospitals in India. Prominent South Asians aided also in the social integration of the community, for in their dealings with others they earned high marks for honesty and reliability.

> I would say that Kapoor Singh and Mayo Singh were the driving forces in our getting into the lumber business right from the start. They weren't the first to own mills, but they were the first to make it permanent. Mill work was a rough business, and in those days conditions were pretty bad everywhere. Even so, Kapoor and Mayo were generally better to their workers than most. They tried not to discriminate against employees because of their race, and in good times had mixed work forces. They also supported local schools and temples.

During the 1920's South Asians also made a tentative move into farming. Virtually all of the pioneers had extensive experience with a very complex system of agriculture, but a lack of labour and capital severely limited their ability to farm in Canada. There were few families, and the option of the family farm was therefore not open to them. In the early 1920's there were only a few South Asian family dairy farms located in the Fraser Valley, all of them on rented land. A couple of others had been established on Vancouver Island. By the late 1920's the number had increased to about forty, some of which were run by partnerships of three or four men.

Farming was never to involve many people until the 1970's, but even in the early years it acted as a vehicle for people moving to new places. A few Sikhs settled near Kelowna as early as 1909, and twenty years later one would have found about a half dozen farms between there and Kamloops. [11] By then a few Sikhs had begun farming in Alberta, one family in Glenmore district, three men near Lethbridge, and a few others around Medicine Hat. [12]

In overview, South Asian entrepreneurial activities were well developed by the 1920's, especially in light of the small size of the community and the disabilities they faced. Already, by 1923, it was estimated that South Asians in British Columbia owned or operated a substantial number of businesses.

TABLE 3

South Asian Businesses in British Columbia, 1923

Type of Business	Number
Logging Camps	7
Lumber Companies	6
Shingle Factories	2
Grocery Stores	2
Fuel Dealerships	60
Farms	25
TOTAL	102

SOURCE: Rajani Kant Das, *Hindustanee Workers on the Pacific Coast* (Berlin: Walter de Gruyter, 1923), p. 27.

By then over 10 per cent of the population was self-employed. At the same time, an occupational concentration among South Asians in wage labour in the province's lumber mills helped them to consolidate further their economic position. By 1924, 609 of 680 South Asian workers were employed there. [13]

The personal incentives to move into sawmill work were primarily economic, for the work paid well. In 1921, South Asians in the mills were making over $1,000 a year. By 1925, South Asian wood workers were being paid 40-50¢ an hour over a nine-hour day or the equivalent of about $1,320 a year. [14] The latter figure was close to the average yearly wage of workers in British Columbia and was about 40 per cent higher than the average annual income of Chinese and Japanese. South Asians established a reputation for hard work in the mills, which allowed them to remain consistently employed throughout the decade. They were still paid 10 per cent less than whites for the same work and continued to be denied positions of responsibility, but their incomes were substantial for the times.

They were even more so in relation to their expenses. Living together and spending little, men were able to save as much as 60 per cent of their income. Of this, perhaps half might be remitted to their families in India. Although public stereotypes of South Asians occasionally still portrayed them as poor and economically ill-adapted to Canadian life, this was far from the truth. By the late 1920's their economic foothold in Canada was considerably more firm than that of many European immigrant groups.

RACIAL DISCRIMINATION

The economic success of South Asians in the 1920's did little to mitigate the many racial restrictions they faced a decade earlier. This was especially true of their legal restrictions under British Columbia law. Central among these remained their inability to vote provincially.[15] The 1920 Dominion Franchise Bill compounded the problem by denying the federal vote to anyone barred from the provincial vote on account of race.[16] And upon their inability to get onto the provincial voter's list hung most of the other restrictions imposed by the British Columbia government.

Canada was chided for this restriction at the Imperial Conference of 1921, where a resolution was passed affirming the right of South Asians in the Dominions to vote. Prime Minister Arthur Meighen was present and agreed to act in support of the resolution in Parliament. Shortly thereafter, however, Meighen was defeated at the polls. Mackenzie King became Prime Minister and Meighen's promise came to nothing.

The issue did not die there, however, for sentiment in India kept it alive. In August, 1921, a three man *ad hoc* group composed of Lord Byng, the Maharaj of Cutch, and V.S. Srinivasa Sastri proposed to go to Canada to investigate the situation of South Asians there.[17] This provoked a flurry of activity as the federal government mustered a defence of its immigration ban and its inaction on the vote. Eventually, only Sastri came, spending the better part of August, 1922, on a cross-country tour.[18] He met briefly with representatives of the community in British Columbia, but his main objective was to lobby federal politicians on their behalf. He was able to elicit considerable support for changes in the federal voting restriction, especially among opposition members.[19] The next year Liberal Montreal MP S.W. Jacobs introduced a resolution in the House of Commons supporting the South Asian vote, which provoked a vigorous debate.[20] Support for the resolution in the East was effectively countered by a violently anti-Asian response from British Columbia. As one British Columbia MP put it:

> . . . we in British Columbia want no more Hindus. . . . We have on the coast of British Columbia Chinamen and Japs running our stores. They are running the white people out. We have the Greeks running our hotels and we have the Jews running our second-hand stores, and now some people want to bring in the Hindus to run our mills. . . . If this country wants to cast British Columbia adrift let her cast it adrift before any more Orientals come in. If they do, we white people out on the Pacific will prevent any more Orientals coming to British Columbia.[21]

To British Columbia politicians all Asian Canadians remained unwanted foreigners, and the MPs were unyielding on the question of South Asian franchise. The federal government deferred action until the forthcoming Dominion Elections Bill reached the House. In the meantime, the British Columbia government reaffirmed its stand by maintaining racial restrictions in the Provincial Elections Act of 1924, which disenfranchised all Asians except Japanese who had fought in World War I.[22]

Sastri had even less luck with the immigration issue. The government claimed that the continuous journey restriction was not specifically aimed at South Asians and asserted that over 75,000 immigrants had been turned back at the international boundary with the United States between 1910 and 1920 for not having fulfilled its requirements.[23]

For the rest of the decade, community attempts to have these racial restrictions removed were few and produced no results. All formal restrictions instituted earlier against South Asians therefore continued in effect. Chinese and Japanese shared this situation with them. They continued also to share the same informal restrictions on work, especially in unionized occupations. Until 1930 the platform of the Trades and Labour Council of Canada contained a resolution supporting the exclusion of all Asians from Canada; under the euphemism of "races that cannot be properly assimilated" this resolution was reaffirmed every year up to 1941.[24] All craft and trade unions were closed to them, and they owed their strong position in the lumber industry to the perception that they could do more work than the Chinese and Japanese and would work for less than whites.

In other areas of life, though, discrimination decreased steadily. There was very little hostility shown to South Asian children by their schoolmates and active taunting and provocation of South Asians became rare. Social interaction with other Canadians increased slightly. A small number of interested whites began to visit the gurdwaras, especially during major celebrations. Renting housing became much easier.

Still, some businesses continued to refuse service to South Asians, primarily movie theatres and high-class restaurants. In the former case the rationale was sometimes that turbans blocked the view of other patrons. Restaurants were generally afraid that having South Asian patrons would lower the prestige of their businesses. These restrictions persisted until the depression, when the need for customers led to their demise.

During the 1920's the general image of South Asians in Canada improved considerably. This reflected their increasing prosperity and roots in the country. South Asians were no longer a novelty; neither were they seen as a threat. Although still referred to as "Hindoos," there was an increasing awareness of their Sikh origins and their contributions to British Columbia society. Media portrayal became less sensational than before, despite a continuing concentration on South Asian violence and crime. Their newspaper image in the 1920's was considerably better than that of the Chinese or Japanese.[25]

COMMUNITY AFFAIRS

After the war community action diffused across more issues than it had when Ghadar was ascendant and the immigration battle raged. People were older and had been in Canada longer. Their concerns were therefore more complex, and without dynamic leaders these concerns were not easily given focus. Leadership in the early 1920's chiefly devolved upon the Khalsa Diwan Society in Vancouver, which had shown itself to be the strongest, most influential, and longest lasting community organization of all.

After the Ghadar disasters of 1914-15, the Khalsa Diwan Society and the community became much more involved with specifically Sikh issues. By then most of the comparatively few Moslem and Hindu pioneers had migrated to the United States or returned home and Ghadarite adventures had removed most non-Sikh leaders. As a consequence, the community was more homogeneous. Ethnicity, religion, geographical origin, class, and common experience were all very similar.

It was only natural that Sikh issues would soon hold sway, and changing conditions in India further emphasized this trend. After the war there had been a general expectation among the Indian elite that the British would recognize the Indian contribution to the war effort by granting Indians greater self-government. Both the Indian National Congress and Mohandas Gandhi had strongly supported the British during the war, and their political credibility was therefore at stake. Many hoped to see Dominion status conferred on India within a few years.

These hopes were soon dashed. Six months after the end of the war the hated Defence of India Rule was to expire, and the general expectation was that this would lead to a restoration of the civil rights Indians had previous to its proclamation. Instead, rather the opposite occurred. The Anarchical and Revolutionary Crimes Act of 1919 gave the government the power to hang or imprison convicted individuals without appeal, to hold suspects without presenting cause, to arrest individuals without a court order, and to continue indefinitely the detention of people held under the Defence of India Rule. Discontent soon led to violent clashes between Punjabis and British authorities. On April 13, 1919, troops under the command of Brigadier General R.E.H. Dyer fired without warning on an unarmed Punjabi crowd of several thousand individuals gathered in a walled public square, the Jallianwala Bagh, in Amritsar. Several hundred people were killed. Jallianwala Bagh became an important rallying point on the road to Indian self-determination. The event shocked Sikh communities around the world and in Vancouver resulted in a petition to the Prince of Wales critical of British rule and the conditions that Sikhs experienced in Canada.[26]

Jallianwala Bagh also gave the remnants of the Ghadar Party in California a boost in their attempt to regroup. By early 1920 it was back in operation, publishing the *Independent Hindustan* and such pamphlets as *Invincible India*. In 1921, Ghadar sent Surendranath Karr to Moscow to establish relations with the new Bolshevik government there. The party was subsequently represented at the fourth conference of the Third International.[27]

This new outburst of nationalist feeling was also felt in Canada.[28] On January 15, 1921, an international meeting of Ghadar was held in

Stockton, California, which was attended by Surian Singh representing Vancouver. The day before, a mass meeting was held at the Vancouver temple to raise funds to support the families of those who went to India in 1914-15. The sum of $13,000 was collected and given over for dispersement to a committee led by Kapoor Singh and Mit Singh. On January 23 250 people met at Fraser Mills to honour Mewa Singh and donated another $900 to the Indian independence movement.

This sort of strong financial support was nothing new to the community. By their own accounts, the Vancouver Khalsa Diwan Society had contributed $295,000 to various social and political causes before 1921.

TABLE 4

Contributions Made through the Vancouver Khalsa Diwan Society, 1908-1920

Sufferers of massacres	$ 4,330
Families of political prisoners	2,100
Sufferers from political activities	30,700
Congress Swaraj fund	3,333
Religious and educational causes	148,000
Komagata Maru case	50,000
Immigration cases	30,000
Deportation cases	12,000
South Asian press in Canada	15,000
TOTAL	$295,463

SOURCE: Tien Fang Cheng, *Oriental Immigration in Canada* (Shanghai: Commercial Press, 1931), p. 228.

By 1925 the Khalsa Diwan Society had autonomous branches in Vancouver, Victoria, Abbotsford, New Westminster, Golden, Victoria, Duncan, Coombs, and Ocean Falls – virtually everywhere that Sikhs lived in any number. They all continued to support Indian independence financially throughout the 1920's.

With the revival of Ghadar, government interest in South Asian political activities also rose and the pre-war system of spying and mail-opening resumed. Ghadarite publications were banned from the Indian mails and could not legally be sent to India from Canada or the United States. From 1924 on, the Canadian government continued at British request to forward information to the Secretary of State for the Colonies on South Asian activities in Canada.

This surveillance increased dramatically in 1926-27, chiefly as a result of the rise of the Sikh Akali Movement in Punjab, whose objective was Sikh control over Sikh religious institutions.[29] Because the gurdwaras were potential seats of Sikh discontent, the British had begun appointing the managers of the more important temples and shrines in the 1880's. This led to the introduction of many unorthodox religious practices. After the war Sikh protest about these conditions began in earnest. In 1920 the Shiromani Gurdwara Prabandak (Central Gurdwara Management) Committee was formed to liberate the Sikh temples.

To accomplish this objective the committee organized its followers into *jathas* – groups analogous to historical Sikh military units. These were organized into the Akali Dal, the Army of Immortals. Following the model of Gandhi, the Akalis were dedicated to passive resistance techniques rather than violence. In their many successful conflicts with the British and their supporters, many Akalis were killed or injured. By 1922 most temples had been secured by the SGPC, and three years later the government passed the Sikh Gurdwara Bill, which placed all historical Sikh temples and shrines under the committee. The Akali Dal has continued to be a potent political force in Punjab right up to the present.

British Columbia Sikhs were powerfully affected by these events and the Canadian authorities knew it. Financial contributions to the gurdwara reform movement had been flowing from Vancouver to Punjab since 1921 to assist the *jathas* and the families of those imprisoned or killed. Money was also sent to fund Punjab newspapers and to set up schools where people could be educated outside of British influence. In mid-1924 eleven Sikhs renounced their comfortable lives in Canada to join the reform movement personally.[30] They participated in at least one of the *jathas* sent to Jaito, an important gurdwara. Mit Singh, who had been active in Vancouver community affairs from the first, led the group and carried with him at least $5,000. He was later arrested, tried, and jailed along with many other Akali leaders.[31]

Although support for Ghadar and the Akalis continued into the 1930's, British and Canadian government fears about the re-establishment of a powerful Ghadar Party in Canada were unfounded. Financial support and occasional personal sacrifice were forthcoming, but the deep commitment that Ghadar evoked before the war never returned. Moreover, Ghadar sympathy never negated support for other Indian causes and political approaches. For example, a steady stream of donations flowed from Canada to the Congress Party, the dominant political organization devoted to the cause of Indian independence. Moreover, Canadian Sikhs harboured a deep respect for Indian religions and cultures. Throughout the 1920's the local community supported visits by a number of Indian philosophers and religious teachers, which helped to keep these sentiments alive among people who had not seen their homeland for almost twenty years. These visits culminated in 1929 with the arrival of the Nobel laureate, poet Rabindranath Tagore. On April 15 Tagore was introduced by Governor General Lord Willingdon to an overflow crowd at the Victoria Theatre; hundreds of community members were there.[32] Accompanying him on his trip to Canada was the missionary and defender of overseas India, C.F. Andrews. Andrews then travelled across the country lecturing about the problems faced by Indians throughout the Empire.

South Asian Canadians found themselves in a somewhat contradictory situation at the end of the 1920's. In 1910 the community was ethnically strong but was socially, economically, and politically marginal. By the beginning of 1930 this had changed, but not uniformly. Ethnic and community solidarity remained high, but people's individual situations and interests became more variable. Their political marginality remained unaltered, yet their public image and social situation improved. Economically, they had done well despite many constraints.

By 1930, most of their concerns were with Canada rather than India and the presence of families promised to make that connection permanent despite discriminatory law and practice. Even so, in retrospect one cannot but be saddened by the social isolation within which all this transpired – and by the psychological burdens this imposed. By 1930, South Asians had laid their tile in the Canadian ethnic mosaic and guaranteed its survival. Racism assured that the tile continued to remain peripheral to the whole.

NOTES

1. Tara Singh to R. Borden, June 7, 1919, PAC, RG 76, #536999, part 12.
2. A.L. Jolliffe to F.C. Blair, July 28, 1920, PAC, RG 76, R.O., part 1.
3. PC 1094 of May 7, 1920.
4. F.C. Blair to anonymous, January 3, 1924, PAC, RG 76, R.O., part 3; F.C. Blair to Lt. Col. C. Campbell, Simla, July 5, 1923, PAC, RG 76, #536999, part 13.
5. Das, *Hindustanee Workers*; Cheng, *Oriental Immigration*, p. 199.
6. Sadhu Singh Dhami, "Discovering the New World," *Queen's Quarterly*, 76 (1969), pp. 200-12.
7. Das, *Hindustanee Workers*; Yusuf Dadabhay, "Circuitous Assimilation among rural Hindustanis in California," *Social Forces*, 33 (1954), pp. 138-41.
8. George H. Lowes, "The Sikhs of British Columbia" (B.A. honours essay, University of British Columbia, 1952); Button, "Sikh Settlement in the Lower Mainland."
9. Das, *Hindustanee Workers*, p. 27.
10. *India and Canada*, 1, 3 (1929), pp. 1-4.
11. A. Joy and V. Dusenbery, "Being Sikh in British Columbia: Changing Definitions of 'Self' and 'Others,' " paper presented at the annual meeting of the Canadian Asian Studies Association (1980, mimeo.), p. 9.
12. Personal communication with Kawal Singh Littar, July, 1978.
13. British Columbia Legislative Assembly (1927).
14. Cheng, *Oriental Immigration*, p. 167.
15. Chapter 72, Revised Statutes of British Columbia, 1911, clause 7.
16. Statutes of Canada, 1920, Chapter 46, Sec. 30.

17. Lord Byng to the Colonial Secretary, August 20, 1921, PAC, RG 76, #536999, part 13.
18. See PAC, RG 25, G 1, v. 1300 f, 104 p, for details of his trip.
19. A. Meighen to H.H. Stevens, September 6, 1922, Stevens Papers, HH-20; Sastri's report, 9 pp., Stevens Papers, HH-22.
20. House of Commons, *Debates*, 1923, pp. 4073, 4640-8.
21. M.P. MacBride, *ibid.*
22. Revised Statutes, 1924, Chapter 76, Sec. 1.
23. F.C. Blair report, July 31, 1922, PAC, RG 25, G 1, v. 1300 f, 1011 p.
24. Trades and Labour Council (Canada), *Proceedings*, 1930-41.
25. Indra, "The Portrayal of South Asians."
26. *Vancouver World*, September 29, 1919, p. 1.
27. Josh, *Hindustan Gadar Party*, vol. 2, p. 211.
28. Malcolm Reid to W. Cory, January 27 and 28, 1921, PAC, RG 76, #536999, part 2, British.
29. For more details on the Akali Movement, see Mittal, *Freedom Movement in Punjab*; Ruchi Ram Sahni, *Struggle for Reform in Sikh Shrines* (Amritsar, n.d.).
30. *Victoria Daily Colonist*, July 18, 1924, p. 1.; Mittal, *Freedom Movement in Punjab*, p. 174.
31. Josh, *Hindustan Gadar Party*, p. 231; Sahni, *Struggle for Reform*, pp. 245-8.
32. *India and Canada*, 1, 1 (1929), p. 3.

SIX

Small Gains

The 1930's in Canada were a time of profound social and economic dislocation. This was especially true of British Columbia. The province's resource-based economy was almost entirely dependent on United States and eastern Canadian markets – markets that disappeared with the onset of the Great Depression. By 1931 unemployment was rife and the average British Columbia wage had dropped over 20 per cent. Unemployed Asians found it hard to get work because white job-seekers were willing to accept Asian pay scales. Job insecurity among white workers in turn led to an increase in anti-Asian attitudes during the decade. Such feelings led to a British Columbia minimum wage law, which attempted to protect white employees against being undercut by Asians and unemployed whites; thereafter, minimum wage rates in the mills were set, with a provision that 25 per cent of employees could be paid 25 per cent less.[1] These were invariably Asians.

The 1930's were hard years for South Asians, but several strategies developed earlier stood them in good stead. Their concentration on mill work turned out to be an advantage, for their reputation as good workers often led to Chinese and Japanese being let go before them. This was not so in other working-class occupations, where South Asians were virtually eliminated by the mid-1930's. In 1934, almost all South Asian wage labourers in British Columbia were in the mills. Unemployment increased, but not to the extent that it did among the Chinese and Japanese.

Some of those with work continued to earn about $100 a month – only a little less than they had in the prosperous late 1920's.[2] Considering that prices had dropped at least as much, this select few weathered the depression with few difficulties. Steady work, however, became rarer. In the mills about one-fifth of the usual South Asian work force might be unemployed at any one time. In addition, many men were employed by mills at far below the minimum wage – sometimes less than 20¢ an hour. Average yearly income for most men decreased significantly.

South Asian entrepreneurs suffered, too, but perhaps less than one might expect. South Asian mill owners were as hard-pressed to make ends meet as their competitors, and several were forced to close down. Mayo Lumber Company's mill burned in 1933 and was not rebuilt for two years. In contrast, fuel dealers were affected only insofar as the price they could ask for their product decreased; few of their customers could do without their services. Small farmers reduced their operations to virtually a subsistence level.

What made it relatively easy for South Asians to wait out the depression was their extensive system of mutual aid, which, though severely taxed, did not fail them. South Asians in British Columbia were rarely on relief during the 1930's.[3] This was so despite the rapid aging of the community, which was being required to support an increasing number of men who were sick, injured, or too old to work. The depression made impossible the rapid accumulation of savings characteristic of the previous decade. Families in particular felt the pinch because of their comparatively higher living expenses.

Still, South Asians adjusted rather well to the new demands of the depression years. Communities in both the cities and rural areas remained fairly stable, save for the comings and goings of people to and from India and the arrival of some men illegally from the United States. This account of conditions at Paldi (near Duncan) where a community had arisen near Mayo Mills is fairly representative:

> After Mayo Lumber Company's mill burnt down there was very little work around. Only two mills remained open, the Hillcrest Lumber Company and the Yuba Lumber Company. The bunkhouse, cookhouse, and temple remained open, so many of us stayed at Paldi even without work. Right around 1930 quite a few men went off to India, where they knew that they could at least wait out the depression on family farms. They began coming back to Canada around 1934.
>
> About fifty people from Paldi got jobs at Hillcrest, where they worked nine hours a day, six days a week for ten cents an hour. Those who weren't working had all saved money, and so could wait for things to get better for a long time. They did what they could to keep things around Paldi in order – tidied up the temple, cleaned up rubbish, and fixed buildings. Still, mostly they could do little but sit around.

For those who continued to live in camps, life went on much as before:

> Sikhs in the camps continued to live together right through the 1930's and 1940's. Most men lived in workers' barracks; conditions were pretty bad, but no worse than for other workers. Sikhs always got together and supported a cookhouse for themselves. Usually, a full-time cook was hired to run it; workers usually paid him one day's wages each month. Two other people were usually elected to order, buy, and collect groceries for the cookhouse.

Any visitors that might come by were fed without charge for up to seven days. If they stayed eight days or more, then they would be charged for the whole time. It was a pretty cheap way to live, and with occasional work and savings people got along. You could never find a Sikh in a soup kitchen lineup. Some were poor enough, but it was too humiliating.

Even in the worst years of the depression there was more to life than just the struggle to survive. Visiting between communities remained an important and frequent event:

Way back in the 1920's the temples across the province began "specializing" in certain celebrations. Victoria would stage a big event for the birthday of Guru Gobind Singh, while Vancouver would celebrate Sikh Martyrs Day in May. People planned in advance to travel to wherever one of these big celebrations was happening, even sometimes going right across the province. These were opportunities to visit with old friends and to discuss local problems. They were especially important to women, who were otherwise often very isolated.

Other forms of recreation also developed:

In 1933 I was working in a Vancouver sawmill for ten cents an hour. Every Saturday I went off to see a show at the Royal Theatre. I budgeted ten cents for the show, another ten cents for a milkshake, and five cents to play a game in the lobby. I was raised and went to school in Vancouver, so for me the screen characters I saw were second nature. Many older men still didn't know much English, but this didn't stop them from going to the movies. In the 1920's it was easier for them, since the films were all silent. Still, they kept right on going when sound movies came in. It was one of the few things that they did for recreation that involved "whites" in any way. We still were not welcome in many beer parlours.

Despite economic hard times, a drive for the elimination of all the restrictions still placed on South Asians was begun in the 1930's: the inability to vote, the various restrictions of rights that went with it, and the ban on immigration. By 1948 these objectives would be achieved, due in good part to the efforts of the local community. As before, these changes required certain preconditions, most notably in regard to Canada's relationship to India and India's to Britain. Almost equally important were fundamental changes in the political milieu of British Columbia during the same period.

ILLEGAL IMMIGRATION

Community resources were first mobilized in regard to illegal immigration – an issue that might at first seem to bear little relationship to the expansion of South Asian rights. In actuality, the connection was very close. The question of illegal South Asian immigration created a broad coalition to fight against deportations, which then turned to address these other issues. It also publicized South Asian racial restrictions, both nationally and internationally.

The inequities of the continuous passage regulation were a licence for prospective South Asian immigrants to try to beat the system. The depression made immigration even more difficult, for in reaction to it the federal government enacted several further restrictive regulations. In September, 1930, an Order-in-Council (PC 2115) was passed to prohibit the landing of all Asian immigrants except the wives and dependent children of legal residents or those dealt with by special treaty. Even Syrians and Armenians were affected by it. In the spring of 1931 another Order-in-Council (PC 695) prohibited the immigration of all people except British subjects from Great Britain, United States citizens "with means," and agriculturalists with capital. With this, Canada's immigration program came to a screeching halt, not to begin again in earnest until after World War II.

South Asian schemes to circumvent the immigration ban took several forms. The most prevalent involved simple deception. This had been used on a small scale since the mid-1920's by individuals making application for young men to come from India who falsely were claimed to be their sons. This process picked up considerably by the early 1930's. From 1930 to July, 1933, South Asians in Canada applied for the immigration of 173 relatives. Of these, 137 were for sons and 36 for wives.[4] Many of these so-called "sons" were actually either other relatives or sons of their friends. About the same time others began to smuggle men across the Washington-British Columbia border.

The government became aware of illegal immigration when it learned of a third scheme, which involved the purchase of false Indian government papers stating that individuals were the relatives of Canadian residents. Letters opened by the RCMP claimed that an appropriate paper could be had in Singapore for less than $10. The Canadian government response was to tighten its interpretation of immigration regulations. Thereafter, South Asian men who stayed out of Canada for even three days longer than the three-year limit were denied entrance.

The controversy first surfaced in a serious fashion in 1937, by which time there were about 300 illegal South Asian immigrants in British Columbia. The local community had become alarmed by an RCMP investigation of Ghadar-related Communist activities in Bombay, which had uncovered a system of passport fraud.[5] The Vancouver Khalsa Diwan Society immediately formed a committee, collected funds, and got a lawyer to deal with the possible repercussions. In Victoria, mill owners Kapoor Singh Siddoo and Mayo Singh contributed heavily to a similar fund, which soon reached $1,500. By December, 1937, the two groups had amalgamated as the Canada-Indian Association with a fund of $6,000.

In early 1938, Kapoor Singh and Mayo Singh enlisted the aid of Dr. Anup Singh Dillon, an American resident with a Harvard doctorate in political science. Anup Singh had been involved peripherally with Ghadar from its inception until about 1930 and had thereafter been in India researching the Congress Party. He was then the secretary of the India League of America. Anup Singh was sent to Ottawa in March to intercede with the Canadian authorities on behalf of the illegal immigrants. He was accompanied by Dr. Sadhu Singh Dhami, who was then teaching at the University of Alberta.[6] In Ottawa they talked briefly with the Superintendent of Immigration. Local immigration officials conspired with their American counterparts to try to deport Anup Singh to India upon his return to the United States. While he was eventually released, this ploy removed him from the dispute brewing in Canada.

In British Columbia the situation became much more serious due to a new set of events. From 1931 on, concern had been building that local Japanese had developed a massive scheme for bringing in illegal immigrants. In fact, a 1931 trial had determined that as many as 2,500 Japanese had been brought in illegally between 1915 and 1931 through a system of forged documents.[7] In 1938, Prime Minister Mackenzie King appointed a board of review to investigate the situation. The board held extensive hearings, yet uncovered only nineteen possibly illegal Japanese immigrants from the post-1931 era. On the other hand, fifty-nine South Asians were informed on, largely by other community members.[8] The issue had split the community, with the consequence that it activated grudges lying dormant for a long time. Illegal immigrants who were the friends or relatives of someone else's enemies were the unwitting victims. Two of those singled out were immediately deported and another fifteen were held. By mid-1939 this list had grown to twenty-seven.

These events resulted in redoubled efforts on the part of the community to resolve the issue. In March, 1939, Ishar Singh wrote to the government with an admission that there were perhaps fifty to sixty illegal South Asian immigrants in British Columbia. He asked that they be allowed to stay in the light of their few numbers and relatively long residence in Canada.[9] Shortly thereafter he travelled to Ottawa with D.P. Pandia. Pandia had the reputation of being a private secretary to Gandhi and had just come from the United States, where he had helped to secure a congressional decision to naturalize the 3,000-odd South Asians in the United States who arrived before 1924.[10]

At that time Canada had two international concerns involving India that it did not want interfered with by something as small as this. In the Pacific, the growing expansionism of Japan was giving the government worries; also, Canada did not wish to disturb British India's loyalty in the light of growing tensions in Europe. At the same time, Canada was negotiating a preferential trade agreement with India. Because of these considerations, the government quickly agreed not to deport any illegal South Asian immigrants who were willing to come forward and register. [11] It was decided to announce the deportation stay in such a way as to deny credit to Pandia, who by then had visited Ottawa once more. This was done to keep groups like the White Canada Association in British Columbia from getting the impression that the government was caving in to South Asian pressure. [12] The deadline for registration was to be January 31, 1940, by which time 225 people registered instead of the predicted sixty.

These individuals could stay in Canada without fear of deportation but could not apply to bring their wives and children here. This consequently became the next challenge, which was launched with the help of Margaret Crang, a lawyer from Edmonton. She visited Ottawa on this point in June, 1940. [13] In the meantime the RCMP and the Indian secret police set out to limit Pandia's activities, which they saw as a threat to the racial status quo that had developed in the interwar years. Pandia soon left Canada to investigate the conditions of South Asians in Trinidad. Following Canadian directions, the British India Office then refused to grant him a permit to visit Canada and he remained in Trinidad until 1946. [14] In 1941 Margaret Crang got the government to accept forty-three more recently registered illegal immigrants but could do nothing about getting them the privilege of having their families here. It was not until April, 1947, that Lester Pearson suggested that these individuals be granted normal Canadian passports. [15] The issue had already been decided by the time the Vancouver and Victoria Khalsa Diwan Societies sent Pandia to Ottawa in June, 1947.

THE VOTE

The vote was the other central issue of the 1930's and 1940's. [16] In the long term it was far more consequential than the question of illegal immigration, because the achievement of legal equality for South Asians in British Columbia depended on it. Without the vote they were second-class citizens regardless of their economic success or their commitment to Canada. All legal liabilities except the immigration ban were dependent on the denial of the vote. Achievement of the franchise would be a powerful argument for changing the continuous passage restriction.

By the 1930's it was time to mount a fight on this issue. A substantial number of families had been established, and parents did not wish to see their children inherit their own marginal status. By 1935, about 300 people in the community had been born in Canada and several hundred others had immigrated as children or adolescents. In addition, the economic elite in the community were affronted by the anomalous position in which they were placed by their disenfranchisement, for they could not fully exercise the privileges that wealth usually granted.

Several things paved the way for a fight for the vote. One was the rise of the provincial CCF, which consistently supported Asians on the vote issue. The 1930's also saw the liberalization of the racial policies of several important unions. For example, in 1931 the Japanese-based Camp and Mill Workers Union was able to get the Canadian Trades and Labour Council to support the Asian vote in British Columbia.[17] Later, the International Woodworkers of America would become actively involved. As well, the status of India was changing, and by the mid-1930's that country was clearly on a course toward independence. Earlier concerns about the international effects of anti-South Asian discrimination were to become revived in a much more powerful form as Indian independence approached.

It should be recalled that South Asians had been promised the federal vote by Arthur Meighen in the early 1920's, but Mackenzie King's slim majority made the political risks of acting on it too great. At the 1923 Imperial Conference the Prime Minister remained verbally committed to the idea but did not see it through; in 1925 the Parliamentary Committee on Privileges and Elections failed to support such a change.[18]

In 1933 Sir Atul Chatterjee of the India Office, London, began agitating for a change in the discriminatory legislation. Prime Minister R.B. Bennett replied that he had no basic objection to South Asians having the vote, but did not know how to get British Columbia to change its legislation.[19] The issue arose once again at the Commonwealth Relations Conference held that year in Toronto. Federal government inaction subsequently prompted a query by the Indian representative of the League of Nations. This also came to nothing.

The controversy then shifted to the provincial scene. In British Columbia, the Liberals and the CCF had already been debating the issue, the latter advocating the extension of the vote to Asians. In 1935, Clive Planta (Liberal, Peace River) attempted to put forward a motion in the British Columbia legislature reaffirming the disenfranchisement of Asians in the province. This was attacked by Harold Winch (Vancouver East) of the CCF and was ruled out of order. Similar skirmishes occurred every year up to 1938, when the new Dominion Elections Act was proclaimed; once more, it did not reinstate the federal vote for Asians. British Columbia's revision of its Election Act in 1939 retained all the discriminatory clauses of the previous Act.[20]

The outbreak of World War II did not moderate government position on the vote. The key problem was that the public could not easily separate the question of South Asian franchise from that of the Japanese. Animosity toward Japanese in British Columbia was deepening and Mackenzie King was unwilling to take the issue under consideration during the first years of the war.[21] Even the intervention of H.S.L. Polak, a long-time associate of Gandhi, did little to affect government opinion. Polak had been on a lecture tour in central Canada and was brought to British Columbia through the efforts of Kapoor Singh Siddoo, Mayo Singh, and Kartar Singh Hundal. While in Canada he corresponded with

Mackenzie King, who agreed to an eventual change in the relevant federal legislation. In January, 1942, Polak met with Premier John Hart of British Columbia, who was unwilling to consider the question of provincial franchise. Pearl Harbor had already had a devastating effect on white attitudes toward the Japanese in British Columbia and this was quickly reflected in a hardening of the government position on this question. On February 21, 1942, Polak was informed that Mackenzie King would not consider the vote in the light of the imminent removal of Japanese Canadians from coastal British Columbia. [22]

From this point, community participation in the drive for the vote increased steadily. Unbeknownst to them, the federal government's concern about the situation in India was very real. In early 1942, the British had agreed to grant India Dominion status after the war. Mackenzie King became interested in the constitutional evolution of India and for the rest of the war attempted to lobby the British government to accept Indian independence. [23] Even so, he remained reluctant to grant South Asians in British Columbia the freedoms he so vigorously advocated for South Asians in India.

South Asians were unwilling to let things ride any longer. In March, 1943, a twelve-man delegation was sent to Premier Hart to argue for the vote. In addition to Nagindar Singh Gill and other leaders of the Khalsa Diwan Society, they brought along Harold Prichert, the district president of the International Woodworkers of America, Sir Robert Holland, and Harold Winch of the CCF. By 1943 many South Asians in Canada were becoming IWA members and the union was very supportive of their cause. They also brought with them tangible evidence of their commitment to Canada – a veteran of World War I (Bahoo Singh) and two Sikhs recently enlisted in the Canadian Army (Phagan Singh and G.S. Badall). They pointed also to the several hundred thousand dollars in war bonds to which community members had already subscribed; this figure would reach $496,730 by the end of the war. Hart refused to act until the war ended.

This did not dampen the community's desire for the vote, and there were other ways of applying pressure for it. One way was to oppose military conscription on the grounds that a country not allowing some of its citizens to vote could not ethically ask them to fight. As early as January, 1940, a number of South Asian Canadians were registered accidentally because their surnames appeared to be European. By the end of 1942 several South Asians had already been called up and fifty more had been called for a medical. [24]

The government was required to make some sort of policy statement, for although Japanese Canadians had already been "exempted" from service, South Asian conscription had not previously been an issue. On racial grounds the government did not really want to call them up in any case and several options, such as alternative service or postponement of service because of the strategic importance of their mill jobs, were considered. Through mid-1943 the community kept up the pressure and found a strong supporter for their "no vote-no war" policy in Elmore Philpott, managing editor of the Vancouver *News-Herald*. Most were more than willing to serve if the vote issue could be resolved, and they did not realize that their pressure was pushing the government toward an unexpected decision. When a Toronto Sikh with a surname of Gill requested a month's deferment of his call-up date, the government decided to exempt all South Asian Canadians from service for the duration of the war.[25] Another round in the fight for the vote had been lost.

In 1944 Mackenzie King faced a federal election and did not want to risk alienating voters by supporting the South Asian franchise. Such strong feelings had arisen over the issue when the CCF brought it up in the provincial legislature that Labour Minister G.S. Pearson claimed that:

> The Hindu is not helping us to maintain the standard of living we have set up in the province. There is nobody in the province as unreliable, dishonest and deceitful as the Hindus. They break every regulation we have . . . we are justified in excluding them from the full rights of citizenship.[26]

Pearson's remarks sparked the Vancouver community to send a delegation to him and to the provincial Attorney General demanding an apology, but none was given.

Rebuffed again, the community began to try to develop greater public support for their cause. The Vancouver Khalsa Diwan Society delegated Nagindar Singh Gill and Hazara Singh Gurcha to visit all the South Asian communities in British Columbia to collect information on South Asian standards of living, occupations, numbers, and participation in the war effort. The objective was to publicize South Asian contributions to the province. An attempt was also made to form a united front with the Chinese, who were also pressing for the vote.

South Asian public relations efforts began to have their effect as it became clear that the war would be won. The CCF continued to provide strong support, both in the legislature and in the media. In 1944 the British Columbia Provincial Command of the Canadian Legion also lent its support. About that time the federal government decided to conscript Chinese Canadians, which generated a parallel "no vote-no fight" movement among young Chinese.[27] It was agreed that Chinese Canadians who served would be granted the federal vote. In 1945 the CCF presented a resolution in support of the franchise in the provincial legislature, but it was narrowly defeated. As a result, however, all Chinese, Japanese, South Asian, and native Canadians who served in World War II were granted the provincial vote. This parliamentary activity indicated a change in racial attitudes that had been ongoing during the war years. China had been an ally of Canada during the war, with the consequence that public opinion about the Chinese improved considerably. Indian troops had fought alongside Canadians in the Battle of Hong Kong and later were extensively used in the British counter-offensive in Burma; this, too, had an important public relations effect.

Moreover, as both China and India became more independent politically, the denial of the vote to Chinese and South Asians began to be an embarrassment to the federal government. This was made doubly so by Canada's participation in the formulation of the original United Nations Charter; Canada's denial of the Asian vote directly contradicted the Charter. Economic considerations also played a role in changing government opinion. In 1945, M.R. Ahuja was sent to Canada by the government of India to serve as India's Trade Commissioner in Toronto. Canada had high hopes of developing large-scale trade with India and was sensitive to Ahuja's protests about the situation of South Asians in British Columbia.[28] He was soon joined in protest by P. Konanda Rao of the influential Servants of India Society, who had come to Montreal to attend a meeting on international migration. In the fall of 1946 Rao went on a cross-country speaking tour sponsored by the Association of Canadian Clubs and the Canadian Institute of International Affairs, during which he spoke strongly against racial restriction in British Columbia.

Rao's visit coincided with the return of D.P. Pandia, who within a month visited the Director of Immigration in Ottawa about the vote. Pandia, Kapoor Singh Siddoo, Kartar Singh, Ishar Singh, Nagindar Singh, and Gurdit Singh subsequently met with the British Columbia Elections Act Committee. The committee was sympathetic and agreed to recommend that the necessary changes be made in the new Act. The vigorous support of Jawaharlal Nehru, who was in Ottawa in February, 1947, made a positive vote by the legislature a certainty.

The recommendations of the Elections Act Committee were embodied in Bill 85, which amended the Elections Act by deleting Chinese and South Asians from the list of disqualified persons. On second reading an additional amendment was made disqualifying those without "an adequate knowledge of English or French" from voting. The amended bill came to the floor of the legislature on April 2, 1947, and was passed unanimously. The provincial vote had been won. With the provincial vote automatically came the federal vote and the end of all the attendant legal restrictions on South Asians. The South Asian drive toward full Canadian citizenship was almost complete. Only two problems still remained: the municipal vote and the ban on immigration.

The first of these was dealt with summarily. The city of Vancouver was organized under the Vancouver Incorporation Act, which included a clause disenfranchising South Asians. So did the Municipal Elections Act, which governed all other British Columbia municipalities. The community lobbied several mayors, who were due to meet at Harrison Hot Springs, September 7-15, 1947. At that meeting Mayor P.E. George of Victoria put forward a resolution to ask the legislature to change the Municipal Elections Act to allow South Asians to vote.[29] This resolution was moved by Mayor Loutet of North Vancouver and passed with only one dissenting vote, which was cast because the resolution was not extended to native people. On October 23, 1947, the Vancouver City Council was subjected to the same lobbying effort and agreed to ask that the Vancouver Incorporation Act be changed in a similar fashion. Only the immigration restriction remained, and it was to take another twenty years before it was to be entirely eliminated.

A COMMUNITY ON THE EDGE OF CHANGE

The successful conclusion of the fight to get the vote in 1947 also corresponds with the end of an era of South Asian Canadian history – a period of slow growth and consolidation and an even slower march toward full participation in Canadian society. By 1948 these things had largely been achieved. A second generation was growing up, marrying, and having children. In the 1941 census, 424 of the 1,465 people enumerated had been born in Canada.

The war allowed the community to repair quickly the economic damage done by the depression. Full employment was guaranteed to anyone who would work, and wages rose. By the middle of the war, men in the mills were receiving thirty cents an hour working as manual labour, which was frequently two or three times what they were getting a few years earlier. Still, whites working alongside them earned forty-five cents an hour, and workers had no union protection.

During the war the International Woodworkers of America began accepting South Asian members, and a few courageous South Asians began recruiting new members. Many were too scared of being fired to join readily, so recruiters went house to house to make their plea. After a successful strike in 1946 wrung important concessions out of the mill owners, all South Asian workers joined the IWA. They soon were an important force in the union, with many becoming local representatives.

TABLE 5

South Asian Wage Labour, 1946

Occupational Sector	Number
Lumber	492
Wood manufacturing	18
Food product manufacturing	7
Coastal shipping	6
Other	32
TOTAL	555

SOURCE: British Columbia, Department of Labour, *Annual Report*, 1946.

The IWA became the first major organization to break the isolation between South Asians and others.

Although the great majority of South Asian workers continued to be employed in the mills throughout the war, some occupational diversity began to develop.

The resurgence of the wartime economy also gave a big boost to South Asian business activities. Most such businesses remained small – either one-person operations, partnerships, or family-run businesses. Still, there were a large number by 1946, and they supported a significant proportion of the community.

TABLE 6

South Asian Businesses, 1946-47

Business	Number
Fuel merchants	130
Sawmill owners	29
Logging camp operators	10
Farming	75
Miscellaneous	91
TOTAL	335

SOURCE: Based on survey by D.P. Pandia, and Nagindar Singh in 1946-47. See D.P. Pandia to H. Keenleyside, March 16, 1948, PAC, RG 76, #536999, pt. 18.

By 1947 perhaps 5 per cent of the provincial lumber business was in South Asian hands, as was virtually all of the wood fuel business. Independent trucking also became important.

Race relations got substantially better. Despite the ongoing provocations of a vocal minority of white British Columbians, the public image of South Asians continued to improve steadily from the 1920's right on through the war. The derogatory label "Hindu" was replaced by the more neutral "East Indian" in the 1930's. By the end of the war there was little systematic discrimination against South Asians. Changing ideas about South Asians and India, union pressure, and the high demand for labour during the war led to a collapse of systematic wage discrimination. By 1945 few businesses refused to serve South Asians and little hostility was shown to South Asians in everyday life.

Even so, the situation of South Asians in Canada remained anomalous. The effects of forty years of structural discrimination did not automatically disappear overnight. Economic integration and legal equality had been achieved, but many barriers to full social and psychological integration remained. Superficially, South Asian immigrant men gave every evidence of substantial assimilation and integration into Canadian society. They dressed and lived much like other Canadians, spoke some English, worked alongside Canadians, and took on Canadian first names. Even so, four decades of social isolation were only beginning to be broken down by the second generation. Too old to change, most of their immigrant parents were to associate primarily with each other for the rest of their lives.

In 1947, this small community could not possibly predict the radical changes that were to occur in the future. With the vote won, formal restrictions removed, and jobs available, it appeared that stability and equality had finally been achieved; the future would be the same, only better. Perhaps the only important change that was foreseen was a weakening of the immigration ban, so that more families could become unified. Such a simple scenario was not to be. Rather, the very mechanisms that had resulted in their being granted full rights of citizenship were to transform entirely the South Asian Canadian panorama within a few short years.

NOTES

1. British Columbia Statutes, 1934, Chapter 47.
2. Eric W. Morse, "Immigration and Status of British East Indians in Canada: A Problem in Imperial Relations" (M.A. thesis, Queen's University, 1935), p. 169.
3. Canada, Board of Review (Immigration) on Charges Concerning Illegal Entry of Aliens into Canada, *Interim Report and Supplement* (Vancouver, 1938, typescript).
4. List of outstanding applications, Vancouver, PAC, RG 76, #536999, part 14.
5. RCMP Secret Reports, August 31, 1937, and December 24, 1937, PAC, RG 76, #536999, part 15.
6. A.S. Dillon, *Nehru: The Rising Star of India* (New York, 1939); RCMP Secret Report, March 17, 1928, PAC, RG 76, #536999, part 15.
7. Ken Adachi, *The Enemy That Never Was* (Toronto, 1979), pp. 180-1.
8. Board of Review, *Interim Report and Supplement*, p. 24a; Canada, Board of Review, *Report* (Ottawa, October, 1938), p. 10.
9. Ishar Singh to A.L. Jolliffe, March 4, 1939, PAC, RG 76, #536999, part 15.
10. Director, Immigration Branch, for File, July 11, 1939, *ibid.*, part 16. Pandia had come to Canada to lecture to the Theosophical Society of Canada. Re: South Asian American naturalization, see 76th Congress, 1st Session, HR 7110, July 10, 1939.
11. O. Skelton to F.C. Blair, September 9, 1939, PAC, RG 76, #536999, part 16.
12. H. Keenleyside to F.C. Blair, September 21, 1939, *ibid.*
13. M. Crang to F.C. Blair, June 30, 1940, *ibid.*
14. C.I.D. report, December 5, 1940, *ibid.*; H. Division, RCMP, to the Com-

missioner, February 11, 1940, *ibid.*; Stewart Macleod to S. Morley Scott, November 28, 1945, *ibid.*, part 17.

15. Lester Pearson to H. Keenleyside, April 22, 1947, *ibid.*; PC 3312 of August 14, 1947.

16. For an extensive discussion of the vote issue and its international implications in the 1940's, see Hilliker, "The British Columbia Franchise and Canadian Relations with India in Wartime, 1939-1945," *B.C. Studies*, 46 (1980), pp. 40-60.

17. Adachi, *The Enemy That Never Was*, p. 125.

18. Memo on the Admission to the Provincial and the Dominion Franchise of Indians Resident in B.C., c.a. 1937, PAC, RG 76, #536999, part 15.

19. Prime Minister to Sir A. Chatterjee, March 29, 1933, PAC, RG 13, v. 382. H. 484.

20. B.C. Provincial Elections Act, 1939, Chapter 16, Section 5a.

21. See Hilliker, "The British Columbia Franchise," pp. 44-6, for details.

22. Khalsa Diwan Society, *Report of Correspondence and Documents . . .* (Vancouver, 1947); Sir Robert Holland, "Indian Immigration into Canada: The Question of Franchise," *Asiatic Review*, 39 (1943), p. 170.

23. Hilliker, "The British Columbia Franchise," pp. 46-8.

24. Charles Pennock, Registrar, to the Director of Mobilization, November 17, 1942, PAC, RG 27, v. 1486, 2-153-1; A. MacNamara to N.A. Robertson, March 8, 1943. *ibid.*, v. 130.

25. Anonymous to the Registrar, October 7, 1943, and related documents in *ibid.*, v. 999, 2-114-27.

26. *Victoria Daily Colonist*, March 9, 144, p. 1; *Victoria Daily Times*, March 9, 1944, p. 1.

27. Carol F. Lee, "The Road to Enfranchisement: Chinese and Japanese in British Columbia," *B.C. Studies*, 30 (1976), p. 51.

28. M.R. Ahuja to N.A. Robertson, January 18, 1946, PAC, RG 76, #536999, part 18.

29. Khalsa Diwan Society, *Report of Correspondence and Documents*.

PART THREE

The Post-War Era, 1948-1984

SEVEN

Winds of Change

For forty years the circumstances of South Asians living in Canada had been closely tied to international relations. This was chiefly because virtually all of the 400 million people of South Asian origin in the world lived under British imperial rule. Most of these people were to be found in British India, and in Britain's subject princely states, Burma and Ceylon (now Sri Lanka). Those who lived elsewhere were located primarily in British sugar colonies such as Mauritius, Fiji, British Guiana, and Trinidad. They or their ancestors had been taken there as indentured labourers, often supplanting previous systems of slave labour. Others had travelled colonial pathways on their own to the Far East, Egypt, East and South Africa, Canada, and the United States. Only in the U.S were they partially free of British control; everywhere else they were subject peoples whose concerns were rarely reflected in British policy. The end of World War II signalled the beginning of the end of this situation. Within five years independence had been granted to the new states of India, Pakistan, and Ceylon. Within twenty-five years virtually all of the other places where South Asians lived had also thrown off colonial rule. This was to have important effects on South Asian Canadians, as Canadian international relations shifted to address the post-colonial era.

The war also changed Canada's international standing and this, too, had repercussions on Canadian South Asians. Canada came out of the war freer of British influence than ever before. Having escaped the devastation wrought on European countries, Canada had become a major industrial nation. This engendered a new-found confidence in the country, which was reflected in an active, more independent foreign policy. This was quickly manifest in support for the fledgling United Nations and for the independence of European colonies. If Canada was to maintain international credibility she would have to change her racial policies significantly.

INDEPENDENCE FOR THE INDIAN SUBCONTINENT

A key factor in this changing scene was the independence of colonial India. By the end of World War II everyone knew that this was imminent. At the beginning of the war few would have predicted it so soon. In fact, in the previous forty years Indian nationalists had made few gains. In 1909 some participation by Indians in the provincial and central legislatures was allowed, along with minority input into the Viceroy's executive council. These positions were held primarily by the Indian National Congress and the All-India Muslim League.

Indian soldiers suffered over 100,000 killed and wounded during World War I and so much money and material was drained from India during that war that the economy and monetary system were in desperate straits. India's reward was insignificant. It was not until 1929 that the British Labour government came out in favour of eventual Dominion status for India. This eventually led to a new draft constitution for India, which was embodied in the Government of India Act of 1935. Under it, representative government was to predominate at the level of provinces and below, though the British would have a veto over any legislation enacted. India remained a colony, with Dominion status put off indefinitely. Discord between Hindus and Muslims increased as Congress increasingly dominated the political arena, and by 1939 many Muslims were convinced that only some form of national or regional self-determination would protect them from being handed from one political master to another at independence.

When World War II broke out, the Viceroy unilaterally announced that India was at war with Germany. Congress pulled out of all participation in the colonial government and boycotted the British war effort. Into the vacuum produced by Congress's departure moved Mohammed Ali Jinnah, whose Muslim League began to advocate the creation of a new Moslem state – Pakistan.[1]

Despite Indian objections the British shifted India over to a war footing and Indian soldiers were soon sent to fight in North Africa. Still, until 1941 India was peripheral to British war efforts. This changed dramatically when Japan entered the war. India became a major staging area for the Southeast Asian campaign. Worried about Indian discontent, in March, 1942, the British confirmed that India would achieve Dominion status after the war. Virtually every party and national association rejected the offer as insufficient and indefinite. Gandhi was soon back in control of Congress, which initiated the Quit India Movement to remove the British through passive resistance. All major Congress leaders were arrested. While they were held the Muslim League's demands for a separate state had become clearer and their political organization had strengthened. After the central legislative election of late 1945 the Muslim League and the Indian National Congress were so polarized that they could not work together. With their hold over the situation deteriorating, the British government announced in February, 1947, that they would withdraw from India by June, 1948. Independence for Ceylon would follow soon after.

With social chaos mounting and time running out, Congress and the Muslim League endorsed a proposal for the partition of India into two new dominions, Pakistan and India. Each gerrymandered state would have a religious majority that belied tremendous internal problems: large religious minorities, princely states still not officially part of either state, little governmental infrastructure, no clear plan for independence.

Independence came to India and Pakistan on August 15, 1947, yet for many of the 40 million Muslims in India and the 20 million non-Muslims in Pakistan, independence was far away indeed. One of the partition lines between Pakistan and India bisected Punjab, where communal violence among Muslims, Hindus, and Sikhs escalated as Muslims moved to Pakistan and Sikhs and Hindus left for India. Within the year, 12 million people made the journey in one direction or the other and as many as one million others may have died in the wholesale slaughter that ensued. Despite the trauma of their births, by 1950 both Pakistan and India had achieved relative stability and order. Their social and economic troubles were by no means behind them, but they had achieved what two generations of nationalists had striven for – self-determination.

SOUTH ASIAN INDEPENDENCE AND CANADA

The independence of India, Pakistan, and Ceylon did not initially have a great impact on Canada.[2] In 1945, India sent M.R. Ahuja as Trade Commissioner to Canada and the next year Canada reciprocated with a High Commissioner, John Kearny. Basic changes in Canada's racially restrictive immigration regulations were not quick in coming. Indeed, in Mackenzie King's landmark statement on post-war immigration policy he reaffirmed the government's desire that immigration not change the racial or cultural "character" of the Canadian population; this was in particular reference to possible "large-scale immigration from the Orient."[3] In contrast, in 1946 the United States eliminated its total ban on Indian immigration by establishing a quota of 100 people a year.

Pressure for a change in Canadian law began in 1947. Once more, it was spearheaded by the Vancouver Khalsa Diwan Society, which claimed that the ban was racist and in conflict with the UN Charter.[4] What provoked more official concern was Indian independence and its consequences. By then, the (interim) Indian government had a representative in Washington, who suggested a token immigration quota along the lines of the American program. Canada responded that no changes in immigration policy toward India would be forthcoming.[5] The only exception was to allow the immigration of wives and children of illegal immigrants, who themselves had been allowed to stay in 1939. Anglo-

Indians were banned and British immigrants from India were allowed into Canada only through waiving the continuous journey clause in every case.

During 1946-47 it appeared that independent India might become a Dominion in the Commonwealth. This would give Indians preferred-entry status into Canada. Because of this possibility, the Canadian High Commissioner to India suggested that an annual immigration quota be established.[6] The government was reluctant because it could not see how to avoid extending the quota idea to the rest of Asia. It did agree to consider the immigration of South Asian fiancés and relatives of Indian businessmen on a one-by-one basis, a practice that was soon extended to fiancées, husbands, and the children of previous marriages.[7] Visa approval shifted to New Delhi.

Ironically, the treatment of South Asians in Canada was used in India as an argument against Commonwealth status, especially Leo Tolstoy's "Letter to a Hindu" and its 1909 response by Taraknath Das.[8] India became a republic in the Commonwealth in April, 1949, and thus eliminated the immigration threat posed by possible British subject status.

Little changed until 1951, when there were still only 2,148 South Asians in Canada, 1,937 of them in British Columbia.[9] Only ten South Asian immigrants had been accepted during World War II and about 300 had come in the next five years. Community members were dying off almost as fast as they were being replaced. On January 1, 1951, the government initiated a change in policy that was eventually to revolutionize the position of South Asians in Canada. Succumbing to pressure from India, the government initiated a quota system for South Asian immigrants. The quota was set at 150 Indians, 100 Pakistanis, and fifty Ceylonese per year. Once here, these individuals would be allowed the same privileges to support the immigration of relatives that other resident South Asians already had.

At first, this quota system was made use of primarily by Indian citizens who were related to Canadians. In neither Pakistan nor Ceylon had the Canadian government developed the means to process emigrant applications, and with the exception of some Pakistani Sikhs, few people in these countries had contacts with Canada sufficient to initiate immigration. Few Pakistanis or Ceylonese came to Canada under the quota system.

In contrast, all of the quota positions for India were filled every year the system was in place in its original form (1951-56), thus resulting in the immigration of 900 people and their dependants. The Canada-India Immigration Agreement of 1957 raised the Indian quota to 300, one-half of which would be subject to a preference quota giving priority to relatives of South Asian Canadian citizens. In 1958 the government allowed South Asian Canadians to sponsor a wider range of relatives, including mothers over sixty and fathers over sixty-five.[10] By then, the Canadian immigration office in New Delhi had a staff of twelve – 20,000 people had applied

TABLE 7

Pakistani and Ceylonese Immigrants to Canada, 1951-61

Year	Pakistani Immigrants	Ceylonese Immigrants
1951	24	0
1952	81	3
1953	98	9
1954	100	19
1955	84	40
1956	100	24
1957	98	23
1958	54	23
1959	98	12
1960	100	5
1961	64	27
TOTAL	901	185

SOURCE: Figures from the Canadian quota book for 1951-62, PAC, RG 76, not yet catalogued.

by the time the office first opened.[11] By the end of 1961, 2,338 immigrant visas had been given out by the New Delhi office under the quota system and another 2,000 Indian citizens had come to Canada as dependent relatives of resident Canadians.

At first, most of these immigrants were very similar in cultural background to those who had come before. Until 1957 most Indian immigrants were Sikh relatives of Canadian residents. The quota for Pakistan was also primarily taken up by Sikhs who had been trapped in Pakistan at independence. Even so, important changes in the type of South Asian immigrant coming to Canada were already developing. One of these involved the class backgrounds of immigrants. The pioneers had been well-off peasants with some familiarity with British institutions. Some of their relatives who were arriving in the 1950's were professionals – teachers, scientists, doctors, technicians, engineers, and businessmen. Such people would become increasingly prevalent right through the 1960's.

Another change was equally fundamental – an increasing proportion of South Asian immigrants were not Sikh, and as such were the pioneers of their own communities. From India in the 1950's came a small number of Punjabi Hindus and Muslims, and a few more Punjabi Muslims were added by Pakistan. By 1960 a couple of hundred Indian nationals of other ethnic, linguistic, and regional backgrounds had also arrived – a polyglot collection of Hindi-speaking people from Uttar Pradesh, Gujaratis, Bengalis, Tamil-speakers from Madras, and others. Almost all of them were well educated and highly trained. In addition, a few Sinhalese and Tamils arrived from Ceylon and a handful of Anglo-Indians came from Pakistan. As these groups went their separate ways they increased the complexity of the South Asian experience in Canada, which could never again be equated simply with the Sikhs. Finally, these new immigrants began to spread out across the country, starting communities in Toronto, Montreal, and elsewhere.

THE 1950's IN BRITISH COLUMBIA

British Columbia remained the heartland of South Asian Canadian life during the 1950's, and renewed immigration brought many changes there. By 1961 there were 4,526 South Asians in British Columbia.[12] After fifty years in Canada the community had once more reached the numbers it had in 1908. Of these, perhaps 3,000 were in the Lower Mainland and half were post-war immigrants.

Chain migration continued to keep British Columbia's South Asian community homogeneous. A high proportion of new immigants were relatives, and hence shared most of the ethnic, religious, and cultural traits of the Sikh community. Most of the rest were also Sikhs, who found it less isolating to settle in an area where there were already many Sikhs. By 1957 there were fewer than a hundred non-Sikh South Asians in British Columbia.

Nevertheless, the reduction of immigration restrictions led directly to the loss of much of the coherence that had characterized the Sikh community for so many years. No longer was there a geographical centre in Vancouver around which South Asians congregated. The days when everyone knew everyone else were gone. Moreover, despite common Sikh roots, people's backgrounds, interests, and affiliations became more varied. Changing Canadian criteria had already made immigration easier for professional South Asians than for working-class or farming people, and this introduced class divisions into the community by the late 1950's. In addition, renewed immigration brought modern Indians into a community controlled and defined by older men of a different era, and the new arrivals were typically far more Westernized and less traditional. This frequently made their adjustment to life in Canada easier, but often at some cost:

> I immigrated in 1952 from the Indian Punjab. My parents were better off than most, so I was sent right through secondary school. When I came to Canada my sights were set on being an engineer, but I had no money to go to university. None of my close Canadian relatives were very educated, and all the men worked hard in the mills. They did the best they could for me, taking me in and finding

me a job alongside them. Work in the mills was hard but it paid pretty well, so most of my Sikh friends and relatives were content with it. I just wasn't. I saved up my money and set off to the University of British Columbia. Despite objections I took off my turban and shaved my beard in order to better fit in. Eventually I got my engineering degree and began work for a utility company. I never lost touch with my friends and relatives from earlier years, but we don't see as much of each other as we might. Family feeling and Sikhism keep us together, because in other ways we live in different worlds. Many of my close friends are also professionals, and many of them are not South Asians.

In Vancouver this diversity soon resulted in a religious dispute. In contrast to the pioneers of 1903-08, a majority of post-war Sikh immigrant men had decided not to continue the observance of wearing the *Kakkas*, the overt symbols of Sikh religion. This they did with reluctance, in the belief that to do so would allow them to fit better into the Canadian society. Following the lead of their second-generation compatriots they cut their hair, shaved their beards, and put aside the turban. This was a difficult and contentious choice. As one commentator of the period noted:

> The problem of whether to wear the *Kakkas* (especially the beard) is one which has wide implications for the unity, and perhaps even the survival of the Sikh community. Many men coming from India shave their beards and put aside their turbans with mixed feelings. They do it to 'look like other people', for they feel self-conscious with what to most Canadians is a strange and perhaps disquieting dress. At the same time, they feel at least temporarily that they have abandoned part of their heritage. Nobody denies that communal unity is weaker through the absence of the *Kakkas* [for] when the visible evidence [for Sikhism] is gone assimilation to Canadian society is that much easier. [13]

In 1952 this was one of several issues that arose in the Vancouver temple about appropriate Sikh religious practice. In the discussion of these points of conflict the majority sided with the non-traditionalists. The others broke away and founded the Akali Singh Sikh Temple on East 11th Avenue in Vancouver. A similar split occurred in Victoria. Realizing that such a dispute weakened their position vis-à-vis government, Vancouver Sikhs started the East Indian Welfare Association (later, the East Indian Canadian Citizens Welfare Association) to form a bridge between the two groups.

Other differences were a function of the community's growth. For one thing, the caste distribution among Sikhs changed. Whereas virtually all of the pioneers were Jats, this had dropped to about 80 per cent by the end of the 1950's as quota immigration brought non-relatives into the community.[14] Some Rajputs became influential in community affairs, and Jat solidarity was weakened somewhat by the arrival of some members of other Sikh castes – Khatris, Aroras, and others. Although all Sikhs worshipped together and usually associated with each other, this solidarity stopped at the point of marriage – even today few Sikhs in Canada marry out of caste. There was also an increased diversity of area and village origins, which brought with it different cultural values and identifications.

There were nevertheless many important continuities with the past. One of these was work, where the mills continued to be central despite more men going into manufacturing, farming, and the professions; women rarely worked outside the home throughout the 1950's. Another was the importance of the local temples, which continued to be the focal points for community affairs. Religious services continued to bring people together within each community and large celebrations held each year at specific temples helped to maintain inter-community links.

In particular, there persisted a rigorous continuity in family life and marriage. As the population of young unmarried people grew through immigration and the rise of the second generation, a system of match-making arose to find these people mates. For the most part, these were to come through marriages arranged by their families in India. Sometimes, a man or woman would be sent off to Canada without having ever met his or her prospective spouse. For Canadian men it was more common to return to one's home village and place oneself in the hands of relatives:

> I went back to India in 1951 and stayed eight months. Soon after I had arrived, word got around that an eligible bachelor had arrived from Canada. People with daughters started to enquire about me to my relatives in the village. Only one man talked to me directly. He asked me what I wanted in a wife, did I want an educated girl? I said that it would be better if she was, for she would need to read a bit and answer the telephone in English, and it would be easier for her to start wearing a dress if she was educated. He never came back, so I guess that his girl could not read. Several men made bids, and my relatives thought that they were suitable, so we all went to Jullundur, to meet 'by accident'. But you know, I could not see the girls at all clearly, they were either with a whole crowd of people, or else I had to look through one of those windows they have, with bars on. I told my relatives this, and we had one girl come into the same room, but she stood behind me, so that I did not like her. One girl's brother and mother were in favor of me. Her father did not want her to marry a Sikh without a beard, but they told him, 'even if he grows it here for you, you know that he will shave it when he gets to Canada.' He gave in, and that was the girl that I married.[15]

Very few Sikhs of either sex married non-Sikhs, a pattern that has continued to the present.

Some other continuities were less positive. Selective, low-level discrimination continued to be a problem in the 1950's in employment and education; most private schools in Vancouver did not accept South Asians until the 1960's and job discrimination against those women who wanted to work outside the home was quite strong. [16] Sikh fears about acculturation continued to make many suspicious about the value of extensive education for their children and about associating too closely with non-Sikhs. These concerns sometimes developed into sharp conflicts between parents and children, husband and wife, young and old. These familial stresses were to be mirrored time and time again as other South Asian groups subsequently came onto the scene.

NEW FRONTIERS, NEW PEOPLES

The post-war expansion of Canada's industry created a demand for labour that the government intended to fill through immigration. Once more, the government was required to weaken its cultural criteria in order to tap pools of appropriate overseas labour. Soon peoples traditionally considered to be culturally marginal (such as Italians) were being solicited in great numbers. As the 1950's unfolded the government made several attempts to stiffen the economic criteria for immigration; enough unskilled labour had been secured, and the goal was to set up a system of selective immigration in high-demand occupations.

In addition, Canada was under pressure from the international community to remove its racial immigration restrictions. Token national quotas for India, Pakistan, and Ceylon aside, racial restrictions continued in force. Throughout the 1950's Canada continually upped the occupational criteria through which it selected South Asian quota immigrants. As a consequence, the proportion of South Asian professional, managerial, and technical workers among immigrants rose steadily, from about 32 per cent in 1951 to 55 per cent in 1961. [17] Labourers dropped from 46 per cent to 29 per cent during the same period. In the early 1960's the yearly proportion of professionals among immigrant workers from India went as high as 68 per cent.

These changes in the immigration regulations brought to Canada immigrants from a number of South Asian populations who had no prior tradition of immigration to North America. It led also to a geographical expansion of South Asian communities across Canada as skilled, well-educated South Asians went to where job prospects were best. In those days this primarily meant Toronto. A few Sikhs had lived in the Toronto area as early as the 1920's, but Toronto-area settlement really dates from the rise of professional-class immigration in the mid-1950's. During this period a small number of families dispersed across the industrial heartland of Ontario, settling wherever the job market took them; many were teachers or university instructors or became government bureaucrats. Because of their small numbers and Anglicized middle-class

TABLE 8

South Asians in Canada, 1961

Province	Number
British Columbia	4,526
Ontario	1,155
Quebec	483
Alberta	208
Manitoba	198
Saskatchewan	115
Nova Scotia	46
New Brunswick	22
Newfoundland	17
Prince Edward Island	1
Yukon and Northwest Territories	0
TOTAL	6,771

SOURCE: *Census of Canada*, 1961, vol. 1:2.

origins, they rarely formed communities in any real sense. The only exceptions were Sikhs, who were numerous enough to establish a gurdwara in the Toronto area. This became the first substantial South Asian Canadian cultural institution east of British Columbia. By 1961 this process of geographical dispersal was well established.

These immigrants pioneered places where there had been no history of South Asian settlement before; consequently, there were no communities to assist them, no relatives to give support, no social institutions to help in the transition to Canadian life. As with the first pioneers, these were things they had to do on their own:

> When I first came to Winnipeg in 1962 it seemed as if there were almost no South Asian people here at all. I had come to go to the University of Manitoba, and I soon found that there were a handful of other South Asian students there – a few Sikhs, a few Muslims from India and Pakistan, and one or two others. There were also some South Asians on the faculty of the university and perhaps a score of men worked at a variety of other jobs around town. Counting their families, I doubt if there were many more than a hundred of us.
>
> In some ways I think it was harder on us new immigrants then than it was later, especially because so many of us had to figure everything out on our own. Take the winter, for instance. Most of us hadn't ever seen snow close up before!

There wasn't really a South Asian community in Winnipeg in those days. We came from a number of different countries, practised different religions, and spoke different languages. What we had in common was a sense of being South Asian, somewhat similar family and educational backgrounds, and the English language. Already, though, people were beginning to encourage their relatives to immigrate to Winnipeg or to come there from other parts of Canada. Out of this arose the beginning of the many communities we have here today.

Even so, the Westernized middle-class background of these later immigrants and relatively easy access to jobs made adapting to Canadian life fairly straightforward. It should be noted that most higher education in South Asia was then carried out in English. Moreover, long association with the British had resulted in the middle classes taking up many elements of British culture. In a certain sense, many new immigrants were "pre-adapted" to life in Canada. Also, the lack of prior Canadian contact with South Asians often meant that these new pioneers did not have to face the racial bigotry that had characterized earlier South Asian experiences in British Columbia.

The key to these changes would once more be immigration. To be sure, the quota system had its effect, trebling the number of South Asians in Canada within a decade, but those 7,000 people who were here in 1961 were not that many more than were here in 1908. Annual immigration was increasing, but the number of immigrants was still very low.

TABLE 9

South Asian Immigration, 1945-1961

Year	Number	Year	Number
1945-46	1	1954	177
1946-47	8	1955	249
1947-48	167	1956	332
1948-49	64	1957	334
1949-50	54	1958	454
1950	77	1959	741
1951	99	1960	691
1952	172	1961	772
1953	140		
TOTAL			4,532

SOURCE: Michael M. Ames and Joy Inglis, "Conflict and Change in British Columbia Sikh Family Life," *B.C. Studies*, 20 (Winter, 1973), p. 19, from Department of Citizenship and Immigration annual statistical reports. South Asian here refers to ethnic origin, as volunteered to immigration authorities.

TABLE 10

South Asian Immigration to Canada by Last Country of Permanent Residence, 1962-71*

Country	1962	1963	1964	1965	1966	1967	1968	1969	1970	1971	Total
India	529	737	1,154	2,241	2,233	3,966	3,229	5,395	5,670	5,313	30,467
Pakistan	55	121	282	423	566	648	627	1,005	1,010	968	5,705
Sri Lanka	14	23	80	126	144	112	76	179	167	218	1,139
Other South Asia	0	0	0	0	4	5	9	10	21	14	63
Uganda	2	3	7	18	54	68	62	69	90	149	522
Kenya	9	18	46	112	114	239	359	363	245	289	1,794
South Africa	5	9	23	55	89	137	92	60	65	73	608
Tanzania	3	7	17	42	75	115	135	54	49	180	677
Guyana	40	80	200	487	502	589	658	1,492	1,672	1,907	7,627
Trinidad	32	64	160	390	565	1,170	1,210	2,816	2,395	2,075	10,877
Fiji	25	50	125	304	271	172	253	590	776	721	3,287
Mauritius	0	1	3	6	19	59	59	81	146	132	506
TOTAL	714	1,113	2,097	4,204	4,636	7,280	6,769	12,114	12,306	12,039	63,272

* Estimating South Asian immigration is difficult, and these figures should be considered approximate. Country of last permanent residence is a weak indicator of South Asian origin, inasmuch as there are substantial South Asian populations in countries where the majority is not South Asian. This table is based on the following assumptions: (1) that all immigration from India, Pakistan, Sri Lanka, Afghanistan, Uganda, Tanzania, Kenya, Fiji, and Mauritius was South Asian during 1962-71; (2) that 80 per cent of immigration from Guyana and 60 per cent of that from Trinidad was South Asian; (3) that 10 per cent of South African immigration was South Asian; (4) that immigration from Uganda, Kenya, South Africa, Tanzania, Guyana, Trinidad, and Mauritius rose during 1962-64 at the same rate of increase as Fiji. During this period South Asian migration from other places (chiefly the U.S. and Britain) must add several thousand more to the overall total.

SOURCES: Canada, Department of Manpower and Immigration, *Immigration Statistics* (1962-71); John R. Wood, "East Indians and Canada's New Immigration Policy," *Canadian Public Policy*, 4, 4 (1978), p. 552.

113

Fundamental changes in immigration were afoot, though, which would change this forever. In 1962 the Canadian government removed almost all racial and national restrictions from its immigration regulations. Five years later the federal government made socioeconomic immigrant selection criteria much more rigorous and eliminated all racial, national, and ethnic restrictions. This resulted in an exponential increase in South Asian immigration. Immigration during the decade 1962-71 was over *twelve times* what it had been in the previous decade. It was nine times the total resident population in 1961. The 1961 census had shown a small population still concentrated primarily in British Columbia, but the census of 1971 showed a strikingly different picture: the geographical distribution of South Asians in Canada had been transformed. There were now more South Asians in Quebec than there had been in British Columbia in 1961; Ontario had increased its South Asian population twenty-seven times; there were more South Asians in Edmonton (915) than there had been in Vancouver in 1951.

Rates of immigration remained high right through the 1970's and early 1980's. From 1971 to 1982 at least 200,000 South Asians came to Canada, making them one of the largest immigrant flows of the period. There were about 310,000 people of South Asian origin in Canada at the end of 1982, representing about 1.2 per cent of the Canadian population.[18] Taken together, South Asians are now one of Canada's largest

TABLE 11

South Asians in Canada, 1971	
Province	*Number*
Ontario	30,920
British Columbia	18,795
Quebec	6,510
Alberta	4,400
Manitoba	3,205
Saskatchewan	1,625
Nova Scotia	1,345
New Brunswick	465
Newfoundland	460
Prince Edward Island	135
Yukon and N.W. Territories	0
TOTAL	67,860

SOURCE: *Census of Canada*, 1971, vol. 1:2.

TABLE 12

South Asian Immigration, 1972-82

Country	1972	1973	1974	1975	1976	1977	1978	1979	1980	1981	1982	Total
India	5,049	9,203	12,868	10,144	6,733	6,772	5,110	4,517	8,464	8,256	7,776	84,892
Pakistan	1,190	2,285	2,315	2,165	2,173	1,321	1,159	1,117	878	731	868	16,202
Sri Lanka	240	405	527	369	235	168	146	117	144	223	182	2,756
Bangladesh	103	151	158	104	79	164	110	50	76	73	58	1,126
Other South Asia	5	28	12	12	11	9	11	4	13	38	79	222
Uganda	5,021	2,056	423	112	29	248	43	16	7	16	45	8,016
Kenya	320	1,193	2,394	2,477	1,202	540	227	319	360	345	277	9,654
South Africa	44	77	115	157	161	246	165	134	137	143	99	1,478
Tanzania	1,105	1,688	2,024	2,188	1,299	790	361	535	450	664	514	11,618
Guyana	1,581	3,846	3,224	3,515	2,744	1,978	1,802	1,978	1,818	2,269	2,789	27,544
Trinidad	1,370	2,569	2,401	1,909	1,180	776	595	393	477	477	496	12,643
Fiji	636	987	1,530	2,323	1,081	713	552	518	637	699	818	10,494
Mauritius	127	123	247	253	286	198	147	190	277	186	304	2,338
Britain	600	800	1,000	1,200	1,400	1,350	1,100	1,000	1,000	1,000	650	11,100
TOTAL	17,391	25,411	29,238	26,928	18,613	15,273	11,528	10,888	14,738	15,120	14,955	200,083

SOURCES: The assumptions and sources used in preparing this table are the same as for Table 10.

115

ethnocultural populations and they continue to be one of the fastest growing.

Changing immigration criteria during the 1970's also increased the ethnocultural and occupational diversity of South Asian Canadians. A score of linguistic, ethnic, national, and religious groups were soon established across the country, weakening the traditional preponderance of Sikhs.[19] Up until about 1972, Canadian immigration preferences remained strongly biased in favour of professionals, managers, and skilled white-collar workers – occupational skills that for many people in India, Pakistan, and Sri Lanka were very underutilized because of fierce competition for available jobs. Such people were representative of immigrants until the early 1970's. Nevertheless, occupational criteria of immigrant selection were already changing. Compare the professional-oriented occupational distributions of immigrants from 1967 (Table 13) with those from 1974 (Table 14).

By the late 1970's this occupational distribution had been transformed once again. Economic recession resulted in a general restriction in the number of people coming to Canada. Occupational immigrant demand factors for most occupations were lowered and this hit prospective independent immigrants hard. The result was that from 1975 on the proportion of sponsored (now called family-class) South Asian immigrants has predominated. In 1982 only 11 per cent of immigrants from India were independent immigrants. This has contributed to a shift in the oc-

TABLE 13

Occupations of Indian and Pakistani Immigrants, 1967

Occupation	India	Pakistan
Management	48	13
Professional	1,213	233
Clerical	144	36
Transportation	12	3
Commerce	26	3
Service	22	9
Agriculture	18	2
Construction	12	3
Manufacturing	163	31
Labouring	99	1
Other	45	6
Total to work force	1,802	340

SOURCE: Canada, Department of Manpower and Immigration, *Immigration Statistics* (1967), pp. 14-15.

TABLE 14

Occupations of Indian, Tanzanian, Fijian, and Guyanese Immigrants, 1974

Occupation	India	Tanzania	Fiji	Guyana
Managerial	77	175	19	70
Professional	863	101	14	117
Clerical	198	112	67	270
Commerce	82	30	16	64
Services	77	8	25	73
Transport	14	—	4	7
Agriculture	268	11	12	3
Manufacturing	416	46	104	217
Other	200	2	11	73
Total to work force	2,195	485	272	894

SOURCE: Canada, Department of Manpower and Immigration, *Immigration Statistics* (1974), pp. 34-37.

cupational background of South Asian immigrants, especially among South Asian groups like Sikhs with a strong tradition of sponsorship. A greater government preference for skilled blue-collar immigrant workers has similarly affected South Asian immigration. That there are now larger communities of South Asian Fijians and Guyanese and Trinidadian Indians in Canada can be attributed primarily to these changes in immigration preferences. By the late 1970's the occupational range of South Asian immigrants was very wide indeed.

Even today, though, the worldwide flow of South Asian immigrants to Canada cannot be entirely accounted for by such things as the occupational skills of prospective immigrants or their varying interests in coming to Canada. Rather, many anomalies in this flow seem to stem from political, bureaucratic, or other factors that are not technically supposed to be part of the selecting process. Consider, for example, that Bangladesh (population: over 80 million) sent fifty-eight immigrants to Canada in 1982, while Fiji (population: 600,000) sent 818; neither the regulations nor the strength of immigration demand can account for the fact that a Fijian is almost 2,000 times more likely to immigrate than a Bangali. Similar imbalances exist among other countries. There have also been sharp swings in the yearly number of immigrants from particular countries (see Table 12), and many South Asian Canadians are convinced that the reduction by two-thirds in overall South Asian immigration between 1975 and 1979 was consciously done in the hope of reducing the level of prejudice against South Asians and backlash against federal immigration policy.

It is now very hard to immigrate to Canada from South Asia, in part

117

TABLE 15

Occupations of Indian, Tanzanian, Fijian, and Guyanese Immigrants, 1979

Occupations	India	Tanzania	Fiji	Guyana
Entrepreneurs	15	2	—	3
Managers	124	9	5	29
Physical sciences	127	10	9	43
Social sciences	16	1	—	5
Teaching	19	1	2	7
Medicine	57	4	5	20
Performing arts	27	—	2	6
Clerical	317	90	35	198
Sales	83	33	7	36
Service	26	7	8	77
Farming	76	3	3	30
Processing	19	1	2	11
Machining	31	3	7	41
Fabrication	49	8	20	136
Construction	14	2	14	38
Transportation	9	4	4	7
Material handling	10	1	—	18
Other	646	18	54	148
Total to work force	1,665	197	177	853

SOURCE: Canada, Department of Manpower and Immigration, *Immigration Statistics* (1974), pp. 36-41.

because access to the application process is difficult. There is only one Canadian immigration centre in India and it also handles Sri Lankan applications. In 1979 there were seven centres in the United Kingdom alone.[20] The application procedure can take years and the probability of success is low. Those who can, seek out relatives in Canada to sponsor them, even when they would prefer to apply independently. Enterprising individuals sometimes move temporarily to European countries where they know that the chances of being accepted by Canadian immigration officials are better. A few try to qualify for entrance as businessmen-entrepreneurs by converting all their assets into cash. Others seek marriage mates in Canada.

Despite recent cutbacks, South Asians will unlikely ever comprise less than 10 per cent of Canada's yearly total of new immigrants. For one thing, there are continuing reasons why the demand for immigration will remain strong wherever South Asians live. Hundreds of thousands of well-qualified people in India, Pakistan, Bangladesh, and Sri Lanka remain underemployed or are otherwise dissatisfied with their economic situation. South Asians in East Africa, Fiji, and Guyana face limited economic prospects and great political uncertainty. Those in South Africa remain racially oppressed through the government's policy of apartheid. Others in Britain wish to escape racial discrimination and marginal economic situations. There are so many South Asians with such a wide variety of backgrounds that no future changes in the immigration regulations could possibly result in there not being a vast number of qualified South Asian people upon which to draw. Strong ties of kinship will continue to guarantee that prospective South Asian immigrants will take every advantage of the possibilities of sponsorship. Short of a complete termination of Canada's immigration program it is hard to envision anything that could result in there being less than 10,000 new South Asian arrivals each year for the rest of the century. By the year 2000 South Asian Canadians will in all probability number between 600,000 and 750,000. South Asians will then be one of the largest ethnic groups in Canada.

Even so, the early 1980's can be looked back to as the end of a third phase of South Asian Canadian history – the phase of rapid expansion and establishment, of building a foundation for life in this country. Between 1965 and 1982 over a quarter of a million people of South Asian origin experienced the risks and rewards of making Canada their new home. They were drawn from a wide range of cultural, national, and ethnic backgrounds. Instead of one group with a single culture there were first a few groups, then half a dozen, then a dozen, then more. The next chapter introduces these many groups and some of their commonalities and differences.

NOTES

1. The name Pakistan was coined by Chaudhuri Rahmat Ali in 1933. P represented Punjab, A, Afghanistan, K, Kashmir, S, Sind, and Tan, Baluchistan. Afghanistan was not part of British India, but Muslim nationalists then envisioned a state including it.
2. There were some small administrative changes made to allow the children of South Asian Canadians to come to Canada even though they had come of age during 1941-47; the rationale was that because of the war and subsequent turmoil, they had been unable to come as dependent minors.
3. Freda Hawkins, *Canada and Immigration: Public Policy and Public Concern* (Montreal, 1972), pp. 91-8.
4. Petition to the Minister of Mines and Resources, March 3, 1947, PAC, RG 76, #536999, part 17.
5. G.L. Mann to Escott Reid, May 16, 1947, *ibid.*; H.L. Keenleyside to the

Undersecretary of State for External Affairs, January 5, 1948, *ibid.*, part 18.

6. John Kearney to the Secretary of State for External Affairs, May 17, 1948, *ibid.*

7. Cabinet memo for file, June 18, 1948, *ibid.*

8. Y. Nasenko, *Jawaharlal Nehru and India's Foreign Policy* (New Delhi, 1977), pp. 67-8; Taraknath Das, *An Open Letter to Count Leo Tolstoy in Reply to his "Letter to a Hindoo"* (New York, 1909).

9. In 1951 there were seventy-six South Asians in Ontario, sixty-one in Quebec, twenty-seven in Alberta, and twenty-three in Nova Scotia. *Census of Canada*, 1951.

10. PC of January 2, 1958.

11. David C. Corbett, *Canada's Immigration Policy: A Critique* (Toronto, 1957), p. 181.

12. *Census of Canada*, 1961, vol. 1:2.

13. Adrian C. Mayer, *A Report on the East Indian Community in Vancouver* (Vancouver, 1959), p. 8.

14. *Ibid.*, p. 14.

15. *Ibid.*, p. 17.

16. Jennifer G. Munday, "East Indians in British Columbia: A Community in Transition" (B.A. honours essay, University of British Columbia, 1953), p. 39.

17. Michael M. Ames and Joy Inglis, "Conflict and Change in British Columbia Sikh Family Life," *B.C. Studies*, 20 (Winter, 1973), p. 26.

18. We believe that this is the best substantiated estimate made so far of the number of South Asians in Canada. It accepts the 1971 census figure of 67,860, adds all South Asian immigration for 1971-82, compounds this total at an annual rate of 3 per cent to allow for natural increase, adds 10,000 people for early South Asian immigration from Britain and another 10,000 for illegal immigration, and subtracts 20,000 for outmigration.

19. Even so, Sikhs still account for two-thirds of Indian immigration, 20 per cent of East African immigration, and at least half of South Asian immigrants from Britain. See John R. Wood, "East Indians and Canada's New Immigration Policy," *Canadian Public Policy*, 4, 4 (1978), pp. 547-67.

20. Doreen Indra, "The Relationship Between Canadian Immigrant Flows and Source Country Populations, Wealth and Trade," in K.V. Ujimoto and G. Hirabayashi (eds.), *Visible Minorities and Multiculturalism: Asians in Canada* (Scarborough, 1980), pp. 163-80.

Gurdit Singh Sarhali (far left, front) his son, and others aboard the Komagata Maru *in Vancouver harbour, 1914. (From* Literary Digest, *July 18, 1914, p. 95)*

The Hong Kong Regimental Contingent in Victoria, on their way to and from (below, left) Britain, 1902. (From Victoria Daily Times, *June 4, Sept. 8, 1902)*

New South Asian arrivals camped on the sidewalk on West Hastings Street in Vancouver, November, 1905. The temperature was below freezing. (Courtesy Vancouver City Archives)

Lumber workers in the Queen Charlotte Islands, B.C., 1910-1914. (Courtesy B.C. Provincial Archives)

Pioneer South Asians often lived under very rough conditions: these are living quarters at a Todd Inlet lumber mill. (Courtesy B.C. Provincial Archives)

South Asian and fellow loggers at a Sikh funeral service at Todd Inlet around 1909. (Courtesy Victoria City Archives)

WILL THE DIKE HOLD ?

This newspaper cartoon appeared during the Komagata Maru *incident in 1914.*
(From Literary Digest, *July 18, 1914, p. 96)*

The Komagata Maru *anchored in Vancouver harbour.*
(From Literary Digest, *July 18, 1914, p. 95)*

Guarding food destined for the Komagata Maru, *1914. (Courtesy B.C. Provincial Archives)*

Mewa Singh on his funeral pyre soon after being hanged by Canadian authorities for the assassination of William Hopkinson.

A meeting held in the Vancouver Sikh temple during the drive to secure the vote, 1946. (Courtesy Vancouver City Archives)

The Vancouver Sikh temple on Christmas night, 1943. (Courtesy Vancouver City Archives)

*Mayo Singh, a major Sikh industrialist during the period 1920-1950.
(Courtesy Victoria City Archives)*

A send-off photograph at a celebration marking the emigration of a family from Sri Lanka (Ceylon) to Canada, 1955. (Courtesy Multicultural History Society of Ontario)

Sikh dancers participating in the Vancouver Folk Festival Parade, 1974. (Courtesy Vancouver Sun)

A South Asian business area in East Vancouver. (Courtesy Vancouver Sun*)*

CANADA CUSTOMS AND IMMIGRATION

Clamp down, Immigration, before things get worse

STOP AND REPORT

Newspaper objections to Asian immigration arose again in the mid-1970's. This anti-immigration column is from the Vancouver Sun, *May 31, 1975. (Courtesy* Vancouver Sun*)*

Cab drivers and others demonstrate against racism in Vancouver during the height of anti-South Asian prejudice, 1980. (Courtesy David Clark, Vancouver Province*)*

South Asian and other Muslims participating in a prayer meeting at the CNE, Toronto, 1976.
(Courtesty Ontario Archives)

Sri Lankan Buddhist temple in Toronto, 1976.
(Courtesy Multicultural History Society of Ontario)

Ismaili Centre in Burnaby, B.C., designed by architect Bruno Freschi to treat traditional Islamic architecture in a contemporary manner. (Courtesy Ismaili National Council)

South Asians demonstrating against racism, City Hall, Toronto, 1977. (Courtesy Multicultural History Society of Ontario)

Tin Paiser Pala, *a Bengali version of Bertolt Brecht's* Three Penny Opera, *performed in Toronto in 1980. (Courtesy Multicultural History Society of Ontario)*

Sinhalese drummer leading a Sri Lankan New Year parade in Toronto, 1983. (Courtesy Multicultural History Society of Ontario)

South Asian women in Vancouver taking a course to familiarize themselves with Canadian life, 1984. (Courtesy Vancouver Sun)

Anne-Marie Gaston (Anjali), an internationally known performer of South Asian dance. (Photo by Tony Gaston)

Indian dance at the Heritage Day Festival in Edmonton, 1984. A Bharathanatyam pose (left) and children performing Bhangra (right). (Courtesy S. Padmanabhan)

Marc Lalonde addressing the 1984 NACOI Conference in Montreal. (Courtesy S. Padmanabhan)

Offering puja *(worship) at the Saint Thyagarija Music Festival. (Courtesy S. Padmanabhan)*

Saint Thyagarija Music Festival, Edmonton, 1984, organized by the Edmonton Tamil Cultural Association. (Courtesy S. Padmanabhan)

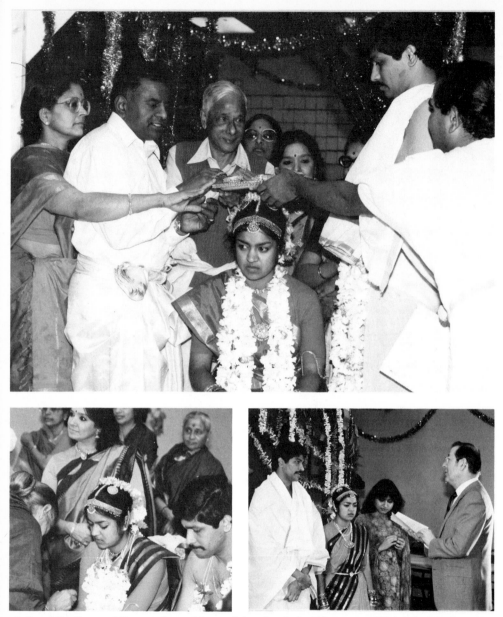

A South Indian wedding performed in traditional style in Edmonton, 1984. The Hindu priest was flown in from Toronto for the occasion. After the Hindu religious ceremony the couple was married by a commissioner. (Courtesy S. Padmanabhan)

EIGHT

Diversification and Expansion

A sharp rise in immigration during the 1960's and the early 1970's led to enormous changes in the South Asian Canadian experience. One of the most important of these changes was a substantial increase in the range of cultural, ethnic, and national backgrounds of South Asian immigrants. Previously, the dominant theme of South Asian Canadian culture was Sikh; thereafter, Sikhs became only one (albeit the most evident) variation of a South Asian cultural theme involving many other groups. This chapter outlines a few elements of this diverse South Asian cultural heritage within a general unity of values and practices. As such, it begins with what may at first appear to be rather obvious questions. What do we mean by the term "South Asian"? What do people so categorized have in common? This in turn introduces a series of brief sketches of today's many South Asian Canadian ethnocultural groups.

THEME AND VARIATIONS ON BEING SOUTH ASIAN

There are basically three quite different ways to approach the question of what is meant by "South Asian," and each has important consequences for the people concerned. Perhaps the easiest of the three to describe is to ask how South Asians are viewed by other Canadians. In other words, do Canadians generally see people, say from Punjab in India and Kandi, Sri Lanka, as being in some ways the same? This was certainly true in early British Columbia, where the term "Hindoo" was once used to refer to all immigrants from the Indian subcontinent regardless of their ethnic or religious roots. Ethnic stereotypes of the day took little account of such variation and, indeed, were largely based on popular British prejudices against Indians, not on local immigrants. It was only in the 1930's and 1940's that people understood that their fellow British Columbians were Sikhs. Naturally, as the *Komagata Maru* incident faded from memory, almost no one outside the province was aware of Sikh Canadians at all.

This situation changed as South Asian immigration increased in the

1960's and 1970's. As is detailed in Chapter Twelve, this increase in immigration did eventually catch the public's eye across the country, and it led to some parallels with what had occurred earlier in British Columbia. People then (as now) knew little about South Asia and were consequently unaware of the important differences between one South Asian immigrant group and another. To most Canadians they all became "East Indians," a term that came to be applied rather casually without distinction to everyone who appeared to be from South Asia. Eventually a negative stereotype of East Indians arose, which gave further support to the notion that such people were culturally very similar to each other. It has only been in the past few years that most Canadians have caught even the smallest indication of the ethnocultural diversity of South Asians.

Popular misconceptions about South Asians and South Asian cultures still abound. Accordingly, they cannot be dismissed even though they are at such variance with reality. People of South Asian origins have had to live and adjust to these misconceptions. Popular stereotypes and widespread ignorance of South Asia have created a certain degree of commonality in the lives of all South Asian Canadians. One result has been a made-in-Canada consciousness of being South Asian among people who might not have thought much about it before. In this sense, South Asians *are* those whom others call South Asian.

Another approach to the question of what "South Asian" means is to consider it from the point of view of South Asians themselves. Doing so produces a rather complicated result. To most people of South Asian origin, the term has about the same sort of meaning as does "European" to those who can trace their roots to Europe. While recognizing broad commonalities with other South Asian ethnocultural and national groups, members of any particular group are primarily identified with their immediate group. Just like Europeans, South Asians usually hold an overlapping set of identities: perhaps with respect to family, village or town, caste, religion, ethnic group, language, nation, South Asian culture, and the world. Commitment to those identities closer to everyday life is naturally the most important.

This makes a good deal of sense. The cultural differences between one South Asian and another are often very great. Consider the heartland, South Asia. A continent in itself, it has a greater population than Europe, North America, South America, or Africa. From this alone stems much variability; it is a vast area populated by many different peoples. Moreover, the region was never exposed to centralized political or military control long enough to fully reduce the social and cultural differences between these groups. In this regard, South Asia differs from China, where centuries of central rule widely disseminated Han culture and society.

As a result, South Asia is an unparalleled region of human diversity where political, religious, linguistic, regional, class, caste, and physical distinctions abound. The area is politically subdivided into the Muslim states of Pakistan, Afghanistan, and Bangladesh, predominantly Hindu India, and Buddhist Sri Lanka. All across India's international boundaries, basic cultural conventions and oral languages are continuous, but religion and group identity change dramatically; culture, religion, and identity, for example, all differ between India and Sri Lanka.

Within each of these countries there is a diversity of languages and one level of identity follows this. Prior to partition in 1947 the Linguistic Survey of India found 179 languages and 544 dialects in India.[1] Even though most of these are spoken by very few people, there are fourteen languages in modern India spoken by two million people or more (Table 16). Each of these defines broad cultural and language-based identities at least as sharply as those between anglophones and francophones in Canada. Similar linguistic cleavages exist in Pakistan (between Urdu, Punjabi, Pushtun, Baluchi, Sindi, and other languages) and Sri Lanka (between Sinhalese and Tamil).

There are also substantial religious divisions. Perhaps 100 million Muslims still live in India, as do Sikhs, Christians, Jains, non-Hindu

TABLE 16

India's Major Languages, 1961

Language	Number (millions)
Indo-Aryan Group	
Western and Eastern Hindi and Urdu	157.0
Bengali	33.9
Marathi	33.3
Gujarati	20.3
Bihari	16.8
Oriya	15.7
Rajastani	14.9
Punjabi	10.9
Assamese	6.8
Kashmiri	2.0
Dravidian Group	
Telugu	37.7
Tamil	30.6
Kannanda	17.4
Malayalam	17.0

SOURCE: W.H. Morris-Jones, "Languages and Region Within the India Union," in P. Mason (ed.), *India and Ceylon: Unity and Diversity* (London: Oxford University Press, 1967), p. 54.

tribal peoples, and others. Pakistan, Sri Lanka, and Bangladesh all have their corresponding Hindu minorities.

South Asia has been invaded continuously for the past 2,500 years, and each major invasion has added to its cultural complexity. When the Aryans moved into northern South Asia around 1000 B.C. they imposed a cultural overlay of their language, beliefs, and society on the indigenous peoples. Even today, Aryan influences can be seen in the foundations of Hindu thought and in the linguistic split between the Indo-European, Sanskrit-based languages of north and central South Asia and the Dravidian languages of the south. Over 2,000 years later the great world expansion of Islam was manifest in the consolidation of Mogul rule over northern and central South Asia. Through the Koran and *dowa* (teaching), Islam made many converts. It also spread Mogul and Islamic customs among the non-Muslim population of the area. This effect was very uneven; some regions were completely Islamicized while others were virtually untouched.

The Mogul empire eventually weakened and the British moved into the political vacuum this created. Like their Mogul counterparts, the British set about transforming India in their own image. Also like the Moguls, their effects were unevenly felt. Some small urban groups took up English as their first language and subscribed to British customs to as great an extent as a colonial people could. In other rural areas few people ever saw a British person in their whole lives.

This regional, linguistic, religious, and cultural variability is further compounded by sharp class and caste distinctions that are the rule across most of South Asia. Much social interaction is framed by class considerations. Marriage, friendship, occupation, status, and identity are determined by it. In Hindu areas of South Asia this has been made explicit in the notion of caste – endogamous status groups are often linked to traditional occupations. There are many hundreds of distinguishable castes and subcastes in Hindu South Asia, and it is not uncommon to have twenty to thirty different castes represented in a single village; they "live together separately" in a universe filled with fine distinctions of inter-caste etiquette and status.

This social complexity results in the self-identity of people from South Asia being very situationally specific. An individual will only feel South Asian when interacting with non-South Asians. In interaction with Pakistanis, he or she will be Indian; with Gujaratis he or she will be Punjabi, with Punjabi Hindus he or she will be Sikh. Among other Sikhs he or she would be a Jat from a good family in Patiala. Being "South Asian" to most people from South Asia is only relevant when they leave the area.

To this complex picture must be added those whose ultimate origins are in South Asia but who live elsewhere – Fiji, the Caribbean, East and South Africa, and Mauritius. Beginning in the mid-1800's the British began to indenture Indians for work on colonial plantations. In theory, the terms were contractual and clear. Typically, a worker would receive free passage to the colony in question. Once there, he or she would receive one shilling a day for achieving specified tasks. The contract was for five years, at which time the individual could reindenture himself or herself, settle in the colony, or be given free passage home.

Practice was far different. Indentured labour overseas was usually viewed by South Asians as a last recourse and most who went had been detached from their traditional roots by family or village conflicts. Labour contractors found people where they could and paid no heed to regional, ethnic, religious, or caste distinctions. This resulted in an extremely varied indentured population, which at first shared little except their indentured condition. Conditions under indenture were harsh. Death rates were commonly 5 per cent per year and workers were often not paid, either because they could not fulfil their daily tasks or because of fines for being absent from work or off the plantation.[2]

Indentured labourers went out to Fiji, South Africa, Mauritius, British Guiana, Trinidad, and a host of small Caribbean islands. In almost every instance, the consequence of introducing Indian indentured labour was racial conflict between Indians and the populations already established there. In Fiji, the primary division was between Indians and native people. In Mauritius, Guyana, and Trinidad it arose between blacks and Indians, while in South Africa the conflict was chiefly Indian-white. As

TABLE 17

Approximate Overseas South Asian Populations Deriving Primarily from Indentured Labour, 1970*

Country	Number
South Africa	614,000
Mauritius	520,000
Guyana	360,000
Trinidad	360,000
Fiji	241,000
Surinam	101,700
Grenada	9,500
St. Vincent	3,700
TOTAL	2,209,900

* This table does not include similar populations that have arisen in South and Southeast Asia. There are about 1.2 million Indian Tamils in Sri Lanka, over 800,000 South Asians in Malaysia, and 272,000 in Burma.

SOURCE: Yash Tandon, *Problem of a Displaced Minority: The New Position of East Africa's Asians* (London: Minority Rights Group, 1974), p. 4.

125

competition between these groups developed after independence, it eventually created a strong incentive for Indians to leave. Generations of living outside of South Asia have largely severed allegiances of these populations to their continent of origin and have created among them strong identifications with their birthplaces. Few people feel that they have much in common with those who come from South Asia itself. There are now approximately two million people of South Asian origin living overseas whose ancestors emigrated during the period of indentured labour.

To a lesser extent, this divergence of identities of South Asians deriving from a history of indenture from those in India can also be seen among those who emigrated from South Asia on their own. Thus, Sikhs who went to what are now Uganda, Tanzania, Malawi, Zambia, and Kenya between 1895 and the 1940's as labourers and traders soon developed a certain distinctiveness. So did the Hindu and Muslim populations of East Africa, who were attracted there by business opportunities. Most of the many overseas minority communities created by "free" immigration were able to keep language and custom relatively intact.

TABLE 18

Approximate Overseas South Asian Populations Deriving Primarily from "Free" Immigration, 1970*

Country	Number
United Kingdom	270,000
Kenya	182,000
Singapore	125,000
Tanzania	105,000
Uganda	76,000
Indonesia	27,600
Thailand	18,000
Israel	23,000
Madagascar	12,350
Malawi	11,300
Zambia	10,700
Zimbabwe	10,000
TOTAL	870,950

* This table does not include Canada and the U.S., each of which had about 70,000 South Asian residents in 1970. The number of South Asians in the United Kingdom has subsequently increased to well over a million.

SOURCE: Tandon, *Problem of a Displaced Minority*, p. 4.

When people of South Asian origin come to Canada their relations with others activate their identities as South Asians. Even so, their primary ethnic identities remain those with which they were familiar before emigration. Personal social networks typically will follow such lines and most organizations will be based on them. The common belief that South Asians now form a homogeneous community in Canada is entirely false. For example, there are far fewer social contacts between Vancouver Sikhs and Fijians than there are between either of these groups and other Canadians.[3]

UNITY IN DIVERSITY

At the same time, there *is* something that can be broadly termed South Asian culture – something that partially transcends regional and other group differences. Isolated by mountains from both China and the West, South Asia is the heartland of one of the oldest continuous cultural traditions in the world. For more than 3,000 years most people in South Asia have participated in a complex, village-based agriculture that has made its mark on belief and behaviour across the region. From the earliest days, this form of village life made the household the most important social unit. The household was typically made up of an extended family and was the basic unit of production, distribution, and consumption. It held land, provided most of the labour to work it, and shared in the results of labour. It was also a political unit: individuals were weak but households were strong.

Today, all of South Asia is rapidly urbanizing and many people no longer live in villages. Nevertheless, this has not diminished the importance of households or of the extensive kin links that radiate out from them. A limited dependence on family and kinship remains an important requisite for security and success.

The importance of the family is parallelled by several other cultural uniformities. The most important of these is the influence of Hinduism on South Asian thought and practice. Not all of South Asia is Hindu, but Hindu religion and its secular culture have had profound effects everywhere. These effects transcend regional, linguistic, and even religious boundaries.

Over the past 2,000 years Hinduism has influenced every aspect of life. It has provided the basis for folk philosophy all across South Asia. Hinduism has also been inextricably intertwined with South Asian history; most of the major religious texts are also historical documents that have served to connect the present with the past. Great epic poetry like the Ramayana is part of the folk tradition everywhere. Thus, Hinduism and the social contexts that supported it provided a certain ideological and behavioural uniformity across South Asia.

Hinduism has always stressed the importance of the family, perhaps to a greater extent than any other world religion; it gives religious legitima-

127

tion to the fundamental social unit of South Asian society and provides models for ideal familial and village roles. Hinduism often legitimated male domination over women; it gave authority to the old and to the upper classes; it supported the caste system through its doctrines of reincarnation, *karma*, and *dharma* and thus helped maintain a keen sense of social difference among South Asians. Even so, it provided a universal code of proper behaviour that has been deeply infused into South Asian culture.

South Asian cultural uniformity was strengthened subsequently by more than a century of British colonial rule. There were never many British in South Asia and British domination was maintained through the extensive use of South Asians in the lower ranks of the military and the civil service. Legions of South Asians were trained to carry out this work. By the 1930's a growing class of anglicized South Asians had arisen, some of whom took British culture to extremes not often seen in Britain itself. For some, English became a first language and it was a *lingua franca* across South Asia. Higher education and government were carried on in English. British cultural influence on South Asians was particularly heavy on urban populations. These are the same people from which Canada draws immigrants; while differing in traditional culture and identity, these individuals therefore have much in common. They share this British heritage with South Asian immigrants from overseas communities, who come from ex-colonies where British cultural influence was very strong. It should be noted that South Asian immigrants share more than just a veneer of British culture and language. Britain set down the formal infrastructure of their countries of origin – basic political forms, legal and educational systems, the structure of the bureaucracy, and basic economic relations.

In overview, then, the term "South Asian" is full of paradoxes. To many Canadians it is a covering term for a culturally homogeneous ethnic group. However, most people thereby identified as South Asian see themselves primarily as Sikh, Fijian, or Sinhalese. General commonalities of culture and experience nevertheless exist. These shared values and beliefs create a unity in diversity of a very complicated sort.

CANADA'S MANY PEOPLES OF SOUTH ASIAN ORIGIN

Among South Asian Canadians are over a score of distinct ethnic, national, linguistic, and religious groups. So diverse have been their respective experiences that it is useful to introduce a capsule summary of each of these groups and their settlement in Canada.

Sikhs

Sikhs no longer monopolize South Asian immigration, but they outnumber substantially any group.[4] It is estimated that two-thirds of Indian immigrants are Sikh, a proportion that is unlikely to fall in the future.[5]

Some Sikhs also come from other places in the world. Perhaps three-quarters of South Asian immigrants from Britain today are Sikhs, many of whom came originally from India and settled there in the 1960's and early 1970's. Sikhs also make up 5 to 10 per cent of South Asian immigrants from East Africa and a few come from Fiji and East Asia. Sikhs in Canada presently number roughly 80,000 to 100,000, or about 30 per cent of all South Asian Canadians.[6]

Throughout all of the post-1945 changes in immigration, Sikhs have continued to make use of available options to sponsor their relatives. The most immediate consequence of this has been that most Sikhs today have a number of relatives also living in Canada, often in the same city or town. Many other local Sikhs will be related through marriage or through friendships established long ago between their respective families. Many others share common town or village roots. Immigrant sponsorship consequently has provided a powerful support for community relations, which continue to be at least as important to Sikhs as to members of any other South Asian community.

An automatic consequence of this enormous increase in the Sikh Canadian population has been a substantial broadening of their backgrounds and interests. Sikhs in India have maintained their tradition of resourcefulness and are now widely distributed throughout the economy. Their success with cash-crop agriculture has given them the resources to become one of the better-educated and skilled groups in India. Consequently, the emphasis on professional-class immigrants in the 1960's and 1970's did not reduce Sikh immigration. Rather, it shifted the odds in favour of educated, urban Sikhs at the expense of their rural counterparts. More recent changes in the selection criteria have shifted the odds back somewhat. Today, immigrant Sikhs can be found from virtually every walk of life.

On top of comparatively sharp class differences are compounded several others. For example, politics in Punjab is serious business, and differences developed there continued to divide people here. Similarly, there are several sects of Sikh religion and substantial regional distinctions are made between people from different parts of Punjab. In addition, Sikh communities in Canada exhibit generational differences and substantial differences between immigrants and the Canadian-born. Many recent Sikh immigrants live in an orbit of Sikh friends and acquaintances, but the situation is almost the reverse for some of the second-generation Sikh Canadians.

Hence, the Sikh communities present an ongoing paradox. On one hand, religion, strong ethnic identity, common culture, kinship, and friendship combine to make Sikh communities stronger and more sharply bounded than communities in almost any other ethnic group. On the other hand, differences of class, politics, religion, region, and personal incompatibility often result in communities with deep social cleavages, political factionalism, divergent religious practices, and weak

129

overall consensus on important community issues. Here is a small example:

> There are now hundreds of Sikhs driving cab in this city. Being a "black" cab driver is sometimes no fun. We often have trouble with customers who refuse to ride with us or who call us names. Some have been victims of racist attacks.
>
> What can we do? The most important Sikh organization in town is the executive committee of the big Sikh temple. They are all doctors and engineers, who don't have to face the kinds of prejudice that we see all the time. They keep saying that discrimination is going away or that incidents are not part of any pattern. We want protection and they talk about the need to educate the public. I think that it won't be long before we working people form our own Sikh organization.
>
> We members of the executive committee have to take into account the long-run interests of the whole community. I know that Sikh cab drivers are extremely worried about racism – we all know it. The chief problem is that the cab drivers don't know how the system works here. They want vengeance, an eye for an eye. They think that the police should do something, when discrimination isn't even covered by the Criminal Code. The only way we're going to reduce racism in the long run is to change the attitudes of the public about Sikhs. In this regard we are working with the schools, the Human Rights Commission, and the police right now.

It is therefore more difficult to generalize about Canadian Sikhs than it once was. For example, consider their present geographical distribution. British Columbia continues to have the largest provincial Sikh population, now estimated to be somewhere between 45,000 and 50,000. Most of these people live in or adjacent to the Lower Mainland, but the smaller communities in Victoria (4,000), Duncan (1,000), and Nanaimo (500) also experienced rapid growth in the 1970's. Elsewhere in the country Sikh Canadians have settled wherever work is available in an urban context; like all South Asian ethnocultural groups, Sikhs strongly prefer living in cities.

Today, relatively large Sikh populations can be found in every city of any size from British Columbia into Quebec. In the urban corridor from Metro Toronto to Windsor are spread at least 20,000 Sikhs in a South Asian population of over 100,000, and in the whole province of Ontario there are about 25,000 Sikhs out of roughly 130,000 South Asians.

In the Prairies perhaps 4,000 Sikhs live in both Edmonton and Calgary; 2,000 are in Winnipeg, 500 each in Saskatoon, Regina, and Brandon. Another 500 are sprinkled across the small towns of Alberta, Saskatchewan, and Manitoba. In Quebec, Sikhs have congregated primarily in Montreal, where they have become part of the anglophone minority; there are about 1,500 Sikhs in the Montreal area and 500 elsewhere in the province.[7] There are very few east of Quebec; the largest Maritime Sikh population is in Nova Scotia, where there are perhaps about 500.

Pakistanis

The term Pakistani properly applies to a citizen of Pakistan rather than a specific ethnic group.[8] Pakistan has a population approximately three times that of Canada and encompasses many ethnic, linguistic, and religious groups. In an ethnocultural sense, Pakistani immigrants consequently vary more than do Sikhs.

Before its creation in 1947 the people of Pakistan were governed as part of colonial India. In that era, overseas emigration from what is now the Pakistani part of Punjab was considerable. In this sense, Pakistani immigration to Canada dates from the earliest times. It should be recalled that the contingent of British South Asian troops that came through Canada in 1902 on its way to the coronation of Edward VII was headed by a Muslim officer from Western Punjab. Perhaps 200 early pioneers were Muslims from what is now Pakistan. Within a few years the majority of these Muslim pioneers returned home or left for the United States. Those who remained in Canada got along well with their Punjabi Sikh compatriots and participated in most of the important events of the era. They were too few to be able to create their own separate community but did maintain a makeshift mosque in Vancouver for a period beginning around 1908. The 1907 immigration ban applied to all people of South Asian origin and immigration from what is now Pakistan was stopped almost entirely until after World War II.

Few people emigrated from independent Pakistan during the 1950's and most of those were Sikh. Only in the late 1950's did this begin to change as quota places were most frequently taken up by extremely well-educated professionals. They proved to be the vanguard of an exodus of professional Pakistanis who came to Canada in the 1960's (see Table 13). Pakistan has produced a surplus of certain kinds of skilled and educated people, especially university-trained professionals. There has been a strong incentive for such people to leave.

Almost without exception, immigrants in the 1960's and early 1970's came from the urban elite of Pakistan – educators, doctors, engineers, accountants, and scientists. For example, in 1967 about 70 per cent of all Pakistanis destined for the Canada labour market were professionals. Most of them went to Ontario or Quebec. A high proportion of these highly skilled Pakistanis were Punjabis or Muslims who had emigrated from India at the time of partition.

By the 1970's the range of Pakistani immigrants changed considerably. In the mid-1960's a pattern of sojourner migration became well established between Pakistan and Britain. By 1970 there were at least 180,000 people of Pakistani origin in Britain.[9] Today there must be over 300,000. At first, the majority were young single males whose objectives in going to

131

Britain were short term – to work hard, save money, and return home. As immigration to Canada became somewhat easier a similar pattern developed between Canada and Pakistan. This resulted in an initial disparity between the number of men and women who emigrated from either country, which is only now being redressed. This second wave of Pakistani immigration was composed primarily of skilled and semi-skilled working people rather than professionals.

Pakistanis are now one of the largest South Asian Canadian populations after the Sikhs. While only 750-1,000 Pakistanis had come to Canada by 1960, in the next ten years the population rose to 6,000. At the end of 1983 it stood at about 25,000.

Most Pakistanis share with Sikhs the need to associate with co-religionists. Over 85 per cent of Pakistani Canadians are professed Muslims who have supported energetically the establishment of Islamic religious and community institutions all across the country. Islam is a world religion encompassing people from scores of countries and hundreds of ethnic groups. It differs from more ethnically based religions like Sikhism. This is nowhere more evident than in the history of the establishment of mosques and Islamic centres in Canada, for they have frequently been started, supported, and used by people of very diverse nationalities. While this means that Pakistani religious institutions are not ethnically exclusive, religion nevertheless brings Pakistanis together across Canada.

Pakistanis share many cultural values with people from adjacent parts of India. Urdu is the national language of Pakistan, a language understood by many Punjabi Indians. The memories of partition and subsequent hostilities between India and Pakistan are, however, still strongly felt and these cultural similarities rarely find expression in strong social bonds between Punjabi Pakistanis and Indians in Canada. In contrast, links between middle- and upper-class Pakistanis and their Muslim counterparts from other parts of north India are often quite substantial.

Islam is of course more than a religion. It provides the foundation for some culture patterns that are very different from classical Hindu norms; in these respects, as we shall see, Pakistani, Bangali, and Indian Muslims are quite distinct from other South Asians. Islam specifically discourages caste and as a rule South Asian Muslims do not recognize it. Family relations and practices also differ. Perhaps most importantly, Islam has partially separated its South Asian adherents from the folklore, values, myths, and history of Hindu South Asia. Muslims in South Asia have been strongly influenced by Arab and Persian culture, a fact reflected in architecture, philosophy, poetry, and language.

Pakistanis have tended to prefer city life once they come to Canada and the great majority of Pakistani immigrants come from urban areas. Pakistanis have concentrated even more in the cities than Sikhs and most have gone to the industrial heartland of Ontario (about 10,000) and to

Montreal (5,000). Several thousand are in Vancouver, Edmonton, and Calgary, and perhaps 1,000 live in Winnipeg.

South Asians from Africa: Ismailis, Gujaratis, Sikhs, Goans, and South Africans

Another of the largest South Asian groups in Canada is the Ismailis.[10] Ismailis are also Muslims. Shortly after the death of Muhammad, Muslims divided into two major sects over the issue of who would be the prophet's religious successor. These two sects are today termed Sunni and Shia. Sunnis are the dominant force in the Arabic-speaking world, Pakistan, Bangladesh, Muslim India, Afghanistan, and Indonesia. Sunni religious practice does not acknowledge central religious authority, nor does it hold that religious leaders are necessary for the salvation of the individual believer. Shia Muslims are the majority in Iran and are a minority sect in many other Islamic countries. Shia Muslims place greater emphasis on the role of religious leaders, who are often involved in the secular affairs of adherents.

Ismailis are one of the many branches of Shia. They acknowledge a continuous line of religious leaders, or *Imam*(s), through Muhammad's son-in-law and cousin, Hazrat Ali, down to the present day Aga Khan IV, Mowlana Shah Karim Al-Husayni, the 49th hereditary *Imam*.[11] Ismailis existed for over 1,000 years as a minority group and this developed among them strong community organization co-ordinated through a network of religious leaders. Iran was the centre of Ismaili culture at that time.

The Mogul expansion into South Asia brought Ismaili proponents to India, where they made many converts. In 1848 the 46th *Imam*, Hassan Ali Shah, moved to India, thereby shifting the religious centre of Ismailis to that country. The next century was to be one of great change among Ismailis. Many Ismailis from Gujarat emigrated to East Africa beginning in the late nineteenth century, following Sikhs and other Punjabis who had gone there to do railway work. This settlement was encouraged by the British, especially in Uganda, where they had not been able to attract British settlers in any number. South Asians there quickly acquired a dominant position in retail and wholesale trade, transportation, small-scale manufacturing, and lower-level government jobs.

Under the guidance of Sir Sultan Muhammad Shah, Aga Khan III, Ismailis embraced many aspects of Western culture and modernized rapidly.[12] Soon Ismailis in East Africa and South Asia had developed a full range of community institutions: schools, hospitals, welfare societies, and religious institutions. Religious organization was made more effective by the creation of a hierarchical set of regional councils and boards.

Few Ismailis came to Canada before the 1970's. Those that did came directly from India and followed the general pattern of 1960's South

Asian immigration. Most were professionals or business people who settled in Vancouver or Toronto. Developments in East Africa beginning around 1970 initiated Ismaili settlement in Canada. South Asians in East Africa had moved into middleman positions between the British colonizers and the indigenous peoples of the area; the former controlled the government, the military, and the large-scale aspects of the economy and the latter supplied the labour necessary for the developing colonial infrastructure. South Asians did much of the rest. When the British relinquished control over political and military institutions to the indigenous African majority, South Asians were placed in a difficult political position. Their highly visible place in the economy was much resented by local people, who saw South Asians as parasitical, foreign, and standoffish.

As independence came, the position of South Asians quickly deteriorated. This was especially so in Uganda. In 1962 they were asked to take out Ugandan citizenship. The 15,000 Ismailis in Uganda immediately applied, but few of the other 60,000 South Asians in Uganda did so. In the late 1960's this was followed by the application of trade and employment restrictions on non-citizens. South Asians began to leave Uganda. Hundreds arrived in Canada, often via Britain. In August, 1972, Idi Amin ordered all South Asians to leave Uganda. Because of their strong support for Muslim institutions in the country and their early declaration of citizenship, Ismailis thought they would be exempt, but this was not to be. Within months, 29,000 Ugandan Asians entered Britain. The Canadian government also took in 6,000 as political refugees. Most of them were Ismailis.[13] Many others went to Tanzania, Kenya, or India. By the end of 1973 there were only a few thousand South Asians left in Uganda.

Refugees from Uganda were allowed to bring only a small amount of wealth with them when they left. Since the expulsion order had come with little warning few people had taken the precaution of moving money out of the country. Some were able to convert a portion of their holdings into cash or jewelry and smuggle these out of Uganda, but many arrived in Canada with nothing at all and with no psychological preparation for life in a new country. In this respect, Ugandan refugees were distinct from any other group of South Asians who have come to Canada before or since. Because they were political refugees with no relatives here, they wound up being distributed across Canada by the Department of Manpower and Immigration. Virtually every large city west of the Maritimes received at least a few hundred refugees.

Considering the dramatic conditions of their exodus, Ismailis were soon able to get their bearings and establish a measure of stability in their new homeland. In this they were helped by their background resources and skills as well as by initial government assistance. Fully half had been involved in business and 30 per cent were professionals. Most of the rest were skilled workers. Although they came under very disadvantageous circumstances, most soon found employment, though not at the levels they had experienced before. Those who were lucky enough to bring money with them frequently went into business in Canada, chiefly in services or real estate. Ismailis had already developed a tradition of women going overseas for education and training, which made it relatively easy for women to find work here. Within two years very few Ismaili refugees were in need of any form of government support. They have subsequently become one of the most organized and self-supporting South Asian groups in Canada. Once established, Ismaili refugees began to sponsor the immigration of relatives in Britain, Kenya, and Tanzania. As a result, the Ismaili population of Canada has grown steadily to its present level of about 30,000. Most of these live in Vancouver, Calgary, Edmonton, and Toronto. Canada is now a major world centre of Ismaili life.

Expulsion from Uganda brought other people to Canada who were not Ismailis, although at first they were relatively few. The highest proportion of these were also Gujarati speakers, who were either Hindus or Sunni Muslims. The Hindu and Sunni Muslim communities of Uganda had been far more variable in economic and social status than were the Ismailis, and they were not as well organized. When the expulsion order came they were therefore at a considerable disadvantage in finding a new home. Like Ismailis, few other Gujaratis wanted to go to India, for most were African-born. Many were taken in by Britain.

Among those who remained in Uganda, Ismailis were at an advantage in gaining Canadian political refugee status for they were better educated, more skilled, and more fluent in English than their Hindu and Sunni Muslim counterparts.[14] This partially accounted for Ugandan settlement going far more smoothly in Canada than it did in Britain, where one-quarter of all refugees remained below the government poverty line in 1975.[15]

Those who could not migrate overseas wound up chiefly in Tanzania and Kenya. The status of South Asians in these countries had also been deteriorating for a long time. By the 1960's there were about 200,000 South Asians in Kenya and 90,000 in Tanzania. In Kenya, 70-80 per cent of these were Gujaratis, the majority being Hindus. The rest were primarily Punjabis, most of whom were Sikh. In Tanzania the proportion of Muslims, especially Ismailis, was somewhat higher. As in Uganda, South Asians in these countries were disliked for their dominant place in the economy and their social separateness.

At independence the new leaders of Kenya and Tanzania stressed that South Asians must take out citizenship if they were to expect equal treatment with Africans. Aside from the Ismailis few did, and the Kenya government began to impose economic restrictions on non-citizens in the late 1960's. South Asians began to leave, mostly destined for Britain. A parallel flow to Britain had also developed from neighbouring Tanzania. Thus, by the time of the Ugandan exodus perhaps half the South Asians in Kenya and Tanzania had left. After the British restricted South Asian immigration in 1968 emigration to Canada sharply increased.

South Asians in Kenya and Tanzania could not easily claim political refugee status. Consequently, they had to come to Canada through normal immigration channels. Having relatives in Canada made people more aware of the option of coming here and made it easier to pass the hurdles of immigration selection. Because of this, disproportionately more Ismailis came to Canada from Tanzania, Britain, and Kenya than other South Asians from these countries. Several thousand Sikhs have also benefited from having relatives here despite their having been only a small fraction of the South Asian population in East Africa.

Some of those who were accepted by Canada as political refugees in 1972 were Gujaratis but not Ismailis. They, too, have sponsored relatives from East Africa, Britain, and India. Today one can find small Gujarati Hindu and Sunni Muslim communities from Vancouver to Montreal. These communities are composed of both East Africans and Indians. Non-Ismaili Gujaratis in Canada may now number 10,000.

Immigration criteria preferentially selected other highly Westernized people from East Africa. The Goans, who originated in the former Portuguese Indian colony of Goa, are one of the most interesting of these groups. The Portuguese cultural influence on this coastal Indian colony was very strong, for Portugal ruled there for over 400 years. Many Goans became Catholics and extensively assimilated to Portuguese language and culture. For many years thereafter, Goans moved through British India looking for ways to put their typically high skills and education to use. Some followed the British to East Africa, where they became well entrenched in the civil service and in education. Few came to Canada during the Ugandan exodus but hundreds subsequently came from other parts of East Africa and from Goa itself, which is now part of India. There are now about 2,000 Goans in Canada. Because their culture, language, and religion are unique among South Asians, Goans also form separate communities, although many have formed extensive networks of friends with other Canadians and with Christian South Asians from Kerala and elsewhere.

Although South Asian immigration from East Africa peaked in the mid-1970's, a small flow continues, particularly from Kenya. Most immigrants who were originally from East Africa now come from Britain, where they have found economic conditions harsh and the social environment hostile. Gujarati and Goan immigration from India itself continues at a relatively low rate.

Finally, some mention should be made of South Asians who have come from South Africa. The racial restrictions that whites have imposed on blacks in South Africa also extend to the 750,000 South Asians who live there. Actually, some of the first racist legislation in South Africa was directed at South Asians.[16] This occurred well before World War I, and Gandhi first became a political activist protesting the restrictions. South Asian immigration into South Africa was banned in 1911. In 1948 the Nationalist government introduced the policy of apartheid (racial separation), which severely limited the rights and privileges of blacks, Indians, and coloureds on the basis of race.

When Canadian immigration regulations were liberalized in the late 1960's a small flow of South African Indian immigration began. South African Indian immigrants tend to be highly anglicized, middle- and upper-class people with strong occupational and educational backgrounds; most South African Indians lack the education or skills to gain entry. About 2,000 South African Indians are sprinkled across the country today. Their class and cultural backgrounds are such that most associate primarily with non-South Asian Canadians and community-based social networks are weak.

South Asians from Fiji, the Caribbean, and Mauritius

There is considerable justification for treating South Asian Fijians and those from the Caribbean and Mauritius together, for their experiences have been quite similar.[17] Fijian Indians as well as those from Guyana, Trinidad, and Mauritius are largely the descendants of indentured labourers who arrived there before 1920. Plantation labour under abject conditions on British sugar estates was their common heritage. So, too, was British rule.

After the abolition of the indenture system in 1920 the paths of these people began to diverge. In Fiji the plantations were disbanded and most sugar was soon being grown by Indians farming sugar company or native Fijian land. Caught between a company sugar monopoly and uncertain land tenure, Fijian Indians in this period were very poor. Conflict and competition with Fiji's large native population was low, for the latter were largely relegated to their villages by British policy. Beginning in the 1950's, Indians began to develop an economic base in retail trade and transportation.

Sugar was also the backbone of colonial British Guiana. As in Fiji, Indians make up about 50 per cent of the population, but about 40 per cent of the Guiana (now Guyana) population is black or mulatto. Native people in Fiji make up about 40 per cent of the population, but indigenous people in Guyana are a very small minority.[18] During colonial times a single company largely controlled British Guiana sugar production. Few Indians were able to move out of plantation labour prior to World War II.

Trinidad's population and economy were more mixed. There, South Asians are about a 35 per cent minority and blacks (at 45 per cent) are the largest "ethnic" group. In the late 1930's, oil was discovered in Trinidad and this broadened the occupational base for both Indians and blacks. By 1945, a growing Indian middle class had been established there.

Indians from Fiji, Guyana, and Trinidad were also subject to the influences of British colonial culture. With increasingly better post-war

137

economic conditions, this was manifest in increasing English literacy, British education, and neo-colonial British culture. Indian culture merged with British and local historical influences to produce uniquely Fijian, Guyanese, and Trinidadian Indian styles of life.

Although it also evolved as an indenture-based island sugar producer, in other respects Mauritius has had a quite different history than Fiji, Guyana, and Trinidad. Because of its proximity to India, South Asian culture remains strong. The influence of the French and the island's Creole elite have lessened the impact of British culture. Also, Indians there enjoy a 70 per cent majority, which gives them a decided political advantage over Mauritian blacks.

Racial conflict arose steadily through the 1960's in Fiji, Guyana, and Trinidad. This had its origins in group-based economic competition and the question of who would control post-independence governments. Trinidad's independence (in 1962) was followed by that of Guyana (1966) and Fiji (1970); in each case, Indians were subsequently relegated to the status of political minorities. Only in Mauritius had the post-1968 independence government been controlled by Indians.

Racial conflict and economic uncertainty soon led to emigration to Britain, Canada, and the United States. By now, one out of ten Fijians has left, a proportion almost matched by migrants from Guyana. Today there are about 14,000 Fijian Indians and a somewhat larger number of Trinidadian Indians in Canada. Guyanese Canadians of Indian origin may number over 30,000. In contrast, Mauritian immigrants total no more than 3,000.

Fijians, Guyanese, Trinidadians, and Mauritians in Canada presently have geographical distributions reflecting the places where the first immigrants from these countries settled. Fijians initially went to Vancouver because they came by sea and it was the Pacific port of entry. Thereafter, over 75 per cent of Fijians have concentrated there as a result of chain migration and the mild climate. Almost 1,000 have gone subsequently to Alberta and the same number live in Ontario. In contrast, Guyanese and Trinidadians are heavily localized in Ontario, as are other people from the English-speaking Caribbean. Only in the late 1970's did their number increase in the West; there are now roughly 1,000 Guyanese in both Alberta and British Columbia. Fewer than half this many Trinidadian Indians have gone to western Canada. Because of their facility with French, most Mauritians have settled in Quebec.

These peoples have very different backgrounds than other South Asian Canadians. Urban Fijians, Guyanese, and Trinidadian Indians have become quite anglicized; most of the young speak English, for it is usually the language of instruction in the schools. This has resulted in relatively easy association with other Canadians, perhaps far more so than among any other general category of South Asian Canadians.

Generally speaking, the class and occupational backgrounds of immigrant Fijians, Guyanese, and Trinidadians are quite different from those of most other South Asian groups. Large-scale immigration from these countries did not get under way until the early 1970's, by which time the immigrant selection criteria had begun to shift away from professionals. Moreover, professionals in these countries usually have less incentive to leave than those who are more in direct economic competition with other groups. The result has been immigrant flows heavily concentrated in skilled and semi-skilled work.

Northern Indians and Bangalis

Hindi- and Punjabi-speaking Hindus. There is no adequate way of categorizing the various emigrant Hindu peoples from India. Hinduism is primarily a religion and way of life rather than an ethnicity. Even so, religion and ethnicity in India reinforce each other, shaping identities, social relations, and cultures. In Canada, people from India who have Hindu and Muslim backgrounds typically have little contact and in this respect there is a certain validity in discussing each separately. At the same time, it is less realistic to discuss all Hindus together than all European Christians, for Hinduism varies widely and does not submerge regional differences in culture and identity.

One of the largest South Asian groups after the Sikhs who have come directly from India are Hindi-speaking people who come chiefly from Uttar Pradesh and surrounding regions in northern India. They are far less of an ethnic group than Sikhs, for they are drawn from a wide range of social situations and a vastly larger base population. Even so, this variability has been limited by selective emigration from the urban middle classes, which have developed a uniform style of life across the region. The vanguard of immigrants from this area arrived in the first large wave of South Asian professionals in the mid-1960's. These people came as independent immigrants and were among the most highly skilled South Asians arriving at that time. Education and training in India remain largely the preserve of the middle and upper classes, and Canadian immigration demands of the 1960's automatically selected individuals from these groups. Many first came to Canada from the United States, where they had been attending university. Subsequent flows directly from Uttar Pradesh and surrounding areas have exhibited a pattern of highly educated middle- and upper-class out-migration. As with other groups, there has been a shift toward skilled clerical and blue-collar work in more recent years. Immigration from this part of India has gone down sharply since 1975, chiefly because independent immigration from India has been drastically reduced. Numerical estimates of how many (Hindu) Hindi-speakers from India presently live in Canada are very uncertain. There were at least 15,000 here by the end of 1983.

Another category of South Asian Canadians with quite similar backgrounds is those who are also Hindu but come from Punjab. Most of them speak Punjabi, an allied language of Hindi. Most of them are also well educated and most of the men know both Hindi and English. Punjabi Hindus have come primarily straight from India, but some have also made their way here from East Africa. There are certainly more than 5,000 here at present.

Punjabis and Uttar Pradeshis often develop strong social and economic links with Canadians of similar class backgrounds. In a certain sense this is an extension of an ongoing process in India whereby middle- and upper-class people across the country are amalgamating into a national elite that transcends language and region. At the same time, Punjabis and Uttar Pradeshis in Canada have not divorced themselves from their cultural and religious heritages. In the 1970's Hindus from these regions were the driving forces in the creation of Hindu societies all across the country. These societies have been developed to maintain some elements of Hindu religious practice and culture in Canada.

Bengalis. For thousands of years Bengal has had a distinctive culture and language from those of north central India. Successive waves of invaders from Iran and Afghanistan and many subsequent years of Mogul rule in Bengal produced a religiously mixed society, with Hindus predominating in the west and Muslims in the east. Under British colonial control, Bengalis quickly moved to the forefront of education, the bureaucracy, and the arts. Bengali literature in particular flourished; the Bengali Nobel laureate, Rabindranath Tagore, remains India's best-known poet. Ramakrishna (1836-86) and Vivekananda (1863-1902) were Bengalis whose Hindu religious ideas powerfully affected Western thinking. Bengalis were also very active in politics, especially in the rise of Indian nationalism.

In this political capacity, Bengali immigration to Canada dates back to the earliest times. A high proportion of Indians studying overseas at the turn of the century were Bengalis, and they played a major role in the rise of overseas Indian revolutionary activity. Taraknath Das and Hussain Rahim, both driving forces in the Vancouver community before 1914, were Bengalis.

At the time of independence Bengal was partitioned, more or less according to the geographical distribution of Hindus and Muslims. The eastern part became East Pakistan, the western, the Indian state of Bengal. As in Punjab, there was a massive shift of population at that time, particularly of Hindu Bengalis to the new Indian state.

Bengalis have not had a strong historical tradition of overseas migration and immigration to Canada was insignificant until the 1970's. Even today Bengalis (not including those from Bangladesh) in Canada only number a few thousand. Nevertheless, Bengalis in Canada have been quite active in maintaining ties with each other. Because of their distinctive culture and language they generally tend to create their own associations, much as do Gujaratis. A high proportion of Bengalis live in Ontario, but small communities have been established in Montreal, Calgary, Edmonton, and Vancouver. Like so many other Indian immigrants, Bengalis are quite skilled and well situated today. Bengalis and people from Bangladesh (see below) share a common language and associate with each other to a considerable extent.

Bangalis.[19] The creation of the state of Pakistan created a number of anomalies, the greatest of which was the existence of East and West Pakistan separated by a thousand miles of India. Political control centered in the West, which was much resented in the East; Bengali Pakistanis shared little but religion with Pakistanis from the West. This led to a violent civil war, which resulted in independence for East Pakistan in 1971. The new country was called Bangladesh, and its people, Bangalis.

Bangali immigration goes back to well before independence. A number of immigrant Bengali citizens of India were born in what is now Bangladesh and a handful came directly from East Pakistan during 1960-65 as part of overall Pakistani immigration. Most Bangalis came to Canada shortly after independence; a goodly number of these came via European countries. The primary motives were economic and political uncertainty. There are now about 1,000 Bangalis in Canada, most of them in Ontario. Bangalis are among the most educated of South Asian immigrants. A high proportion have technical training, especially in engineering.

Like many other South Asian groups, Bangali culture, language, and religion crosscut those of other groups, which results in complex networks of association. Bangalis have a strong national consciousness and keep in contact with each other. They share language and many cultural commonalities with Bengalis and a considerable degree of inter-group contact takes place. Almost all Bangalis are Sunni Muslims and consequently associate with other Sunnis in religious contexts. One outcome of the war of independence is that few Bangalis have cultivated relations with Pakistani Canadians.

Southern Indians

There exists a great north-south cultural and linguistic division in India roughly corresponding to the distribution of Sanscritic and Dravidian language groups. Several thousand South Indians have come to Canada over the past twenty years, though no single group of them is at present very large.

Perhaps the Tamil-speakers from Madras comprise the largest of these groups. Like Bengal, Madras was one of the earliest areas of South Asia colonized by the British. Unlike pre-partition Bengal, Madras was overwhelmingly Hindu. Madras produced a large Western-educated class, which performed important roles in the British India administration. After independence, Madrasis (and other South Indians) have found themselves politically subordinate to the Delhi government, and this has increased regionalist feeling. This and language differences have also made it more difficult for Madrasis and other southerners to find skilled employment in other parts of India. Some have therefore decided to emigrate. A few Tamils came to Canada in the early 1960's. Many were teachers, who spread across the country filling positions in rural areas where it was difficult to secure Canadians. A high proportion of subsequent immigrants have also been teachers.

Madrasis are very different from North Indians. They do not understand one another's language; their food is quite distinct, as are their respective histories, family structures, and values. They are, however, all former citizens of India and in Canada, Madrasis and other South Indians acknowledge this through limited participation in pan-Indian associations. They have been an important force in the development of the Hindu religion in Canada. Madrasis are too few in most parts of the country to form associations. Informal links between Madrasis are nonetheless strong, as they occasionally are between them and Tamil-speakers from Sri Lanka.

Immigration from Kerala is quite similar to that from Madras. Here again, one sees a political division roughly follow a linguistic one, for most people in Kerala speak Malayalam. People from Kerala also moved into the British colonial bureaucracy at an early point and established a tradition of pan-Indian migration. When Canadian immigration became available in the 1960's, Malayalees extended this process here. Again, many came as school teachers and settled in rural areas, particularly in the West. Others were health professionals, accountants, and engineers. Most immigrants in the 1970's also headed primarily to areas where they could get jobs. Of the several thousand Malayalees in Canada, most are in Ontario, Alberta, or British Columbia. Today they may well have the highest proportion of professionals of any South Asian group in Canada.

Immigrants from Kerala are almost exclusively from those classes that have had a hundred years of dealing with the British. As a consequence, they operate well in the context of British-based Canadian culture. Many immigrants are Christians, and some used English as a first language before they came to Canada. They have integrated smoothly into the Canadian social system. Malayalee communities are always small, but informal social relations in them are typically strong. Since 1975, organizations of Malayalam-speakers have sprung up across Canada.

Beyond those from Kerala, Madras, and Goa, relatively few South Indians have come to Canada. The states of Mysore (Kannanda-speaking) and Andhra Pradesh (Telugu-speaking) have large populations but have not yet contributed many immigrants. Telugu-speakers are represented across Canada, but there are unlikely more than 1,000 of them in all. This pattern of high immigration rates from some parts of India and not others can be extended right across the country. For example, the central and northern states of Maharashtra, Orissa, Madhya Pradesh, Bihar, Rajasthan, and Kashmir are virtually unrepresented in Canada.

Sinhalese, Ceylon Tamils, and Others from Sri Lanka

The island of Ceylon (now Sri Lanka) has always been partially isolated from the history and culture of the South Asian mainland.[20] The largest group in Sri Lanka is the Sinhalese, who derive from Aryan invaders who arrived about 500 B.C. The Sinhalese speak a Sanscritic language (Sinhala) related to those in North India and presently make up 70 per cent of the population. By 200 B.C. most of the Sinhalese had become Buddhist. Ceylon subsequently established itself as the centre of Theravada Buddhism, one of the two great Buddhist traditions that continue today. Over the next thousand years Hinduism slowly eliminated Buddhism from most parts of India, but not from Ceylon. Even so, over the centuries a constant Hindu Tamil presence continued in Ceylon, particularly in the north. This was the result of the entry of Tamil-speaking people from South India, who arrived in Ceylon slightly after the Sinhalese. By the fifth century A.D. Tamils controlled the island, as they would on and off for the next 500 years.

The great Mogul invasions of India never had sufficient momentum to reach Ceylon. The same could not be said of European invaders. The Portuguese arrived in Ceylon in the early 1500's. By 1600 much of the island was in Portuguese hands. As in Goa, the Portuguese extensively intermarried with local people and introduced lowland Ceylon to Portuguese culture. Many Sinhalese became Catholics. The Portuguese were soon expelled by the Sinhalese and the subsequent Dutch rule resulted in another mestizo class, the Dutch Burghers, who along with Portuguese Burghers continue to exist as an ethnic group. Burghers were given preferential access to jobs and education and became an important force in the country. Over this period Ceylon also developed through immigration a substantial Muslim population, who are locally termed Moors. They now make up 7 per cent of the population. Most are the descendants of Arab traders.

The Dutch were supplanted by the British, who controlled Ceylon from 1796 until independence in 1948. Throughout this period, Sinhalese and Ceylon Tamils largely continued as separate groups, divided by language, religion, culture, and occupation. The British also brought in several hundred thousand plantation workers, chiefly from Tamil-speaking areas of India. Tamils in Sri Lanka now make up 20 per cent of the population.

Post-independence politics has chiefly followed ethnic lines. The Sinhalese quickly used their numerical majority to support Sinhalese culture and language. Sinhala became the national language, Sinhalese settlement in Tamil areas was encouraged, and quotas were established to reduce Tamil access to education.[21] Explicit legislative discrimination against Ceylon Tamils continued until 1978, and there remains much distrust among Tamils of the Sinhalese majority. Bitter Tamil-Sinhalese clashes in 1983 illustrate how deep-seated these differences are.

143

Because of the early initiation of a Canadian quota system, immigration from Sri Lanka dates from the early 1950's. For almost a decade those who came were primarily Burghers, who like Anglo-Indians in post-independence India felt that they had become an exposed, marginal minority. They were soon followed by Sinhalese and Tamil professionals. Some of these were dissatisfied with ethnic or political relations in Sri Lanka, while others saw economic difficulties on the horizon.[22] Immigration increased steadily in the 1970's. Sri Lankan immigrants come from a wide variety of occupations, from semi-skilled blue-collar workers to professionals. There are now about 5,000 in Canada. The proportion of these who are from the various ethnic groups is difficult to assess, but Sinhalese are certainly in the majority, followed by Tamils and Burghers. Over half of the Sri Lankans are in Ontario. Montreal was an important early immigration destination, but more recent immigration is shifting to the West, to Alberta and British Columbia.

Immigrants from Sri Lanka form complex and varying social networks influenced by ethnicity and class. The polarization between Buddhist Sinhalese and Hindu Tamils in Sri Lanka is difficult to eliminate, especially because the split is religious, linguistic, cultural, and political. Most associations have tried to bridge the gap between Sinhalese and Tamils, but this goal has been difficult to achieve; such organizations have difficulty holding Tamil members. In some areas, Sri Lankan Tamils have begun to establish their own associations and they occasionally support Tamil-language associations that have both Sri Lankan and Indian members.

Others

Few South Asian immigrants come from places other than those mentioned above. Almost no Afghanistanis have come to Canada, nor have any of the South Asian peoples of western Burma. The largest group of "others" are not an immigrant category at all. They are second-generation South Asian Canadians. Except for those of Sikh origin, most of the second generation will not reach adulthood until the mid-1980's. As we shall see in subsequent chapters, they are likely to be very different from their parents and the degree to which they will affiliate with the culture and ethnicity of their parents is still an open question. In the future they will be the leading edge of change, and they, rather than their immigrant parents, will be the main determinators of what it means to be a Canadian of South Asian origin.

South Asians today exhibit a greater degree of cultural, linguistic, and religious diversity than any other ethnic population in Canada. When circumstances allow it, this diversity surfaces in a multitude of distinct communities, organizations, and cultural programs. On the other hand, South Asians face two sets of contraints that make their adaptation to Canada much more uniform than it would be if this cultural diversity were given free rein. One is the economic and social demands of settlement, which bear equally on all South Asian immigrants. The other is the common concerns about preserving some aspects of South Asian culture. In the drama of settlement these dual constraints at times support one another, and sometimes they do not. How Canadian individual and family life and South Asian cultural concerns have been reconciled with establishment in Canada is the subject of the next chapter.

NOTES

1. W.H. Morris-Jones, "Language and Region Within the Indian Union," in P. Mason (ed.), *India and Ceylon: Unity and Diversity* (London, 1967), p. 54.
2. Hugh Tinker, *A New System of Slavery: The Export of Indian Labour Overseas, 1838-1920* (London, 1974).
3. N. Buchignani and D. Indra, "Inter-group Conflict and Community Solidarity: Sikhs and South Asian Fijians in Vancouver," *Canadian Journal of Anthropology*, 1, 2 (1981), pp. 149-57.
4. On recent Sikh Canadian history and social organization, see Ames and Inglis, "Conflict and Change in British Columbia Sikh Family Life"; F.M. Bhatti, "East Indian Immigration into Canada, 1905-1973" (Ph.D. thesis, University of Surrey, 1974); Buchignani and Indra, "Inter-group Conflict and Community Solidarity"; Button, "Sikh Settlement in the Lower Mainland"; James G. Chadney, "The Joint Family as Structure and Process," *Journal of Social Thought*, 7, 1 (1975), pp. 17-22; Chadney, "The Vancouver Sikhs: An Ethnic Community in Canada" (Ph.D. thesis, Michigan State University, 1976); Dodd, "Social Change in Two Overseas Sikh Communities"; V. Dusenbery, "Hierarchy, Equality and the Assertion of Sikh Identity in North America," paper presented at the annual meeting of the Central States Anthropological Association (1980); Dusenbery, "Canadian Ideology and Public Policy: The Impact on Vancouver Sikh Ethnic and Religious Adaptation," *Canadian Ethnic Studies*, 8, 3 (1981), pp. 101-20; Indra, "The Portrayal of South Asians in the Vancouver Press"; Joy and Dusenbery, "Being Sikh in British Columbia"; R.S. Pannu, "A Sociological Survey of Teachers from India Teaching in Alberta, 1958-65" (M.Ed. thesis, University of Alberta, 1966); Ram P. Srivastava, "Family Organization and Change Among the Overseas Indians with Special Reference to Indian Immigrant Families of British Columbia, Canada," in G. Kurian (ed.), *Family in India: A Regional View* (The Hague, 1975); Wood, "East Indians and Canada's New Immigration Policy"; John R. Wood, "A Visible Minority Votes: East Indian Electoral Behavior in the Vancouver South Provincial and Federal Elections of 1979," in J. Dahlie and T. Fernando (eds.), *Ethnicity, Power and Politics in Canada* (Toronto, 1981), pp. 177-201. For an excellent comparative study of Sikhs in Britain, see Arthur W. Helweg,

Sikhs in England: The Development of a Migrant Community (Delhi, 1980). For a detailed analysis of Sikh society, see E. Marenco, *The Transformation of Sikh Society* (Portland, 1974).

5. Wood, "East Indians and Canada's New Immigration Policy."

6. These and subsequent estimates of South Asian ethnic and regional populations are not fully based on official statistics and should be considered to be very approximate. They are derived from national immigration statistics, the 1981 census, and estimates by community leaders.

7. B. McDonough, "A Study of South Asian Immigrants in the Montreal Metropolitan Region" (1978, mimeo.).

8. For more details, see *A History of People of Pakistani Origin in Canada* (1976), published by the Canada Pakistan Association of Ottawa-Hull. See also Sadiq Awan, "The People of Pakistani Origin in Canada, Their First Twenty-five Years," in Ujimoto and Hirabayashi (eds.), *Visible Minorities and Multiculturalism;* R.B. Quereshi, "The Family Model as a Blueprint for Social Interaction Among Pakistani Canadians," in K.V. Ujimoto and G. Hirabayashi (eds.), *Asian Canadians and Multiculturalism* (1980, mimeo.); Muhammad Siddique, "Patterns of Familial Decision Making and Division of Labour: A Study of the Immigrant Indian and Pakistani Community of Saskatoon" (M.A. thesis, University of Saskatchewan, 1974); C. Siddique, "Changing Family Patterns: A Comparative Analysis of Immigrant Indian and Pakistani Families of Saskatoon, Canada," *Journal of Comparative Family Studies*, 8, 2 (1977), pp. 179-200; C. Siddique, "Structural Separation and Family Change: An Exploratory Study of the Immigrant Indian and Pakistani Families of Saskatoon, Canada," *International Review of Modern Sociology,* 7, 1 (1977), pp. 13-35; P.A. Wakil, "The Immigrant Indo-Pakistani Family: A Case Study Research Note," paper presented at the VIIIth World Congress of Sociology, Toronto, 1974.

9. Hugh Tinker, *The Banyan Tree: Overseas Emigrants from India, Pakistan, and Bangladesh* (Oxford, 1977), p. 166.

10. On South Asians in East Africa, see Hugh Tinker, *Separate and Unequal: India and the Indians in the British Commonwealth, 1920-1950* (London, 1976). More details on Ugandan refugees in Canada are provided by C. Pereira *et al.*, "Canadian Beliefs and Policy Regarding the Admission of Ugandan Asians to Canada," *Ethnic and Racial Studies*, 1, 3 (1978), pp. 353-64; B. Adams *et al.*, "Ugandan Asians in Exile: Household and Kinship in the Resettlement Crisis," *Journal of Comparative Family Studies*, 8, 2 (1977), pp. 167-78; M. Twaddle (ed.), *Expulsion of a Minority: Essays on Ugandan Asians* (London, 1975); Benson C. Morah, "The Assimilation of Ugandan Asians in Calgary" (M.A. thesis, University of Calgary, 1974); Ranvir Moudgil, "From Stranger to Refugee: A Study of the Integration of Ugandan Asians in Canada" (Ph.D. thesis, SUNY, Buffalo, 1977); Freda Hawkins, "Uganda Asians in Canada," *New Community*, 2 (1973), pp. 268-75; M. Bristow *et al.*, "Ugandan Asians in Britain, Canada and India: Some

Characteristics and Resources," *New Community*, 4, 2 (1974), pp. 155-66; Tissa Fernando, "East African Asians in Western Canada: The Ismaili Community," *New Community*, 7, 3 (1979), pp. 361-8.

11. Those Ismailis who follow the Aga Khan are technically called Nizari Ismailis to differentiate them from the other sect of Ismailis, the Mustalian Bohoras.

12. In 1937, Sultan Muhhamad Shah was elected president of the League of Nations.

13. Canada, Department of Employment and Immigration, *Annual Immigration Statistics* (Ottawa, 1977).

14. Pereira *et al.*, "Canadian Beliefs and Policy."

15. Tinker, *The Banyan Tree*, p. 161.

16. P. van den Berghe, *South Africa: A Study in Conflict* (Berkeley, 1970); A. Lemon, *Apartheid: A Geography of Separation* (London, 1976); E. Brooks, *Apartheid: A Documentary Study of Modern South Africa* (London, 1968).

17. On Fiji, see K.L. Gillion, *Fiji's Indian Migrants: A History to the End of Indenture in 1920* (Melbourne, 1962); Adrian C. Mayer, *Peasants of the Pacific*, 2nd edition (London, 1973); Ernest K. Fisk, *The Political Economy of Independent Fiji* (Canberra, 1970). For more details on Indians in the Caribbean, see A. and J. Niehoff, *East Indians in the West Indies* (Milwaukee, 1960); B. Brereton, *Race Relations in Colonial Trinidad* (Cambridge, 1979). On Mauritius, see Burton Benedict, *Indians in a Plural Society: A Report on Mauritius* (London, 1967). Fijians in Canada are addressed by Norman Buchignani, "Immigration, Adaptation, and the Management of Ethnic Identity: An Examination of Fijian East Indians in British Columbia" (Ph.D. thesis, Simon Fraser University, 1977); Buchignani, "Social Identity Formation and Interpretation: Recent East Indian Immigration to British Columbia," in J. Elliott (ed.), *Two Nations, Many Cultures* (Scarborough, 1979), pp. 325-37; Buchignani and Indra, "Inter-group Conflict and Community Solidarity."

18. C. Jayawardena, "Culture and Ethnicity in Guyana and Fiji," *Man* (September, 1980); Jayawardena, *Conflict and Solidarity in a Guyanese Plantation* (London, 1963).

19. On Bangalis in Canada, See M. Ahmed, "Adaptation of Bangladeshis in Canada: A Case Study" (Toronto, 1978, mimeo.).

20. On Sri Lankan ethnic relations and history, see B.H. Farmer, *Ceylon: A Divided Nation* (Oxford, 1963); R.N. Kearney, *The Politics of Ceylon (Sri Lanka)* (New York, 1973); A.J. Wilson, *Politics in Sri Lanka, 1947-1979* (London, 1980). On Sri Lankans in Canada, see the following detailed report: E.R. Appathurai, "The Sri Lankans in Eastern Canada" (Ottawa, 1980, mimeo.).

21. Appathurai, "The Sri Lankans," pp. 18-19.

22. *Ibid.*, p. 47.

NINE

Setting Down Roots

Even today South Asians are primarily an immigrant population; most have come to Canada since 1974. For an increasing majority the initial phase of establishment is now behind them, but they are still undergoing long-term adaptation and remain part of the process through their involvement with the immigration and settlement of more recent arrivals. Settlement therefore continues to be an important element of South Asian Canadian life.

South Asian settlement is a variation on a Canadian immigrant theme. Many of the challenges, constraints, possibilities, and problems faced by South Asians are those of immigrants generally. At the same time, South Asians have values, resources, objectives, and difficulties that are in some respects unique. To outline these, we have divided recent settlement history into three basic aspects: individual and familial adaptation; community and institutional development; and inter-group relations. By individual and familial adaptation we mean the process of achieving the basic socioeconomic goals of life and the consequent responses that individuals and families have made to this process. This is the subject of this chapter. Another level of settlement involves the development of informal community and of community-based institutions such as organizations, churches, and businesses. This is covered in the two subsequent chapters. The final chapter deals with individual and collective relations between South Asians and other Canadians.

INITIAL SETTLEMENT

Immigration is particularly challenging for those who, like South Asians, come from substantially different cultural contexts. It is particularly so for those who are dependent on their own personal resources. Such people must be self-reliant for everything – money, learning where to stay and get a job, developing social relations with others, mitigating family problems, and finding their way generally. Some South Asians have gone

148

through this exacting process on their own, but only during the 1960's and early 1970's was it prevalent. This was the era when immigrant professionals created the first South Asian presence outside of British Columbia. These people went to places where there were few people from similar backgrounds and for most it was a big cultural and social transition. Although they quickly achieved economic security, many immigrants from that period characterize their settlement experience as being alienating and socially limited, as evidenced in this account from a Fijian:

> One of the things which most people in Fiji don't appreciate about immigration is how different will be their family and social life in Canada. Immigration changes everything before you even realize it's happening. At least now immigrants can learn from the successes and mistakes of those who came earlier. When I arrived there were only a handful of people from Fiji here, and most of them hadn't arrived so very much earlier than me. Fortunately, I travelled with a few friends, and we stuck together until we got settled. Even so, in looking back we had to overcome really big difficulties. We didn't know a thing about Canada – how to find work, where to live, what a good wage was. We didn't have many people to turn to in order to find out, and had no relatives here to help us in the meantime. If we had brought our families over when we first arrived I don't know how we would have made it financially.
>
> Perhaps the worst thing was the loneliness. You can't imagine how strange it was for us, living away from family and friends. It was something that we were not prepared for and could do little to change. In Fiji we were pretty poor by Canadian standards, but we certainly were rich in other ways. Until we got established we shared the worst of both worlds.

Most South Asians have not immigrated in such isolation from each other, largely because of the chain migration and the development of strong social links between individuals from the same ethnic background.[1] Where the first pioneers went and what their backgrounds were often set the pattern for subsequent immigration, for chain migration quickly became established in the sixties. For example, the first four Fijian Indians set sail for Vancouver in response to a newspaper article on Canadian immigration in the early 1960's. Subsequent letters to relatives and friends led to others applying and the momentum built quickly. By 1976 almost 9,000 Fijians had emigrated and virtually all of them went to Vancouver.

Patterns of chain migration for other groups developed out of similar chance circumstances. In some cases the process was begun by male university students or professional couples who had been attracted to places outside of Vancouver and Toronto; secondary migrants from these cities subsequently initiated immigrant flows to many other places in Canada. Arrival of the Ugandan refugees in 1972 began chain migration to Canada by a number of East African South Asian groups. Immigration restrictions in the late 1970's if anything accentuated the importance of chain migration to South Asians. The great majority of South Asian immigrants are now sponsored.

For South Asians chain migration does much more than determine who comes and who does not. Chain migration allows individuals to tap accumulated family and community resources. Having the support of Canadian relatives expedites the process of immigration. Immigrants sometimes are loaned air fare by Canadian relatives; for many prospective immigrants, travel costs would otherwise be prohibitive. Furthermore, because South Asian immigrants tend to settle where they have friends and relatives, communities of South Asians are quickly established. In many immigrant South Asian communities individuals have far more relatives and friends the moment they arrive than other Canadians will develop in their lifetimes. Community becomes an important support group, which cushions the transition between cultures.

South Asians move to Canada using several strategies. Those who are married would prefer to come as a family unit, but are often precluded from doing so by the high initial costs of settlement. Consequently, husbands frequently travel first in order to prepare the way and earn a little money. In the mid-1970's, thousands of young unmarried men came as the sponsored relatives of people already here; the expectation was that they would only marry and settle permanently in Canada if things turned out well. Whether one individual or a whole family, immigrants are usually met at the airport. Usually they then are brought to a relative's home or to a prearranged apartment. This keeps initial settlement costs down and allows quick access to information about jobs, places to stay, schools, and Canadian society in general. Individuals then slowly shift over to their own independent resources. Within a month or two, men have generally secured their first job. If they have come with their families they will have found their own apartment and placed their children in school. The following account is fairly typical.

It isn't really hard to explain how we wound up in Calgary. We first came to Canada from Uganda during the Canadian airlifts of 1972. The government sent our family and several hundred other Ismailis to Winnipeg. To say that we had a hard time getting established is an understatement. We were all suffering the shock of being thrown out of Uganda, and were deeply worried about relatives in East Africa and Britain. There were few jobs and even fewer business possibilities available in Winnipeg. We did what we could, but like most other Ismailis we eventually left the city for greener pastures.

In our family's case that meant Calgary. Many Ismailis had already been attracted here by jobs; it was rapidly becoming one of the biggest Ismaili communities in Canada. What was more important was that both I and my husband had relatives here who seemed to be doing well. After some correspondence, we moved to Calgary, staying originally with my husband's brother's family. You can't imagine how much easier it was to get established this second time around. Having the support of relatives and friends was an important reason for why this was so. In less than a year we had our own house. Since then we have had two other family members staying with us as they got established here. My husband's friend even gave one of them a lead that led to his first Canadian job. We are now trying to arrange for the immigration of my husband's mother. If we are successful, she will stay with us permanently.

MAKING A LIVING

The advantages of chain migration are substantial but limited. Obviously, such a strategy can do nothing to change the major outlines of Canadian economic, political, and social life. This is notably so in the job search, for few South Asians work for South Asian employers, and places where South Asians make up a substantial proportion of the work force are rare. Outside of these exceptions, community contacts do not usually help to secure jobs.

South Asians have several recurrent difficulties in securing employment. As with most immigrants, they face a demand for "Canadian experience," and it is not always easy to convert their occupational records, skills, and education into Canadian equivalents. The federal and provincial governments have become much better at establishing these equivalencies than they once were, and most people's formal qualifications are now being evaluated somewhat more objectively by employers. Problems in these areas nevertheless remain.[2] South Asians also face ethnic and racial discrimination in employment, which is a case for great community concern.

South Asian families have devised ways to counter these employment difficulties. One initial economic strategy is to get work of some sort as soon as possible. Even in better economic times many men had to accept initial jobs unrelated to their skills. In today's depressed economy half of all newly immigrated South Asian men may follow this pattern. By no means content with this situation, families have attempted to compensate by developing additional family incomes. As a rule, South Asian women have not worked outside the home before they came to Canada. Once here, this situation is reversed, for most women eventually try to secure employment.

The present occupational distribution of South Asian women is quite different from that of other Canadian women. Many South Asian women find it difficult to get any but the most unskilled and low-paid jobs. South Asian societies have restricted women's access to education, occupational training, and work outside the home, so some women are ill-prepared to compete for anything else. They also must contend with the same sexual prejudices that face other women in the labour force. Many South Asian women are locked into dead-end jobs in clothing manufacturing, clerical and secretarial work, retail sales, and agricultural labour.[3] At the same time, a growing number of South Asian Canadian women from elite backgrounds are represented at the opposite end of the occupational spectrum as teachers, doctors, and middle-level civil servants. Either way, income derived from women's jobs frequently makes the difference between just making ends meet and enjoying a comfortable lifestyle:

> I have been working the night shift at this sewing job for the past three years. We make the little emblems that you see on people's caps and jackets. About half of the women here are from one or another South Asian group, while the rest are Chinese and Portuguese.
>
> I have never liked working here. I had the equivalent of a good twelfth-grade education and a few years of bookkeeping experience before I came to Canada. Still, with everyone else looking for work, too, I never even got an interview for a job like that. House payments were going up every year, so I took a job here. When I think about the bad wages and the fact that some of the other women here aren't even literate I feel very frustrated. On the other hand, the night work allows me to have more time with my children and the income *is* important. Without it we might have lost our house.

Other income options are sometimes available to South Asian families. If a working relative or friend is staying with a family, he or she will contribute something for his or her room and board. Men usually pay a small sum while women help around the house. Adult children, especially sons, often help support the family as long as they live with their parents. Alternatively, it is not uncommon for men to take on two jobs during their first few years in Canada.

These strategies have allowed many South Asian families to become economically secure in short order. South Asian family incomes are already above the national average. Even so, the emphasis on quickly securing jobs and on high pay has locked many South Asians into low-status work far below their past occupational experience.

South Asians are now found in every sector of the economy. They are well represented in the professions, particularly in medicine, the sciences, engineering, post-secondary education, and accounting. They have also developed a considerable entrepreneurial tradition in Canada, which will be discussed later.

South Asians are little more able to change the range of goods and services provided by the Canadian economy than they are the job market. They have generally accepted this and have embraced Canadian material culture. The major exception has been food practices, in which they have been culturally conservative. South Asian consumer priorities in general, however, are different from those of other Canadians. This is best illustrated by South Asian housing patterns. Like Italians, Greeks, and Chinese, South Asian families place great stress on home ownership, for it has traditionally signified permanence, household security, and establishment. South Asian families in Canada have tried to secure their own homes by severely restricting the purchase of other consumable goods, by having many people work, and by purchasing inexpensive first homes:

> I guess I'm pretty unusual in being forty years old, South Asian, and unmarried. I certainly didn't need the room, but wanted to buy a house from the very first. In my own house I don't have to worry about neighbours and can do what I want. I bought one with a basement suite, which I rented out to help cover the mortgage. A friend moved in with me and also helped with the expenses. Three years later I bought this place, largely because it's newer. At present two teen-age sisters from our community who are having trouble with their family are staying with me. Both work, so they help a bit with the costs. I don't expect that this unusual arrangement will last, so I am building a rental suite in the basement. There are many families in the community who can't yet afford their own houses but don't like to live in apartment blocks. I don't think I'll have any problem renting it out.

Up until 1978, many South Asian immigrant families were able to achieve home ownership in the West within three or four years; it took somewhat longer in the East. With recent increases in house prices, high interest rates, and an uncertain economy, South Asians have been caught in the same boat as others and the rate of people becoming homeowners has gone down sharply. Apartment living has become a more or less permanent condition for many people, particularly in Metro Toronto.[4]

Perhaps the only other important consumer differences result from many still having close relatives overseas for whom they try to provide some economic and social support. This typically takes the form of cash remittances, which can be quite significant. For example, the economic circumstances of whole villages in Punjab have been transformed by remittances flowing in from relatives in Britain and Canada.[5] People frequently feel the necessity to visit their parents and other relatives or to pay for their relatives to come on visits here. Counting new immigrants, over 30,000 people make the trip between Canada and South Asian source countries each year. This is a significant financial drain on many families.

CHANGES IN FAMILY STRUCTURE

Until recently, South Asians have been able to meet their minimal settlement objectives relatively quickly despite cultural differences and an ini-

153

tial unfamiliarity with Canada. Much of this was achieved through a combination of hard work, cultural flexibility, and the adroit use of systems of familial mutual aid and support. Their substantial educational, skill, and class resources were equally significant, for they guaranteed that South Asian immigrants did not typically start at the bottom of Canadian society, even when they arrived here with little money.

This smooth material adjustment to Canadian economic life belies fundamental shifts in individual and family relations that have generated a host of unresolved problems. In particular, immigration and settlement have resulted in massive challenges to traditional South Asian notions of the family. In a typical South Asian extended family, all of the founding couple's sons, their wives, and children will remain together in one large unit. Land or individual incomes may be pooled in the interests of the family at large. The senior couple maintain primary authority and control over household affairs until they are old. Upon the death of the husband, the resident sons and their families often remain together, forming what are technically called joint families. These are places where roles are highly defined and rigidly sexually stratified. These large family units remain vital to individual economic security and continue to be a major social force in people's lives; they socialize and acculturate individuals and protect them against the world. Industrialization and urbanization have only partially weakened the extended family, and, while by no means uncommon, nuclear families like those which predominate in Canada are not most people's ideal.

In contrast, perhaps the only long-term extended South Asian families in Canada can be found among Sikhs, and even there they are rare.[6] The chief reason why extended families are not more frequently found is that people are far more independent economically here than they are in South Asia. Unlike India or Pakistan, there is little long-term economic gain in two brothers and their families or the married adult children of parents living together – certainly not enough to override intra-family conflicts and differences. Many working-class parents would like to have their adult children remain with them and contribute to the household, but most eventually leave. Immigration and migration also limit extended family development:

> I have tried everything I can think of to keep our family together, but it hasn't really worked out. I, my wife, and children came here from India early enough that it was pretty easy to get settled. It wasn't so easy to reform the family. In India my parents, my family, my brother's family, an umarried brother, and two unmarried sisters once all lived together under one roof. I was able to sponsor my married brother, and so he and his family also came to Toronto. They stayed with us for a while, but soon realized that if they worked hard enough and saved enough money they could buy a

house of their own. His wife and mine never really got along anyway, and they eventually left for the suburbs. Now my oldest son has a job and wants to move out to live with some friends. In a few years my father will be old enough to immigrate, so perhaps I'll be able to talk him and my mother into coming here to live with us. My other brother has since married and will take over the family land.

Nuclear families consequently predominate among South Asian Canadians. Less common are nuclear families with one additional adult member, often an elderly parent, uncle, or aunt or a younger, unmarried brother, sister, or cousin; of these, nuclear families supporting retired parents are the most permanent. Although appreciative of the services available to the elderly in Canada, examples of South Asians institutionalizing their parents are as yet almost unknown. Moreover, elderly mothers and mothers-in-law are extremely helpful in reducing household tasks. With both parents working, grandparents often serve as functional parents for young children.

Almost all other forms of quasi-extended South Asian families are transitory. Adult sons and daughters sooner or later marry and leave. So do brothers and sisters, nephews and nieces. Few of what appear to outsiders to be extended South Asian families last more than a couple of years.

Even the nuclear family has been put under stress by immigration and settlement. This is especially true of husband-wife relations. Traditional South Asian husband-wife roles and statuses follow a pattern somewhat similar to those in southern European societies. The ideal image of these two roles portrayed in the ancient Vedas and elsewhere is one of equality in difference, but in practice formal authority has been monopolized by men.[7] Males dominated public roles and the activities of women were very circumscribed. They had authority only over unmarried children and their sons' wives and children. Interaction between household women and men outside the family was sharply restricted. Women generally sought achievement through the activities of their husbands and families.

The effect of immigration on marital relations has been complex and is a function of ethnic and class background, economic social situation, and individual temperament. Despite these qualifications, there have been several consistent changes. Most significantly, immigration has weakened the power of husbands to control family affairs. Working wives are exposed to a variety of cultural influences contradictory to their traditional role and as wage-earners they demand more authority. Husbands often find their family status weakened by their low-prestige jobs and their inability to transfer their status from their source country into Canadian society. Also, they have little outside support for their authority in the family save from their immediate relatives, and the latters' moral force is weakened in the Canadian context.

155

Wives encounter their own particular difficulties in achieving an acceptable role. Almost without exception working wives are expected to do most of the household work as well.[8] Husbands have generally accepted the responsibilities for more "manly" household duties such as cutting lawns and making house repairs, but cooking, laundry, cleaning, and caring for children are rarely done by men. For many husbands this aversion to increasing their household responsibilities appears to be highly symbolic; they have made an adaptation to Canadian life in which, as one observer has noted, they are "Somdash by day, Somadasa by night"; Somdash is an anglicized version of the Sinhalese name Somadasa.[9] This is to say that, while conceding to the assimilative forces of public life, they try to maintain symbolic aspects of South Asian practice at home. In many cases this results in an unending workload for women. Moreover, wives are frequently subject to much more social isolation than their husbands, particularly if they do not work outside the home:

> In Punjab, I and other women had little control over our own affairs. Our responsibilities did not extend beyond everyday household decisions. Most of us had nowhere near the freedom of movement of our husbands. We spent almost all of our time at home; this wasn't too bad, because there were usually other women living in the household and we all visited a lot with other families.
>
> From what I had heard about life in Canada before we came I knew things would be different, but not in the way it turned out. Once we had settled into our own house I found myself terribly alone. My husband worked long hours and spent a lot of time after work visiting with his men friends. We could afford only one car, and I never learned to drive. This meant that all day I usually stayed home – I even had to wait for my husband to drive me to the store. Most other women that I knew were in the same situation. Although no one had intended it, we were all prisoners in our own homes. Some jealous husbands even locked up the telephone when they were away from the house. Maybe Canadian women can stand that kind of isolation, but we just weren't used to it. We all waited for the weekend, when we could at least visit with each other. It's been only in the last few years that some have had their own cars.

Although men have been reluctant to pick up household tasks, they have been more flexible about sharing decision-making with their wives.[10] For example, everyday household finances are often managed by women and there is usually consultation between husbands and wives prior to major purchases. Extensive husband-wife deliberation in regard to family planning is equally common. South Asians have traditionally had many children, but among immigrants one sees a dramatic shift in all classes and groups toward having two or at the most three children.[11]

Traditional South Asian ideologies of ideal womanhood are quite different from their Canadian counterparts. The traditional South Asian woman was supposed to be devoted to her family, selfless, and self-sacrificing, a support to her husband. A great many South Asian Canadian women have been caught between this ideal and Canadian options that stress independence, self-achievement, and equality. Speaking in the most general terms, South Asian women seem to want the best of both worlds. On one hand, they desire a greater range of freedom outside the home and more control over things within it.[12] They rarely see women's success and achievement outside the home as a threat to their relations at home and therefore see no conflict in expanding their domain in both spheres. They want their husbands to change their ideas in order to make these things more easily realized. On the other hand, immigrant wives and mothers continue to ground their identity in the family. Many continue to accept quasi-traditional ideologies of achievement through the success of their husbands and families. They see many Canadian notions about family, marriage, and children as threats to this family-linked identity. At the same time, they value family access to Canadian educational, economic, and social opportunities even though they are aware that these have potential for further weakening what they value about the traditional family.

Conflict in husband-wife relations, however, is far from endemic. Immigrants who have come to Canada after being married for a decade or more inevitably find ways to keep stresses from breaking up the family. Also, professional couples seem to be able to contain family conflict better, in all probability because they are already used to less traditional male-female roles. Problems are particularly severe for young couples, especially those who have married shortly before or soon after emigrating. Having traditional family expectations, unused to resolving marital disagreements, and cut away from possible conflict mediators, they often have a hard time.[13] Marriage breakup and ongoing estrangement are common results, particularly if the couple has not yet had children.

Relations between parents and children experience similar stresses. How should children adjust to their dual Canadian and South Asian roots? Parents frequently are caught in a dilemma. They have high expectations and acknowledge that if their children are to succeed they must do so on Canadian terms. They are therefore keen to provide their children with appropriate education and vocational skills and hope that these will be translated into economic security, marriage, and grandchildren.[14]

However, they have not abandoned the wish that their children maintain certain key elements of their South Asian heritage, particularly in the areas of family authority and marriage. As a result, children of immigrants eventually learn to negotiate two sets of cultural values, those of their peers and those of their parents. This alternation is rarely made without difficulty, for the immigrant culture of their parents and relatives often contradicts the values expressed by their peers, the media, and the educational system.

For most children, these Canadian influences are fast becoming pre-dominant. Relations between pre-adolescent South Asian children and others have been good and such children have moved smoothly into their peer groups. This has resulted in second-generation and young immigrant children strongly identifying with other children and assimilating most of their values and beliefs. Relations between adolescent immigrant children and their peers are similar, but the former tend to be culturally more South Asian and hence more under the control of their parents.

As a rule, second-generation and young immigrant children are under-going massive assimilation and acculturation. As with all other im-migrant populations, parents have few resources to counter this trend. They work hard and long and have little time to devote to teaching children their culture; so many other settlement challenges seem more immediate. Attempts are nevertheless being made to transmit certain South Asian values, beliefs, and practices to their children. Most of these values and beliefs directly concern family relations.

Parental objectives for cultural retention in the family vary tre-mendously, as is to be expected considering their wide range of cultural and class backgrounds, but there are several common themes. One is an attempt to establish parent-child relationships along somewhat tradi-tional lines. Parents in South Asia demand strict obedience to their authority and have far more control over their children's lives than is typical in Canada. Immigrant parents rarely expect or wish to exert this degree of authority here. Even so, South Asian adults see Canadian society as being far too permissive and they see parental authority as one means of shielding their children from this permissiveness.[15] Many parents therefore try to keep their children away from social situations that they believe threaten South Asian moral values. This is particularly so for girls. In more culturally conservative families, adolescent daughters are expected to maintain great social distance from other children, especially from boys and men. Sons are allowed more freedom but are frequently caught between the expectations of their parents and peers.

Translated into practical issues, this conflict most frequently involves dating and marriage. No South Asian culture has a dating tradition; adolescent women are so carefully controlled by their parents that such a phenomenon could not possibly arise. South Asian marriages have typi-cally been arranged between prospective parents-in-law with little input from their children. Here, the prospect of dating is usually the first thing to set parents thinking about what sorts of marriage partners their chil-dren should have and what role they as parents will play in such mar-riages. Clearly, whom their children marry will have a profound effect on the persistence of South Asian communities in Canada. If they marry within their own ethnic group, the group may last a very long time. If they are less ethnically selective and yet tend to marry within the overall South Asian population, this will make the general category more real than it is now. If they opt to marry non-South Asians, then these communities may not persist past the second generation.

There has so far developed a partial dual standard on dating.[16] Parents are generally against the practice and are quite adamant when it comes to their daughters. Sons are often allowed more freedom, especially when parents feel that it will not result in an "inappropriate" marriage. Culturally conservative groups such as the Sikhs tend to enforce dating restrictions rigidly, whereas this is less true of more acculturated groups, such as the Fijians, or professional class ones, such as North Indian Hindus. Some, such as the Ismailis, tend to accept their children dating others from the same ethnic group, but remain concerned about marriage:

> In some ways I think that we Ismailis might be facing some real problems when it comes to this question of marriage. Of course, almost all parents want their children to marry other Ismailis – it's not just blind prejudice, either. Our religion does not presently look for new converts, so a mixed marriage may well mean that they and their children will be lost to both the community and religion. Why the problems? Outside of religious practice, Ismailis have really tried hard to be completely modern and up to date, especially since what happened in East Africa. We try to get our children to mix with those from other backgrounds, too, so how will we get them to marry within the community? So far this hasn't been too much of a problem because most Ismailis of marriageable age were born overseas and so haven't totally "become Canadian." But what of the younger ones? So far, we have tried to make sure that our children have a lot of contact with other Ismaili children of the same age, so that they will "naturally" find their potential spouses among them. Things are more or less working according to plan, but I'm worried about the future.

Worries over dating for most groups are just a prelude to more fundamental concerns about marriage. In all South Asian cultures, marriages are important mechanisms for creating alliances and interdependence between families. Indeed, they are contracts between two families, not two individuals. Only in the past twenty years have self-contracted marriages been at all common and they are largely restricted to the urban middle classes. Moreover, marriage has been traditionally symbolic of equality between the two families concerned; South Asian societies are highly stratified and very diverse, with the result that marriage patterns have tended to be severely restrictive. People usually marry people of the same ethnicity, class, caste (where relevant), and religion as themselves. These practices are so pervasive and have so much importance attached to them that almost all Sikh immigrant parents pressure their children to marry along traditional lines. Virtually all daughters do so, and most have arranged marriages. Even sons almost always marry within their parents' expectations. For both sons and daughters, not following their parents' wishes can result in ostracism.

With their strong ethnic identity and individual orientation to the group, this pattern of ethnic endogamy among Sikhs is quite predictable. How the other South Asian groups will resolve this dilemma is by no means clear. Most of these groups have not been in Canada long enough for many of the second generation to reach marriageable age. Most of those who came to Canada as adolescents have married members of their own ethnic group, but this is not necessarily an indication of what will happen to Canadian-born children in the future. There is some evidence that most parents would allow in principle the marriage of their children to those of other ethnic backgrounds.[17] Even so, reservations are prevalent. To many, an intergroup marriage signals the end of the family line. It is also seen as offering few rewards to parents; they fail to gain allies or create new social connections, and it makes their status ambiguous in the eyes of other community members. It is thought that sons or daughters who marry out will thereafter not fulfil their familial responsibilities. Matches with non-South Asians are not infrequently suspected of being "love marriages" that can bring dishonour to a family. In short, parents consider it best if children marry traditionally and they put pressure on them to conform. The following Sikh account confirms the inherent ambiguity of this situation.

> I was one of those handful of Sikhs who were born and raised in British Columbia before Sikh immigration really picked up. I was born right after World War II in a town in the Fraser Valley. There weren't very many Sikhs around there then, so virtually all my schoolmates were "Canadians" – but then, so was I. I never had any trouble in school with not being accepted, in fact, I think that I was pretty popular. Still, life for me was complicated, because my parents and other local relatives were pretty conservative Sikhs. This meant that I had to learn how to be almost two people: one for my Canadian friends and one for my parents.
>
> The big question arose when I got into high school. My parents did not want me to date Canadian girls; they didn't want me to date Sikh girls, either. This was quite embarrassing for me, because I couldn't really explain my parents' reasoning to my friends. Eventually, I had an arranged marriage with a woman from India. Married life was pretty embarrassing, too, at first, because I just didn't know how I was supposed to act. I was surprised at how well the marriage worked out in the long run. Still, I'm not sure that I would want our children to have arranged marriages.

The parental expectations may be partially frustrated as the second generation comes of age, especially by second-generation men. Children have become so culturally Canadian that few will want an arranged marriage within their cultural group. Many will not even share a common first language with prospective spouses from the source country. There may nevertheless be a considerable degree of endogamy within the second generation. Some daughters have developed neither the social contacts nor the strategies required to make totally independent marriages. In many instances the only men of marriageable age with whom they will come in frequent contact are from similar backgrounds. Among some groups, such as Sikhs and Ismailis where there is a great deal of community interaction and strong religious and ethnic identity, it is likely that the second generation will largely marry within itself. In contrast, among those groups whose ethnic solidarity is weaker or those whose parents live largely outside of ethnic communities, many of the second generation may seek their own marriage partners outside of both their ethnic group and the South Asian population. Only an unlikely rise in racial prejudice and discrimination would seem to be able to stop the development of such a trend in the 1980's.

Important as it is, the question of marriage is just one aspect of continuously changing relations between parents and children. This is particularly true for parental attempts to transmit South Asian culture to their children; the success of such attempts is a strong function of the degree to which parents can exercise authority over their children, and this is very group-dependent.

Sikhs, without question, have been the most effective South Asian group in instilling their culture in their children. Almost all second-generation Sikhs can understand Punjabi, though some cannot speak it well and few can read or write it. In immigrant families, Punjabi is usually the language of the home. Backed up by strong parental religious convictions and well-established religious institutions, children generally become at least nominal believers. Often tied through their parents into dense Sikh social networks, the children find in other Sikhs an important reference group. Parents, community, and religion generally establish in children a substantial sense of Sikh identity.[18]

Other groups have been less effective in transmitting their culture to their children through the family. There are several reasons why this is so. For one, group identity is often not so strong as it is for Sikhs and it is not necessarily associated with a specific inventory of cultural beliefs and practices. Ismailis, for example, have a strong identity, but it centres primarily on religious practice and social association. Ismailis do not therefore see acculturation as a primary threat, as long as the children maintain their religion, keep up their associations with the Ismaili community, and marry within it. The transmission of language, cultural values, and beliefs outside of this orbit is comparatively less important.

In other groups parental identities are less distinct, for many already had a foot in two worlds before they came to Canada. British or British

161

colonial culture has influenced Fijians, Guyanese, Trinidadians, South Africans, and British South Asians, as well as professional-class immigrants from India, Pakistan, and Sri Lanka.[19] In all of these places Western culture is associated with economic and social success. Immigrant parents are therefore ambivalent about instilling their South Asian cultural heritage in their children. Virtually all South Asians have a positive feeling toward the culture and society in which they were born and raised, and they are proud of their origins. On the other hand, they do not want to impede their children's establishment by locking them into a "foreign" culture.

How this dilemma is resolved is an individual family question. As a rule, cultural retention is much greater if the family resides where there is a large community of people from the same ethnic group; Fijian children in Vancouver will learn much more about their parent's culture than will their counterparts in Montreal. It will be more substantial where familial efforts are backed up by strong community institutions.

Most parents, however, are only selectively committed to a program of cultural retention. The result in some groups has been a substantial cultural loss in less than a single generation. For example, among Fijians, Guyanese, Trinidadians, and South Africans, second-generation children frequently do not understand their parents' language. They know little of the places from which their parents came and their values and beliefs are little different from those of their non-South Asian peers:

> Like most Fijian couples, we speak Hindi to each other at home. Somehow, we have never tried to speak Hindi to our children. Oh, they know a few words of it, but that's about all. Because we both work, our son and daughter spend more time with their Canadian friends and *Sesame Street* than they do with us. There's a lot about our style of life in Fiji that I wish that they could enjoy, but I'm not too sure that many of those things were part of our Fijian *Indian* heritage – there were things that everyone in Fiji shared to one or another in some degree.

> When our grandparents and great-grandparents came to Fiji they adapted to life there. We and our children should do the same here. Perhaps the only concern I really have about our children "becoming Canadian" is that they will certainly lose our Hindu religion. We *have* tried to teach them a bit about Hinduism, but already they seem to look on it with outsider's eyes.

To a lesser extent, the same holds true for most groups from South Asia itself. At the same time, as outlined in subsequent chapters, the rise of South Asian ethnic and religious associations in the 1970's has led to the development of many community-based programs aimed at language retention, religious instruction, and South Asian music and dance. These may turn out to have a considerable impact on the second generation in the future.

SOUTH ASIAN ETHNIC IDENTITIES IN A CHANGING WORLD

As with other immigrant groups, only a small proportion of South Asian cultural practices have survived the settlement process. Individually held cultural beliefs and values have not changed as quickly. Among immigrants, many cherished beliefs and values are constantly being contradicted by practical necessity and alternative Canadian ideas. It has become fashionable to use the apparent Canadianization of South Asian Canadian cultural life as evidence that ethnicity is therefore unimportant to South Asians.[20] Nothing could be further from the truth. Even if recent South Asian immigrants rarely *act* South Asian, this should not suggest that they do not *feel* South Asian. Virtually all South Asians are conscious of their ethnicity. Immigration has made them a minority group and they are well aware that many other Canadians have categorized them as ethnically and physically different. Beyond making them conscious of their perceived ethnicity, this augments identification with an individual's specific ethnic, linguistic, and religious heritage.

In fact, the rapid acculturation that South Asians are undergoing has in no way undermined ethnic group *identity* for most immigrants. To be sure, many people become disoriented and frustrated when initially faced with these massive changes and they feel that some of them are morally wrong. In every group there is great nostalgia for valued aspects of their culture that cannot be reproduced in Canada: strong families and communities, the meaning and world view tied to their language, the richness of their religious practice, the general style of life. Despite this, most people have been able to rearrange their ethnic criteria in such a way that a prideful ethnic identity can be maintained despite the fact that most ethnic culture cannot.

One way in which this has been possible has been by using cultural practices that *can* be maintained as symbolic markers of ethnicity. The continuation of South Asian food practices serves this purpose. So, too, does the private and public maintenance of religious and cultural celebrations. A whole range of community institutions also validates ethnicity.

Even so, the most important supports for ethnic identity among South Asian Canadians are *social* rather than cultural. For example, the relative stability of family life supports many ethnic beliefs and values, even when actual family relations are very different from the norm overseas. Similarly, maintaining relations between families and individuals of the same background has been given very high priority. Culture has been difficult to re-establish here, but such social relations have not. South Asians are masters at cultivating and maintaining social relations, having generally come from places where this art is very important. In several South Asian groups these informal community links may be more developed than they are in any other ethnic Canadian population. So important are these relations that they are a major topic of Chapter Ten. Here it suffices to say that the ability to associate with

163

others of similar background who are also undergoing the stresses of settlement goes a long way toward making these stresses more tolerable.

The form and intensity that ethnic identity takes in the second generation will have at least as important an effect on the perpetuation of the South Asian experience in Canada as will the preservation of ethnic culture. Common identity rather than common culture is, after all, the primary basis for social association, and without social association ethnicity disappears. As with so many other things concerning second-generation South Asian Canadians, it is still too early to say much about what types of ethnic identities they will have or about which situations will activate these identities. One thing is certain. It is unlikely that any second-generation South Asian Canadians will grow up without some sort of identification with the ethnic roots of their parents; they may not know the language or much about the culture, but they will have grown up in a family and community who knew these things well. They will be the products of two decades of dual South Asian and Canadian experience, and although the cultural impact of the latter is so powerful, they will still be influenced by the social strength of the former.

There is already evidence that, in the second generation, ethnic identity will not necessarily be strongest in the most culturally conservative groups. The depth of community relations may have a profound effect. For example, second-generation Fijians in Vancouver may be highly acculturated, but they live in a place where most have scores of relatives, all of them Fijian. Even if they marry non-Fijians they will maintain associations with other Fijians for the rest of their lives. In addition, the development of community institutions capable of attracting the second generation may also have a significant impact.

It is often said that ethnic awareness follows a three-generation cycle, in which the immigrant first generation is vitally concerned with ethnicity, the second generation rejects it, and the third generation goes back to look for its ethnic roots. It is not clear that South Asians will follow this pattern. A case could certainly be made that, in cultural terms, the second generation is not very South Asian. On the other hand, this has hardly resulted from a conscious rejection of their parents' culture. On the contrary, neither socially nor in terms of identity is it likely that they will isolate themselves from others who share their heritage. Predictions about the third generation are dangerous, since most of the second generation have not yet even reached marriageable age. If the second generation of many groups intermarries extensively with other Canadians, the third generation will be correspondingly small. Even if they do not, much will depend on the structure of South Asian communities a generation from now. The direction picked by the third generation must remain an open question.

One of the critical unknowns in predicting the future development of South Asian ethnic consciousness is how they will be viewed by other Canadians. At present, there is enough racial and cultural prejudice in

Canada against South Asians to make virtually every individual in each of these South Asian ethnocultural groups acutely conscious of his or her ethnicity. Should Canadian sensitivities to visible and cultural difference not continue to subside, the inevitable result will be the strong persistence of some form of South Asian consciousness in the second and perhaps even the third generation.

Hopefully, this brief look at how South Asian families have adapted to life in Canada negates a number of rather prevalent stereotypic beliefs about them. A common misconception about South Asians is that they come from an entirely different culture from our own; this is only selectively true and only for some South Asian immigrants. Moreover, it is often thought that South Asians are extreme cultural traditionalists, who bring their culture – lock, stock, and barrel – over to Canada. This, obviously, is not so. Even in such a vital area of life as family relations, every South Asian household has been entirely transformed. South Asian Canadian material culture is already close to mainstream Canadian practice. A look at relations between parents and children makes a mockery of this notion of cultural conservatism, for in most basic beliefs and values the emerging second generation will closely mirror their peers.

These are enormous changes, especially considering that they have occurred in less than twenty years, and they have not happened without generating a certain amount of stress, uncertainty, and ambiguity. True enough, immigrant South Asians are generally satisfied with their lives in Canada, but most see the process as one involving important tradeoffs. The gains are often striking: a better and more certain material standard of living; access to a more open society with many educational and occupational possibilities; a more stable political environment; less ethnic polarization; and greater chances for their children.

Individual and familial losses are equally clear and fall chiefly on adults. Like so many other immigrants, they have left social contexts that they understood and identified with, contexts where their own place was reasonably well defined. Closely linked to family, kin, friends, and community, South Asians come to Canada, where extensive social links are uncommon and where other things have partially taken over the role of social relations in defining the individual. Faced with enormous cultural loss, South Asian Canadians have compensated by quickly re-establishing dense ethnic networks of association. In so doing they have created some of the most complex ethnic communities and community institutions of any in Canada. It is to these that we now turn.

NOTES

1. Srivastava, "Family Organization and Change," p. 9.
2. B. Ubale, "Equal Opportunity and Public Policy" (Toronto, 1977, mimeo.).

3. Zohra Husaini, "Social Networks: A Factor in Immigrant Economic Success" (Ph.D. thesis, University of Alberta, 1981).

4. In a national survey, Appathurai, "The Sri Lankans," p. 88, found that 67 per cent of Sri Lankans owned their own homes and that 50 per cent of them had become home-owners within two years of immigrating to Canada. However, a recent Toronto study found that only 10.5 per cent of South Asians owned homes: Wilson Head, *Adaptation of Immigrants: Perceptions of Ethnic and Racial Discrimination* (Toronto, 1981), p. 46.

5. Arthur W. Helweg, "A Punjabi Community in an English Town: A Study in Migrant Adaptation" (Ph.D. thesis, Michigan State University, 1977); Helwig, *Sikhs in England*.

6. Srivastava, "Family Organization and Change," p. 26, notes that in the 1960's most families that appeared to be joint were actually only temporarily so. Today, more or less stable joint residential units among Sikhs are more common.

7. J.C. Naidoo, "The East Indian Woman: Her Potential Contribution to Canadian Society" (1977, mimeo.). See the Bibliography for other articles by Naidoo on male-female relations.

8. On household authority, see Siddique, "Patterns of Familial Decision Making, " pp. 102-3; Saroj Chawla, "Indian Children in Toronto: A Study of Socialization" (M.A. thesis, York University, 1971), p. 41; Srivastava, "Family Organization and Change," p. 31. This is a heavy load for many women, who in their parents' homes had servants; this may be more than half of all women. Chawla, "Indian Children in Toronto," p. 21; Naidoo, "The East Indian Woman," p. 4.

9. Appathurai, "The Sri Lankans."

10. For example, Siddique, "Patterns of Familial Decision Making," p. 122, could find no direct relationship between equality of husband-wife decision-making and length of residence in Canada. See also Chawla, "Indian Children in Toronto."

11. For example, see Appathurai, "The Sri Lankans," p. 68, on children in Sri Lankan Canadian families.

12. On women's issues, see Naidoo, "The East Indian Woman," p. 6-13; Srivastava, "Patterns of Familial Decision Making," p. 30; Naidoo, "The East Indian Woman in Canadian Context: A Study in Social Psychology" (1977, mimeo.), p. 10, Table 4; Naidoo, "South Asians in the Canadian Mosaic," paper presented at the annual meeting of the Canadian Ethnic Studies Association (1981, mimeo.), pp. 9-10, Table 6.

13. Buchignani, "Immigration, Adaptation, and the Management of Ethnic Identity."

14. Naidoo, "South Asians in the Canadian Mosaic," p. 8.

15. Appathurai, "The Sri Lankans," p. 98; Chawla, "Indian Children in Toronto," p. 72.

16. Chawla, "Indian Children in Toronto," p. 77; Dusenbery, "Hierarchy, Equality and the Assertion of Sikh Identity," p. 6; Srivastava, "Patterns

of Familial Decision Making," pp. 16 – 17; Kuldip Gill, "A Canadian Sikh Wedding as a Cultural Performance" (M.A. thesis, University of British Columbia, 1982).

17. Morah, "The Assimilation of Ugandan Asians," p. 110, found 63 per cent of recent Ugandan refugees to be willing to see a mixed marriage; Appathurai, "The Sri Lankans," p. 101, gives a figure of 84 per cent for Sri Lankans.

18. Srivastava, "Patterns of Familial Decision Making," p. 15.

19. For example, Appathurai, "The Sri Lankans," p. 152, found that 81 per cent of Sri Lankan immigrants spoke English at home.

20. A. Marguerite Cassin and A. Griffith, "Class and Ethnicity: Producing the Difference that Counts," *Canadian Ethnic Studies*, 8, 1 (1981), pp. 109-30.

TEN

Networks of Relations

Family life is but one of several key elements of South Asian Canadian social and cultural life, though it is without question the most significant one. Second to family in importance as an element of South Asian ethnocultural development are two intertwined aspects of community.[1] Here we address one of these, the structure, function, and significance of informal South Asian community relations. The next chapter outlines the rise of community institutions such as ethnocultural organizations, businesses, and schools.

Let us begin with a few words on the often abused term "community." Unfortunately, there has been a tendency of late to use community to refer to so many things that it has almost lost all meaning. Sometimes, it is no more than a way of referring offhandedly to a particular set of people, with the assumption that they have something in common. For illustrative purposes, consider the common reference to "the South Asian community of Toronto." What possibly could this mean? Does it have any basis in reality at all? The use of the term "community" seems to refer most commonly to what is technically called an ethnocultural population: an assemblage of people categorized by having some common demographic attribute, say a common language or source country; along such lines, when people refer to Toronto's South Asian community, they really mean the population of all immigrants and their descendants who can trace their roots to one or another place in South Asia. Alternatively, people often use "community" to refer to geographically bounded groups of people, as in the case of a neighbourhood where a particular ethnocultural population predominates.

If we are to have any comprehension of South Asian Canadian community life we must be more specific than this. After all, as was previously shown, South Asians come from a very wide range of ethnocultural, religious, national, and linguistic backgrounds. Their identities and experiences are often closely tied up with a particular group of people who share similar roots, not with all people of South Asian origin. In terms of community relations this usually results in very sharp boundaries between one South Asian group and the others. People who share common roots may indeed associate closely with each other, but they are likely to have far more to do with *non*-South Asians than they will with South Asians with different roots. It is therefore unreasonable and inaccurate to consider the most important level of South Asian community relations to be those enveloping all South Asians in a given place. Rather, wherever in Canada the South Asian population rises above a few hundred, a number of South Asian communities develop side by side. Large cities may have more than twenty such communities. It should be noted that South Asians in any given city or town generally are quite dispersed, so the common assumption that "community" refers to a geographically bounded group does not apply either.

What, then, are we left with? Perhaps the best way to approach community life among Canadian South Asians is to emphasize that such communities are chiefly made up of networks of overlapping interpersonal ties that link one person to others who share a common ethnic identity. This is much less complicated than it sounds. To illustrate, consider Fijians in Vancouver. Like most South Asian Canadians, Fijians have a strong sense of their roots and their common Fijian heritage. They share unique aspects of culture and history and even their Hindi contains a number of elements specific to Fiji. Most importantly, extensive chain migration to Vancouver from Fiji has resulted in most people having many relatives living nearby. These factors result in strong networks of association between most Fijian Vancouverites and others – the kind of informal community referred to above. In contrast, most Fijians in Vancouver have very little to do with Sikhs or other South Asian groups in the area.

Whatever their particular origins, almost all South Asian Canadian immigrants have come from places where social life was far more developed and far more valued than is typical here. In this respect, without their community links, many South Asian Canadians would feel extremely isolated. South Asian community relations are consequently often extensive, strong, and valued. Indeed, in this respect South Asian communities are at least as well developed as they are in any other Canadian ethnic population.

At the same time, the maintenance of these community contacts is partially voluntary. As with other ethnocultural groups, South Asians hardly form communities in a mechanical response to their common roots. Communities develop out of people making choices about whom to associate with, under what conditions, and for what reasons. Such relations are not formed randomly, with the consequence that no South Asian community is socially homogeneous. Rather, many factors divide and subdivide South Asian communities. The following sections address some of the more important determinants of this level of community organization.

THE USES OF COMMUNITY RELATIONS

If for a moment we go back to the historical situation of Sikhs in British Columbia, it is clear that one of the things that gave great support to the development of community relations was the simple fact that associating together produced important gains for the individuals concerned. Living with other community members lowered costs and provided a system of social welfare for those in need. Support of community institutions paid dividends in changing the immigration regulations and in eventually having anti-South Asian legal restrictions removed from the books. Community relations partially compensated for their separation from families and friends in India.

Are there still such substantial benefits to be had from participating in community? There is no simple answer, for the value of community varies considerably from one South Asian group to another. Indeed, this variation goes a long way to explaining why some South Asian Canadian communities are far more developed than others. At the same time, several broad functions of community participation are important to most South Asians. One of the most vital is that such contacts are an important source of psychological support, especially for new immigrants and the elderly. Immigration of necessity places people between two worlds, but many South Asians feel this sort of marginality far more keenly than immigrants from, say, Britain or the United States. Associating with community-based friends and relations allows people to feel at ease with others who share the same values, beliefs, and experiences as themselves, and this lessens the anomie and alienation of the immigrant experience. The importance of such association is attested to in the following Sri Lankan account.

When I immigrated to Toronto it was my first time out of Sri Lanka. I certainly wasn't prepared for how different things were here. All through my previous life I had lived in a large family and we were continually visiting and being visited by relatives and friends. Family and friends were just about everything to us, but few of us fully realized it; you don't appreciate what you have until you lose it.

I got into Canada because my brother in Calgary supported my application. Instead of going to Calgary I stayed in Toronto. I had no "real" [i.e., close] relatives in Toronto and was able to stay temporarily with an old schoolmate and his family. They hadn't been in Toronto very long either and didn't know very many other Sri Lankans. Being pretty lonely, I tried to meet those I could through my friends and then even took to looking up Sinhalese names in the telephone book; I would have looked up Ceylon Tamils, too, but that was just after the [1971] troubles [between Tamils and Sinhalese] at home. There weren't all that many people from Sri Lanka in the Toronto area then, and it took a few months to get together a set of Sri Lankan friends and acquaintances. Eventually, I moved in with two other young men. By then, I felt far more comfortable living in Canada than I did at first. Since then I have never lost my community contacts, even though many of my friends are now Canadians.

For South Asians, community clearly fulfils a need for a much stronger social life than that with which most Canadians are familiar:

I am still amazed at how few people Canadians seem to keep in contact with. Most of my Canadian friends seem to have no more than a dozen or so people that they feel close enough to visit on short notice. That certainly isn't our way! I would say that I know at least five hundred *families* in our community well enough to visit. If I only visited a dozen or so like my Canadian friends many people would think that I was hostile to them or at the very least was a very ungracious person. I like visiting, but it's a responsibility, too.

This need for association is not necessarily expressed in random relations with members of a given community. South Asian individuals tend to develop relations chiefly with kin or with others whose class, age, sex, and social status are similar to their own.

A third important use of community relations is that they are often the source of valuable information. Through community links passes word of jobs, local events, and conditions in the source country. Recent immigrants are especially dependent on such information to get established quickly. While such information is often inaccurate or incomplete, the compensation is that it is readily accessible and is already framed in culturally relevant ways. Here are two personal examples:

I think that it is hard for the non-immigrant to appreciate all of the little things that are important to everyday life that we immigrants have to figure out for ourselves. Just consider the basic things to do with governments: social insurance (not to mention how to get the card), medical coverage, where to go for information about government services, how to get retrained or recertified. . . . Canadians I know grew up here and still don't fully understand all there is to know about these. This is one area where having friends and relatives in an immigrant community really makes a difference. It's not that everyone in our community is so all-aware of these things. In fact, in the early 1970's when so many people were new immigrants it was often a case of the blind leading the blind. The point is that people helped out as they could at a time when there didn't seem to be much in the way of "outside" help available.

I must say that I have never gotten a job with the help of people in the community. However, when I reconditioned this old house I saved a lot of money by having a couple of unemployed carpenters from our community do it. We get our car maintained and repaired at a garage run by Sikhs, too; I don't know if that is really that much less expensive, but we can converse easily, and I am not afraid to take the car back if something isn't right. We also tend to use one or another Sikh travel agent. As far as shopping goes, we do make some use of South Asian food stores, but not all of them are Sikh-run.

Close kin links are also used to secure short-term loans, for example, to pay for a relative's travel costs to Canada or to provide part of a down payment for a house.

Community relations have several other uses, which can only be briefly summarized here. For one, because community members share common values (and often are linked by kinship), people from the community operate in many ways as a moral force on individuals and households. For example, mediation between estranged husbands and wives by respected community members is common. For another, the recreational aspects of community association are sometimes also important. Beyond informal visiting, many South Asian Canadian communities put on a range of more formal get-togethers, cultural performances, and sports activities; some of these are detailed in the next chapter. A few community members can always be found who will try to maintain community cultural practices, especially since the rise of multiculturalism in Canadian public policy, and in many instances groups have put a great deal of effort into the development of religious institutions; these also are discussed in Chapter Eleven.

KINSHIP, FRIENDSHIP, AND COMMUNITY

The household and the notions of kinship that underlie it are an important basis of community organization. South Asian immigrants have far more extensive notions of kinship and stronger feelings of family responsibility than the vast majority of Canadians. Moreover, since they generally come from places where kinship links are vital to the maintenance of one's socioeconomic status, there is an expectation that even distant kinship connections will be maintained through visiting, reciprocal exchanges, and mutual aid. Counting in-laws, it is not at all uncommon for an individual in South Asia to know and keep in contact with hundreds of relatives.

Immigration reduces people's ability to actively maintain so many kinship ties. There is nevertheless a considerable amount of social interaction between relatives, which usually takes the form of extensive visiting and telephoning. Even this, though, varies from community to community. Obviously, the density of kin relations depends on the size and makeup of the local ethnic populations. To take an extreme example, chain migration has guaranteed that many of the 9,000 Fijian Indians or the 30,000 Sikhs in the Vancouver area are related to each other. Most individuals consequently know far more kin than they could ever hope to visit. In such a situation kinship provides a rationale for association but not a guarantee of it. Individuals pick and choose relatives with whom to maintain contact. In this sense, many of their friends are also their kin – something typical of other large South Asian communities. Large local populations and extensive chain migration have made kinship a similarly important basis for community among Ismailis and other Gujaratis, Guyanese, Pakistanis, and several other immigrant groups. At the opposite extreme, most local populations of South Asian professionals founded in the 1960's (e.g., Pakistanis) were made up primarily of independent immigrants, and because job availability dispersed them across the country, people often had few relatives in the same city. The basis of community association in these cases was more commonly personal compatibility and class:

> By 1980 the South Asian population of Lloydminster [on the Saskatchewan-Alberta border] was made up of perhaps a score of families. No particular cultural background predominated; some were from Kerala [in southern India], and there were a few Gujaratis from East Africa, a couple of Sikh families and some others. Still, they formed a community of sorts. True, they did seem to share a general feeling of having common roots, but also were linked because they were virtually all highly educated and skilled people: doctors and the like.

In recent years this distinction between large communities dependent on chain migration and smaller communities of independent immigrants has become blurred by the overall prevalence of kin-based chain migration.

South Asian immigrants are more social than other Canadians, but the priority they place on maintaining social relations of kinship and friendship is considerably tempered by available time and energy:

> When we first came to Vancouver we immediately felt the need to re-establish our ties to our many relatives and family friends who had come here earlier than us. In the beginning I guess we used our back-home Sikh sense of who to visit and how often, but this couldn't work. By such standards we had at least fifty families in the area that we should see every so often. For a while we spent part of Saturdays and most of Sundays visiting, and this didn't include the time that I and especially my wife spent on the telephone keeping up relations with those who we couldn't visit as often as we thought was right. Eventually, we found out that most of our more Canadian-wise relatives understood that things here could not be as they were at home; they wanted to see us, but realized that some sense of proportion was necessary. From then on, we have tended to visit perhaps two or three other families each week. We often meet other

friends and relatives while visiting, shopping, or at the gurdwara. Still, we keep in contact with many people chiefly by telephone.

Don't think that I'm saying that visiting is just a traditional chore that has to be done. If that were true I doubt that there would be very much of it going on. You have to realize that for us Sikhs and for many others from South Asia there isn't a very strong tradition of the kinds of recreational pursuits that are so common here. Hardly anybody there plays golf or goes boating. As a result, visiting is more than social necessity, it is at the heart of our social life. I wonder what will happen to community life as our children pick up new ways to spend their time.

The number of other households visited by a given individual with regularity is rarely more than twenty. Occasional visiting might double or triple this figure, and in the case of highly organized communities, such as the Sikhs in Vancouver, occasional contacts might extend to several hundred households.

Visiting is an important informal social institution in virtually all South Asian populations; it is the essential stuff of community. A given person may only have visiting links with a few score of others, but each of them in turn has a slightly different network of kin and friends. As a result, personal social networks interlock into far larger structures. Thus, in most South Asian populations people are aware of and are influenced by people they rarely if ever meet. For instance, if someone in a large community has won a lottery or is the victim of a racial attack, virtually everyone will hear of it within a day or two even if they do not know the person directly.

Even so, the overlap of personal networks is rarely uniform. People prefer to associate with others that they perceive to be like themselves. Thus, no South Asian community is a seamless whole with a unity of values and goals and a commonality of experience. Kinship itself divides up communities, for not everyone is related to everyone else nor are all relationships equally important. At the same time, there is a good deal of cultural, economic, and social similarity among immigrant kin. Such commonalities are strongest in those relatively small communities founded by professionals and are far weaker in such large communities as the Vancouver and Toronto Sikh populations; in the latter instances chain migration of kin has been so extensive that the backgrounds of relatives can vary dramatically one from the other.

CLASS AND COMMUNITY

Most South Asian communities are divided into a number of class-based subcommunities. Members of the elite associate with members of the elite, working-class people with other workers. This has resulted from people maintaining South Asian ideas about class – ideas that sharply distinguish one class from another. Virtually every place from which South Asians have come is strongly stratified, with enormous differences in wealth, power, and status, little interclass mobility, and very restricted interaction between members of different classes. Under such conditions a friendship, say, between a dockyard worker and a middle-level government bureaucrat would be difficult to establish and almost impossible to maintain.

If most South Asian immigrants had their way they would use class as a primary determinant of community association. However, class criteria are complicated by immigration. For one thing, indicators of class in Canada are different from those in South Asian countries. Occupational status, class, and lifestyle tend to be closely aligned there, while here they are less and less so. There, being a worker in a steel plant would result in relatively low status and would be poorly paid. Here, a South Asian working at such a job may be able to maintain a lifestyle more typical of an individual of a much higher class in the source country. Moreover, immigration has dramatically reshuffled people's life chances, making losers of some previous winners and vice versa; a Fijian motor mechanic who arrived in Vancouver in 1973 when jobs were easy to find and houses were cheap will almost certainly maintain a better standard of living for the rest of his life than a Fijian accountant arriving ten years later. How are their respective class positions to be measured?

> In Kenya I was one of the principal executives in a large Indian trading company. I was well paid, had a style of life that I could not possibly have here, and was well regarded throughout the East African business community. When things began to deteriorate in East Africa I and my family got out. We settled in Alberta, feeling that it offered the best prospects for our quick re-establishment.
>
> However, things were not so simple. I found it impossible to secure a job in business no matter how hard I tried. Perhaps it was because of my lack of Canadian experience, but I feel that discrimination also played a part: I know of very few South Asians who have successfully got back into business life in Canada aside from those who have started their own companies. I eventually became the person in charge of certain kinds of supplies for a local school system. The job is quite routine – nothing like what I was doing in Kenya – but it pays well enough for us to have our own house and keep ahead of our debts. It is hard for me to figure out what my status is among South Asians here. Successful doctors and engineers like those that I would have associated with in East Africa seem to feel uncomfortable with my present situation. On the other hand, I really don't have much in common with working-class South Asians except my present job.

The above example is not atypical. South Asians are frequently in quite different class situations than they were prior to immigration.

Many work at different occupations; often, they do work of lower status than previously. Consequently, class links within South Asian communities are more flexibly determined than they would be in India, Sri Lanka, or Kenya. People whose occupational status has gone down as a result of immigration nonetheless are usually accorded their previous social status, even though they will always be considered more marginal than if they had found better work. People with low-class status in the source country who have done well here are grudgingly accepted into higher circles. At the top are those from professional or business backgrounds who have maintained or bettered their previous occupational status subsequent to immigration. Such individuals form an informal core elite of varying size in virtually every South Asian Canadian community. As a working-class Sikh from Toronto explains:

> One of the things which puts me off about the Toronto Sikh community is how the rich and well-off people control everything. When the government wants to know what Sikhs want they run to the doctors, engineers, and professors. What do they know about discrimination, unemployment, or immigration troubles? Who are they to speak for me? We working people are never heard from.

As with so many other aspects of life, the changing demands of the immigration system have always had a profound effect on the degree to which South Asian communities are stratified. The very first pioneers to set out for British Columbia came from virtually identical class backgrounds. From the Second World War until about 1960 most Sikhs who came were the close relatives of Sikh Canadians and thus little class stratification developed. The emphasis on highly trained and educated immigrants in the 1960's directly selected for South Asians of very high social class. Among Sikhs this resulted in sharp class divisions and severe conflicts over which class would speak for the community and control community institutions. In virtually every other instance the result was the creation of a founding community core of professionals: Pakistani, Bangali, Sinhalese, and most non-Sikh Indian communities began this way. In the 1970's the immigration shifted to skilled blue-collar workers, and this increased the class complexity of most South Asian communities. Among Sikhs it strengthened those opposed to community leadership by professionals. Among some communities founded by professionals it generated a working class with little in common with the established elite. The characteristics of the source population also determined the class composition in some new South Asian ethnic communities. Fijian, Guyanese, and Trinidadian Indian immigrants have been primarily selected from the urban working class. Such communities consequently are far less stratified than are those formed by people coming from South Asia itself.

The other somewhat aberrant case is that of Ismailis, a few of whom were in Canada before Idi Amin's expulsion of South Asians from

Uganda in 1972. Canada's Ugandan refugee program preferentially selected individuals from substantial entrepreneurial backgrounds. Thus, most Ismaili communities were founded by people who were an incipient elite. Subsequent sponsored immigration has considerably broadened the class distribution of all Ismaili communities.

PERCEIVED ETHNICITY AND COMMUNITY

Because community ties are largely voluntary, they are a good indicator of the degree to which individuals value ethnicity and whom they consider to be ethnically the same as themselves. Nothing better supports the point that *the* South Asian is a Canadian illusion than patterns of South Asian interaction. If individuals from the many different ethnic, national, and religious backgrounds called "South Asian" considered it to be a valid category, one might expect frequent association among, say, Sikhs, Fijians, and Gujaratis. In fact, with few exceptions, whenever the size of the local population makes it possible, Sikhs will associate primarily with Sikhs, Fijians with Fijians, and Gujaratis with Gujaratis. In every large population centre one finds many such "real" communities, each largely separate from the others and each firmly based on a measure of cultural, linguistic, and religious commonality.

Like other ethnic communities, each of these communities tends to be further subdivided by criteria of cultural or regional difference. Fijians, for example, still recognize cultural differences between those whose ancestors came from North or South India and this is reflected in relatively few marriages spanning the cultural gulf. Muslim Fijians also formed an ethnic subcommunity. Similarly, Sikhs make strong distinctions on the basis of region of origin, religious practice, lineage, and caste. Pakistanis come from several regionally based ethnic groups and virtually every other South Asian community is also internally differentiated.

As a rule, individuals in these many groups see little reason for associating with other South Asian groups just because Canadians perceive that all South Asians are in the same category. Conversely, they almost always have more friends and acquaintances who are not South Asian than they do from South Asian backgrounds other than their own. There are important exceptions to this generalization, chiefly with respect to particular communities and especially to the elite members of them. South Asian populations outside of Vancouver, Metro Toronto, and Montreal have always been relatively small, and for a long time South Asians in these places were not able to form specific ethnic communities. Instead, they tended to associate with other South Asians who were of similar (professional) class origins, especially if there was a cultural or religious rationale for it. Sikhs and Punjabi Hindus would frequently associate with each other, but neither would have very much to do with Pakistani Muslims; Pakistanis would often develop relations with Indian Muslims; Indian Hindus crossed cultural lines to associate with each other. This sort of intergroup elite association has continued to the present, although the expansion of local ethnic communities continues to make it less likely than before. It should also be noted that there is a great deal of variation among Canada's many South Asian ethnocultural groups in how strongly developed are informal community contacts. For the most part, this variation is accounted for by such things as the strength of group identity, the degree of cultural and linguistic difference between a given community and others, the proportion of immigrants in the community, the development of community institutions, the degree of chain migration, and the size of the community. Predictably, Sikh community networks are more highly developed than Pakistani ones, Pakistani ones more so than those of South African Indians.

AGE, SEX, GENERATION, AND COMMUNITY

As in so many other Canadian ethnocultural populations, age, sex, and generation strongly determine who associates with whom in South Asian communities and under what conditions. Consider how age affects community organization. Because of the comparative newness of most South Asian immigration and because of the immigration regulations' bias against middle-aged people, South Asian Canadian communities have usually been founded by young adults. Today, the people who are the most active in community affairs are still these people, who are now usually married and between the ages of thirty and forty-five.

Many such people have brought over their parents, making use of the provisions of the immigration regulations that allow the parents of Canadian residents above a certain age to join their children without being subject to the point system. In virtually every instance they will live with their children, taking a secondary, though important, role in family affairs. At the same time, such elderly people's situation is often distinct from other adults in the community. Generally, they do not work once they are in Canada, so they are not forced by necessity to learn English or French or associate with people outside the community. Often they live out their lives in a social circle bounded by family and community, quite uninfluenced by Canadian culture and having little contact with other Canadians. The Canadian-born are at the other extreme (if one can generalize at all). Typically, most of their friends and acquaintances are not within the community, and many take part in community life chiefly because their parents and relatives do.

Sex also determines an individual's personal relations and, more generally, the community structure. Most adult South Asian Canadians are married and consequently many of their intra-ethnic friendships are maintained on a couple-to-couple basis. Even so, men usually have a considerably wider and more active network of community relations. Men frequently visit with each other, whereas there is frequently a good deal of resistance to women having equal freedom; often, women do not have direct access to a car and this also restricts their visiting patterns. In addition, much visiting between couples is sexually segregated; men talk with men, women with women. This results in South Asian communities being, to some extent, dual universes – the universe of men and that of women. This separation of the sexes makes the concerns, activities, interests, and access to information of men and women quite different. At the level of community this is commonly reflected in a more subjective quality in women's relations to each other. Men appropriate virtually all public roles and profess to "speak for" their families; men talk of jobs, home country politics, and major community events. Women communicate more about their personal lives, family relations, and things that have occurred in other families; they often talk, as well, of the behaviour of their men, which is frequently seen as ritual display for the benefit of other men. Communication barriers are such that many of women's thoughts rarely become known to men:

> Men in our community are often surprised when their wives complain of loneliness, isolation, or overwork. Just as often, too, they try to minimize such complaints by comparing them to their "real" problems at work or with paying the bills. And yet every woman in the community knows about the special problems which women immigrants face, both as immigrants and as members of our particular community. Such things are discussed constantly among women both through visiting and by phone. Of course, how could men know? When we visit in mixed groups it is common that the men do all the talking except when women can retire to the kitchen. I think that it is unfair that we women always have to consider the concerns of men, while they so rarely involve themselves in ours.

GEOGRAPHY AND COMMUNITY

In earlier days, when ethnic minorities were *de facto* barred from living in more desirable places and when few people had cars, the equation of ethnic communities with neighbourhoods made some sense. Today, there is virtually no discrimination against ethnic house buyers and where one lives is therefore chiefly determined by economic and other practical factors. The car has revolutionized visiting; practically speaking, a person one mile away is as close as one four blocks away. As a result, South Asians do not intentionally form ethnic neighbourhoods and rarely create them. Because of the car, though, they do not have to sacrifice social community to get the kind of house they want. If anything, housing considerations are weighted more highly today than social ones.

South Asians have tried to buy homes soon after arriving in Canada. This has meant that in Vancouver and Toronto, for example, they first moved into relatively old, less well-maintained, less expensive houses.

Nearness to work was also a consideration, especially for those many families where both parents worked. These two factors led to South Asians congregating chiefly in the poorer urban residential neighbourhoods and eventually led to a few areas with a high proportion of South Asians. The most obvious of these is southeast Vancouver, where perhaps one in ten people is South Asian.[2]

Professional immigrants and those otherwise economically better off never followed this pattern and settled almost immediately in the suburbs. In times when mortgages and house prices were lower than today they were soon followed by their working-class contemporaries, who saw their first old urban house as a stepping stone to something better:

> I really have no idea how many South Asians are in Millwoods [an outlying, newly developed suburb of Edmonton] nor do I know what proportion of the people there are South Asian. Canadians certainly believe that a great many of the people there are South Asian – I have heard the bus line to Millwoods referred to as the "New Delhi Express."
>
> I can be a lot more certain why we and other South Asian families chose to live here. It certainly isn't to be near each other. It certainly isn't convenient to work, either, because virtually everyone has to commute into Edmonton, which is very time-consuming. The reason is simple: it offers us the best housing compromise. We would live closer to work if we could but those areas are either too expensive or else are areas with only used housing available; surprisingly, at first few of us can afford used housing, because it requires larger down payments and doesn't qualify for the grants and supports that new housing does. So the ideal pattern is to first buy a small house or townhouse in Millwoods, stay there until one has saved up enough money to buy something better, and then move out.

Today, South Asians are not centralized in ethnic neighbourhoods. To the extent that they are within a reasonable distance by car from each other, this has not substantially weakened social community.[3] Even so, geography does affect community organization, for ultimately some people live too far away to visit each other easily and as a consequence are in more or less separate, broadly defined geographical communities. In this respect it is inaccurate to talk of, say, the Sikh community of Metro Toronto without recognizing that distance has weakened social links between individuals on opposite sides of the city.

The isolating effects of geography reach their extreme between people in distant towns. As a rule, only twenty or thirty miles is sufficient to lead to partially separate communities, as in the case of Sikhs in Vancouver and Mission. Thus, the social isolation of South Asians who now live in small towns can be quite profound and often leads people to migrate to the cities. The majority of South Asian teachers who went to the rural

Prairies in the 1960's did this. Being so few in a population of "others" frequently means that there is no hope of these people forming ethnic communities. Those who remain in such places have compensated by establishing links with South Asians of other ethnic backgrounds and other Canadians.

This should not suggest a lack of interaction between geographically separate South Asian communities. When people travel they inevitably visit others, thus maintaining ties. Members of those ethnic groups with religious commonalities or national organization frequently use these as a rationale for visiting as well. In addition, local Canadian communities are indirectly connected through continual visiting between Canada and source countries. In many communities it is not uncommon for one adult member of a given family to visit "home" once in five years, and at least as many people (primarily relatives) visit with people in Canada each year. New immigrants increase this number still further. Through such international connections a continuity of values and belief is maintained between source countries and Canada. Through these connections, too, people are able to keep track of others who live elsewhere in Canada, especially friends and kin.

In this respect, community links extend out to the world. Virtually every source country and ethnic group that has sent an appreciable number of South Asians to Canada has also sent them elsewhere. In most cases there are almost as many people in the United States as there are in Canada, and Britain now has a South Asian population of over a million. Exiled Ugandan refugees are spread all over Africa and Europe; every European country now has a small South Asian population and substantial numbers of immigrant South Asians continue to live in East Asia, Southeast Asia, and the Arab Near East. All of these overseas communities are tied together by a continual stream of visitors, letters and telephone calls.

POLITICS AND COMMUNITY

South Asians generally pay no more heed to Canadian politics than other Canadians; unfamiliar with the issues and unsure of how such issues affect them, recent immigrants tend to be even less involved. The exceptions are when South Asians have run for political office.[4] In these cases people of the same background will generally vote for them, everything else being equal. Considering their relatively small numbers, South Asians have frequently run for local office, but they are not yet well represented at the federal or provincial level.

This quiescent approach to Canadian politics should not suggest that South Asians are apolitical. To the contrary, politics and political action are important determinants of community structure. Much energy is expended on jockeying for status and leadership positions within local communities. Unable to fall back entirely on one's previous status, it is

181

incumbent on individuals to claim and defend status. Since almost everyone else in the community is doing the same thing, this often results in the formation of cliques and sociopolitical cleavages. Political infighting and factionalism tend to be most endemic in those South Asian communities with the strongest social identities. Paradoxically, factionalism sometimes results in greater long-term community solidarity, for it orients people forcefully toward community issues. At the same time, it seriously weakens a community's ability to organize formally or work toward a unified goal, expecially when the community is not under threat. There is hardly a South Asian community in Canada where a major issue can be approached without it becoming at least in part a confrontation between personalities. Those who take the initiative in exploring an issue, developing community institutions, or speaking for the community are inevitably accused of doing so in their own self-interest. Community work without status rewards is consequently rarely taken on. Control over knowledge can sometimes be great.

Status conflicts are so pervasive that people are often unwilling to support leaders, since they fear that a "spokesperson" will use his or her position to further his or her own ends; thus it is that "spokespersons" often speak for no one, "leaders" often lead few, and "representatives" represent one faction at best. When a particularly important issue aligns major political factions on either side of it, the resultant conflict can be so profound that it creates great turmoil in the community.

Despite such organizational problems, South Asians realize that to resolve issues and carry out objectives they must in some way work together. All across the spectrum of South Asian communities these needs have been expressed through the development of hundreds of formal associations and organizations. In the next chapter we move from informal structure to the level of formal community institutions – to the many businesses, associations, schools, and religious organizations created by South Asians across Canada.

NOTES

1. For detailed examples of South Asian community life, see Buchignani, "Immigration, Adaptation, and the Management of Ethnic Identity"; Chadney, "The Vancouver Sikhs"; Moudgil, "From Stranger to Refugee"; M. Yasmin, "Retention of Ethnic Identity for the Bangladeshi Immigrants in the Toronto Census Metropolitan Area" (M.A. thesis, University of Guelph, 1982); and other works listed in the Bibliography.
2. Wood, "A Visible Minority Votes."
3. This has been the pattern in the United States, where South Asians tend to be so dispersed that community links are quite weak.
4. Wood, "A Visible Minority Votes."

ELEVEN

Community Institutions

A key element of South Asian Canadian life has been the rise of what are commonly referred to as community institutions: ethnic associations, temples, mosques, and other religious organizations, schools, language classes, community-oriented businesses, newspapers and other media, and the arts. Across the spectrum of Canadian ethnocultural groups the way in which such institutions have evolved has had a great impact on community persistence and the maintenance of ethnic identity. Typically, those ethnocultural groups that have for whatever reasons not been able to develop a strong institutional base have had considerable difficulty in holding onto their roots, especially as the Canadian-born second generation has come into adulthood. This only stands to reason, for without community institutions, family practices and informal community ties are weak defences against the enormous assimilative forces of what remains in an institutional sense an essentially bilingual, bicultural country. English and French language and North American culture predominate at work, in the schools, in government, and in the media. Alternative, parallel community institutions are consequently one of the only organizational responses possible to this mainstream uniformity.

South Asian institutional development is already quite substantial in comparison with other Canadian ethnocultural populations. Wherever there are South Asian communities of a few hundred or more, one sees this sort of institution-building going on apace. This is all the more remarkable when one considers that South Asians have faced several formidable obstacles to this development. Unlike Germans or Irish, for example, South Asians are recent immigrants, comparatively new to most parts of the country. In addition, because of their tendency to segment into small ethnocultural communities, they often lack the numerical resources of other groups, such as the Italians in Toronto or the Greeks in Montreal.

ETHNIC ORGANIZATIONS

Prior to the creation of the federal government's multicultural program in 1971, relatively few community-based South Asian organizations had been formed. Most of these were religiously based, of which Sikh gurdwaras were the most common. By then, Sikh religious organizations had existed for sixty years in British Columbia and had recently been founded in Calgary, Edmonton, Toronto, and Montreal. Hindus in Toronto and Vancouver had begun to meet informally in people's homes, while Muslims and Christians generally worshipped with co-religionists from other ethnic backgrounds. In Ottawa, Toronto, Edmonton, Calgary, and Vancouver, small secular associations were formed to bring together South Asians (mostly Indians) from different backgrounds and explain South Asia and South Asians to other Canadians. There were few specifically ethnic, national, or cultural associations in existence.

The present situation stands in dramatic contrast to what it was in 1971. Such organizations were few then but now they proliferate. In Metro Toronto alone there are at least sixty different South Asian organizations. There are another thirty or so in Montreal, forty in Alberta, twenty in Winnipeg, and another forty in the Vancouver area. Altogether, there are now perhaps 250 organizations in the country, with more being founded all the time. Virtually every local community of any size now supports some kind of an association and sometimes has several.

This organizational growth results from a number of factors. Perhaps the most significant cause has been a tendency among South Asians to think of associations primarily in fairly concrete ethnic terms; if Bengalis or Pakistanis envision the creation of a religious association, they will tend to think of it as an association for Bengalis or Pakistanis, not for all co-religionists. Even though national and pan-South Asian organizations have been created on both a local and national level, they have never had the kind of support given to local ethnic-specific associations. Because of the differences between one South Asian ethnocultural group and another, this tendency for Sinhalese, Sikhs, and others to form their own associations makes perfect sense.

This proliferation is also partially the result of provincial and federal governmental expectations. The federal Multiculturalism Directorate and its various provincial equivalents have encouraged the development of community organizations so that the latter can represent their membership to the government.[1] At the same time, aspiring spokespersons gain community status through their associational affiliation, and this, too, becomes an incentive to found new organizations.

Many South Asian ethnic organizations began informally in the early 1970's as vehicles for people to remain in touch with each other while they were undergoing their first experiences in Canada. As such, they served many of the same psychological and social functions as informal

184

visiting. As local ethnic populations grew, people looked toward these incipient organizations as a means of maintaining culture, language, religion, and links with their places of birth. Most eventually became chartered as non-profit associations. These organizations now typically concentrate on one or another basic type of activity.

Religious Institutions

The commitment of people to these organizations varies according to the degree to which individuals see a definite, not easily replaceable, need for them. In this respect, religious organizations are clearly the best organized and most strongly supported of any kind of South Asian association.

It should be appreciated that the establishment of religious institutions by South Asians, so that in cities they are now available to most South Asian Canadians of most faiths, is quite an accomplishment. Unlike immigrants from most other places, South Asians have generally not been able to join congregations already in place either in their faith or in an allied one. Most South Asians are Sikhs, Hindus, Muslims, or Buddhists, not Christians. This difficulty was especially pressing for Sikhs, Hindus, Ismaili Muslims, and Sinhalese Buddhists, for these groups had to establish their religious institutions entirely on their own, without the assistance of established Canadian churches or the help of other ethnocultural groups.

Of all South Asian religious groups, Sikhs have been the most active in the development of community-based religious institutions. Sikhs have formed temporary or permanent gurdwaras in virtually every community with more than a few hundred Sikhs. In larger Sikh centres, such as Victoria, Vancouver, Edmonton, Calgary, Winnipeg, Toronto, and Montreal, there are several gurdwaras to which people affiliate according to such things as particulars of religious practice, commonalities with other practitioners, and convenience in a fashion much like that of Christians picking their parish or congregation of choice. All across the country, Sikhs have given or are in the process of contributing millions of dollars to house their religious services in substantial buildings.[2]

We have seen that, in the past, Sikh temples were never used just for purely religious activities, important though these were. They continue as vital, multi-use community institutions around which much of Sikh social, cultural, and political life orbits. Weekly Sunday services allow people in the community to remain in contact with each other and provide a way for newcomers to become involved in the community's social life. Without exception, Sikh general services and the free meal (*langar*) provided afterwards are completely open to visitors, both Sikh and non-Sikh alike. Out-of-town Sikhs and other South Asians commonly make use of this opportunity to meet people in the local community, as do an increasing number of other Canadians.

Wherever numbers allow it (say, a community base of 1,000-2,000

185

people), temple associations are rapidly developing a range of educational and cultural programs centred on Sikh temples. One common practice has been the institution of Punjabi-language classes for children; all Sikh sacred texts are written in this language, so such a capacity is vital for children to be able to read them. Some gurdwara associations are also supporting a Sikh version of Sunday school, where children are given formal instruction in the tenets of Sikhism. Allied groups and organizations, which support the teaching and perpetuation of Sikh music, song, and dance, can typically be found, while others support Sikh charitable and political causes. By the mid- to late-1980's permanent Sikh centres across the country will be offering a wide variety of such programs, as some already are.

Local Sikh temples in Canada remain entirely independent of each other, each one being supported and run by local people. This does not mean, however, that they are isolated from each other or from the rest of the Sikh world. Where more than one temple exists they usually get on well with each other and sometimes co-ordinate which ones will carry out particular annual celebrations each year. On a more general level, Sikh religious people from India and East Africa can often be found making the rounds of Canadian Sikh temples, and it goes without saying that Canadian Sikhs remain vitally aware of religious and political events in Punjab; for example, significant financial support for the present Sikh independence movement in Punjab has come from Canadian gurdwaras. In addition, since 1979 there have been three national conferences held on Sikh affairs, two in Toronto and one in Calgary. It is the hope of the supporters of these conferences that they will eventually lead to a national organization devoted to the maintenance and propagation of the Sikh faith in Canada.

Ismailis, if anything, have outdone Sikhs in the sophistication of their socioreligious organizations. Ismailis were already well organized in East Africa, and their subsequent expulsion and settlement in Canada gave them the opportunity to refine and modernize their organizations into a complex hierarchical structure that links small local groups into a national organization.[3] Virtually all practising Ismailis are members of local groups that originally formed to secure a place for worship. In larger Ismaili population centres, such as Vancouver, there may be over a dozen such small organizations. So far, only one permanent religious centre has been constructed, in Burnaby, British Columbia. All of the rest are in rental accommodation, chiefly in schools and in church and community halls. Unlike Sikhs, whose local congregations are autonomous, Ismaili socioreligious groups are linked together under regional and national councils, supported primarily by contributions from local congregations. The Canadian national council is tied to other national councils and to the leadership of the Aga Khan. In religious matters Ismailis are almost entirely separate from the larger Canadian Sunni

Muslim population. Perhaps the only exception is when Ismaili men sometimes go to Sunni mosques to attend important celebrations.

Because of their comparatively recent establishment in Canada, the religious practices typical of Ismailis are still under flux. In East Africa, as here, many religious practices centred on the *jamat khana*, the Ismaili religious meeting place. The lay officers of the jamat khana were responsible for arranging marriages and funerals, performing rites, and carrying out celebrations such as on Muhammad's birthday. Social issues and disputes over religious affairs were handled by a hierarchical set of councils and boards. The key religious services were daily prayer meetings and people's progressive initiation into more and more elite religious circles (*mijlases*). Families voluntarily paid a tithe (*zakat*) of 10 per cent of their income for the support of the communities' religious and social institutions. A key family ritual was group meditation early each day.

There is considerable variation in the degree to which individual Ismailis are able to follow these traditions here. Functional jamat khanas have been established, as has a strong set of councils. Varying work practices, however, have sometimes interfered with early morning meditations; some jamat khanas, though, do open each morning to allow individuals to pray there. In addition, Friday is the day when important Ismaili weekly services are carried out – a normal working day for most Canadians. As a consequence, jamat khanas now hold these services on Friday evening.

Like their Sikh counterparts, Ismaili organizations are multi-purpose institutions. Their expressed purpose is the preservation of Ismaili religious practice, but Ismailis have been welded into something of an ethnic group. As such, they see the need for some means of preserving their cultural heritage and identity. Although still in their infancy, Ismaili associations across Canada have begun many language classes for children, while others provide dance and music instruction. They have also used their organizational infrastructure to put on a wide range of cultural events, as well as to provide financial and informational assistance to Ismailis.

In terms of religious organization, Sikhs and Ismailis have an advantage over some other South Asian groups. Both have evolved into ethnic groups out of religious origins. Thus, ethnicity and religion are mutually reinforcing. Virtually all other South Asians' ethnicity and religion crosscut each other. Either a given ethnic group shares its religion with members of other ethnic groups (e.g., Gujarati Hindus) or else several religious subgroups are within an ethnic population (e.g., Fijians). As a consequence, institutions have usually evolved somewhat differently in these communities.

One key example concerns Sunni Muslims of South Asian origin. This group includes most Pakistanis and Bangalis as well as almost all (non-

Ismaili) Indian, Fijian, and Caribbean Muslims. The first of these to arrive in any number were Pakistanis, and the pattern of religious worship they evolved has subsequently been followed by other Sunnis. The basis of this pattern was either to found mosques jointly with other (non-South Asian) Sunnis or to support such mosques already in existence. This is in accord with Sunni practice around the world. Even today it is only for special annual religious celebrations that South Asian Muslims might get together along the lines of ethnicity. In this fashion Pakistanis and other early South Asian Sunni immigrants to Edmonton were able to make use of the Al Rashid Mosque, which had been founded by Lebanese in the 1930's.[4] In Vancouver and Toronto, Pakistanis, Indian Muslims, and others joined their Arab co-religionists in renting halls or other facilities to serve as temporary mosques. Only in the past ten years have any of these groups been able to establish more permanent mosques and Islamic centres. Like Sikhs and Ismailis, Sunni organizations typically expend a considerable amount of effort in teaching religious precepts to the young; since South Asian Sunnis diverge culturally and linguistically from other Sunnis (and from each other), cultural and language instruction are usually taken on by specific ethnocultural associations rather than through mosques and Islamic centres. South Asians do, however, participate in Islamic organizations across the country, as well as in the national Council of Muslim Communities of Canada.

Sunnis and Sikhs share several decided advantages over Hindus and Buddhists in re-establishing their religious practices in Canada. Each of these religions stresses a relatively clear set of basic precepts and practices, and each group has quickly mobilized community resources to put religious institutions in place. However, Sunnis do face certain difficulties in matching their round of religious observances to the Canadian context:

> One of the Five Pillars of Islam that we used to always follow before we came to Canada was to pray five times daily and to attend the mosque on Fridays. Generally speaking, the places from which we came and their style of life was organized in such a way that neither of these posed any real difficulties. What are we to do here, where the work day is so closely regulated by the clock? Some people bring prayer rugs to work and then use their breaks and part of their lunch time for their prayers. Others have had to give up some of their daily prayers. Almost no one has been able to get time off from work on Fridays, so working people generally attend mosque very early in the morning or after work.
>
> Ramadan also poses some difficulties, but of a different kind. During the month of Ramadan [the ninth month of the Islamic year] we are supposed to refrain from all food and drink from dawn to dusk. Again, where we come from the days and nights are about equal, so that with practice this fast goes smoothly. But try it in Ed-

monton, where the late summer days are almost eighteen hours long!

I might add a few other less significant issues. Like Jews, Sunnis do not eat pork and require that any other meat be killed in a certain way. This makes it very difficult for a conscientious Muslim to ever eat out in public; as a rule, they must stick with vegetarian dishes. For home use we can usually obtain frozen *halal* meat through South Asian food stores. The other problem is more difficult to deal with: Muslims, Islamic culture, and religion have an extremely poor public image in Canada, which is a direct result of the biased and uncritical way in which affairs in Iran and the Middle East are covered by the media. Considering their faith and their pride in their culture, this is hard for many Canadian Muslims to take.

Considerably more profound obstacles have faced Canada's 80,000-90,000 Hindus. Unlike Islam, Hinduism has never established a set of unified practices and beliefs shared by all believers. Both practice and belief can vary dramatically from individual to individual and from one ethnocultural group to another. This variation makes it hard for Hindus from different backgrounds to establish common religious institutions. Beyond this, Hinduism is essentially a personal philosophy and religion that is not heavily dependent on public rites and rituals; when the latter occur they are an integral part of local community affairs. Marriage rites, for example, begin and end grounded in social associations established throughout life. It is a family and community celebration and does not occur in a church or temple.

Prior to the arrival of the first Indian professionals in the 1960's there were few Hindus in Canada. The major exceptions were chiefly Canadians who had been attracted to Theosophy or the teachings of one or another Indian guru. For the most part, practising Hindus among immigrants in the 1960's did without the public aspects of their religion but kept up their private observances. Unlike Muslims or Sikhs, they had no pressing need for a place of worship. By 1970, Hindus in many South Asian communities had extended their individual observances to prayer services held in people's homes. These observances were typically ethnic-specific and sometimes reflected a particular approach to Hinduism rather than others. By then, Hindus were beginning to face several secular problems with religious consequences, the most important of which was marriage. Obviously, social situations in Canada were so different from those in India or Fiji that Hindu marriages carried out here would be unlike anything the participants had experienced previously. This aside, there was rarely anyone available to carry out the religious aspects of the celebration, nor was there anywhere appropriate to carry them out. In addition, Hinduism was not a recognized religion and therefore a Hindu marriage ceremony had no legal validity. Similar difficulties arose when Hindus died.

To meet these needs, people banded together to put Hindu religious observances on a firmer footing. One of the earliest organizations to become established was the Vishva Hindu Parishad in Vancouver, founded in 1972; by 1974 it had opened a multi-use temple with a generalized program of worship as well as opportunities for specific Hindu religious and ethnic groups to use its facilities. There are now permanent multi-use institutions in Vancouver, Edmonton, and Calgary as well as several in Ontario. Elsewhere, Hindus continue to depend primarily on temporary arrangements.

Such temples have usually been founded through the contributions and hard work of Hindus from a wide range of ethnocultural backgrounds. In some cases these people are already organized into community-based associations for the purpose of worship; in other cases they are not. Once a permanent centre is established, time and appropriate facilities are allocated among the various Hindu groups to facilitate prayer and other observances in a fashion appropriate to the groups' particular beliefs. General prayer services (*puja*) and religious lectures are usually carried on for all people on Sundays. In addition, individuals may schedule the use of temples for marriages and other rites of passage.

This multi-use concept is a brilliant solution to the difficulties posed by divergent Hindu practice and belief. Nevertheless, it has neither completely unified Hindus nor solved all the hurdles to establishing Hinduism firmly as a viable religion in Canada. For one thing, Hindus with ultimate origins in North India (chiefly Hindi- and Punjabi-speakers) are the most numerous supporters of Hindu temples, and these organizations reflect this. One consequence is that other Hindus, such as Gujaratis, Bengalis, Fijians, several southern Indian groups, and Sri Lankan Tamils, sometimes form distinct religious organizations. It was only in 1983 that the Vishva Hindu Parishad of Vancouver organized a national conference to develop the constitution for a Hindu Council of Canada.

The establishment of Hindu places of worship has been of great benefit to the people concerned. Even so, difficulties continue to arise in transplanting such a community-based religion as Hinduism. In South Asia, Hinduism operates in a social universe composed entirely of believers whose secular lives are organized by Hindu principles. In Canada, Hindus are a geographically dispersed minority. Hindus often claim that rituals such as birth, marriage, and death carried out in Canada have an artificial, impersonal, and discontinuous nature. More serious in the long term is whether Hinduism can be transmitted effectively to the second generation. Being so much a way of life in South Asia, Hinduism has not traditionally been taught by the formal means more typical among Christians or Muslims. Everyday living in a social context dominated by Hindu believers was the major religious enculturative force. Here, many children do not appear to be learning the basic precepts of the religion. Hindu centres are trying to address this difficulty with programs of religious instruction, but it is far too soon to say how successful such programs will be.

> We have two children, one aged ten, born in India, and the other aged eight, who was born in Canada. Right from the beginning our children have gotten along well and have almost no close Indian friends. We occasionally bring the children to the Hindu temple, but despite our explaining what's going on they think it is all very strange. They have some general idea about our private devotional practices at home, but it's clear that they know far more about Christianity than they do about Hinduism. I think that this is a great loss, but don't know what to do. I have looked at some available books on Hinduism, but even *I* don't understand the religion in the way that it's presented there. Many other parents here share my concern.

South Asians who are Buddhist or Christian have usually been too few to develop their own separate religious institutions. The only substantial population of Buddhist South Asians are Sinhalese Canadians, who scarcely number 5,000 altogether. To date they have not developed permanent religious institutions anywhere outside of Toronto.[5] Christians come chiefly from Pakistan, Kerala, and Goa in India, and from Sri Lanka, Fiji, Guyana, and Trinidad. They have tended to become members of established Canadian church congregations.

It should be noted that a wide range of individuals stand outside the above organizations yet represent community institutions that are at least partially religious. For example, astrology remains important to many immigrants. Most larger communities contain people who have astrological expertise, and they are consulted about such things as the auspicious time for a marriage, the appropriate name for a newborn child, or one's future. Muslim barbers are used by some Muslims and Hindus for religious ceremonies commemorating childbirth. In several Hindu communities, individuals have established small religious sects by virtue of their particular training or experiences. Especially among Sikhs, Fijians, and Guyanese, magic and witchcraft remain significant concerns and certain people have become identified as being particularly well able to deal with them.

Community Service Organizations

In the light of the impact that immigration has had on virtually everyone, it may seem odd that only a handful of the several hundred South Asian organizations help South Asians deal with concrete immigration and settlement problems. The most notable of these have been Indian Immigrant Services in Toronto and Indian Immigrant Aid in Vancouver. Both have been of incalculable aid to people in addressing, in a cultural-specific fashion, difficulties such as family conflicts and job recertification. Both organizations, however, have been so constrained by funding that they have less than one field worker for each 5,000 people who might profitably make use of their services. Elsewhere in the country, no such organizations existed before 1983.

Some South Asian immigrants have been able to compensate for this lack of community service institutions by using their extensive informal community links, but many have not. Unaccustomed to Canadian social service agencies, many South Asians are unwilling to go to them with their personal problems, which consequently often go unresolved. This is particularly common among working-class immigrants, who feel less at ease dealing with the bureaucracy than professionals.

The lack of community service organizations is even more striking in view of the depth of professional and paraprofessional expertise that exists in most South Asian communities. It also contrasts with such other recent immigrant populations as the Vietnamese and Chinese. Perhaps this can be accounted for in part by the lack of a tradition of community service, something generally shared by most South Asian groups. As one keen South Asian observer of community affairs put it:

> I have been active in trying to get people to meet community problems for over fifteen years, and so have given a lot of thought to why the response to practical community needs is so poor. I think that at the heart of it few South Asians come to Canada with a strong sense of community responsibility. For most, the family is everything, so much so that they lose sight of community needs. Canadians often effectively get themselves off the social responsibility hook with their ideology of individualism, free enterprise, and hard work: everyone should help themselves and should try to solve their own problems. South Asians tend to replace this with a family ideology: if people in the community have problems they should turn to their relatives or should "go to the government."

The organizational lack has been partially filled by ethnic entrepreneurs, who have made it their business to become middlemen, bridging immigrant needs and various government and private means to meet them. This is perhaps most common in the area of immigration problems, where individuals have assisted in securing admission of people's relatives. Most of these agents do little more than explain the regulations to their clients and mediate between them and local immigration officials. A few have on occasion initiated schemes to get people into the country illegally or to find them marriages of convenience. Others have operated as labour contractors, lawyers to South Asian clientele, or financial go-betweens.

Sociocultural Organizations

The vast majority of South Asian organizations have been formed ostensibly for social or cultural reasons. Socially, they hope to bring people together and provide a rationale for their continuing association with each other. Culturally, they seek to contribute to the maintenance of ethnic cultures and languages as well as to expose other Canadians to them.

No organization does these things in all possible ways and there are so many of them that it is impossible to deal with them individually. In overview, though, they have several common characteristics. First of all, almost all are ethnically or nationally specific. In this way they are a direct expression of the ethnic identities of members. Second, they tend to be created and maintained by a small core of volunteers. Certain association events may turn out a far greater number of people, but these organizations live or die depending on the support of a few. Third, social activities have tended to bring out greater community support than cultural ones; why this is so can be made more clear by a closer examination of these sociocultural activities.

Since establishing an ongoing constituency is always a problem, social events typically rank high on the agenda of these organizations. These range from informal social gatherings held in homes to large-scale picnics, sports events, dinners, and dances. These events rarely have a specific cultural objective beyond the fact that the participants share a common background, which is expressed in conversation, food, and dress. People clearly see such activities as a useful extension of informal community social relations.

Objectives of cultural maintenance are more difficult to formulate, implement, and muster support for within communities. Contrary to popular opinion, South Asians are rarely concerned about cultural maintenance *per se* except in the key areas of religion, language, and family relations. In other words, no South Asian Canadians wish to recreate their traditional culture here in its entirety. If they did, they would not be here at all. A good case in point is in the area of economic behaviour. Economic difficulties in the countries of origin have typically figured high on lists of reasons for coming to Canada in the first place, and they are consequently hardly opposed to adapting to Canadian ways of doing things if this advances their economic position. Moreover, people realize that most aspects of traditional culture in their everyday lives that they value and still practise in Canada cannot be easily taught; immigrant adults need no guidance in such matters, while children can only be taught with difficulty and not by outsiders.

Consequently, the cultural activities of these associations are never aimed at the maintenance of everyday South Asian culture; the only significant exception to this is language training for children, which is now being carried out by scores of associations. Beyond this, many activities that appear to be cultural maintenance also serve quite different functions. For example, there has been a great upsurge in the teaching of South Asian classical and folk dance across the country. Through both associations and private teachers, thousands of girls and young women

193

(and some men and boys) are being instructed in these complex and ancient arts. However, it is unlikely that they or their parents learned such dances as part of their everyday cultural experiences in South Asia. For almost all, these are new aspects of culture, which, it must be argued, serve largely a symbolic function; instead of being part of traditional culture they stand for all that was proper and good in it; they are symbolic supports for a prideful ethnic identity.

Leaving aside the specific functions of such activity, the teaching, practising, and performing of South Asian music and dance are now very important community phenomena. This is especially true for women and girls, who have provided the chief support for these traditions in Canada. In most cities it is now possible to see music and dance from at least a dozen South Asian traditions, and instruction is available in playing most common South Asian musical instruments.

Folk and classical dance are becoming more and more popular among women who are not South Asian. This represents the first systematic exposure to South Asian culture among any group of Canadians. One Canadian woman, Anjali (Anne-Marie Gaston), has established an international reputation for her South Asian dancing. A few Canadians have also become proficient at playing South Asian musical instruments.

Music and dance are rooted deeply in the cultures from which they have sprung and are not intelligible without some understanding of that cultural milieu. Many interested Canadians have realized this and through South Asian music and dance have learned a great deal about South Asian culture; besides a handful of academics, missionaries, world travellers, and practitioners of South Asian religion, they are the only Canadians, as yet, who have.

Like Canadians, South Asians value traditional folk and high culture but do not often participate in it. Most South Asian immigrants are from urban or semi-urban backgrounds and their musical and dance traditions are quite different from those of people in rural villages. Much "traditional" artistic and musical culture among South Asian immigrants is of very recent origin; all South Asian cultures and nations have strong poetic song traditions in which vibrant new works are being created constantly. These enjoy long-lasting popularity and have a far greater audience than South Asian classical traditions.[6] These are greatly augmented by popular romantic songs, many of which derive from India's enormous film industry.

Many associations actively support this popular musical tradition by providing encouragement and an audience to amateur performers and by bringing in professional entertainers from overseas; booking the latter has become an important entrepreneurial activity and in most large urban centres there are many such performances each month.

Because of their widely varying backgrounds, South Asians from different ethnic populations are assimilated, acculturated, and integrated to a varying degree. This is reflected in what sociocultural associations tend to emphasize in different South Asian communities. Communities with high ethnic solidarity rarely need a community organization to provide further support for social interaction and social solidarity. More weakly bounded communities do; they are consequently much more likely to emphasize social events, such as sports events and picnics, which bring people together. Conversely, the former are more deeply worried about the loss of everyday ethnic culture in the second generation and are more likely to wish that associations would combat it.

Nevertheless, even the most culturally conservative people realize that nothing an association can do can completely negate the acculturative forces of Canadian society. As such, associations are usually called upon to address rather specific issues of cultural maintenance. Perhaps the most common of these is the loss of language facility in the second generation. No South Asian immigrant parents are entirely at ease with their children not learning their first language. Language is the great reservoir of cultural meaning and parents believe that monolingual French- or English-speaking children will be monocultural as well. Many communities have used their associations (or religious organizations) to develop classes for children to combat language loss. In most instances these classes are in conversational speech, both parents and teachers alike conceding the loss of the children's ability to read and write the relevant script. The exception to this is in Sikh communities, for, as mentioned, their religious teachings are in gurmukhi script; more attention has therefore been attached to learning how to read than in most other communities. At present, these voluntary, community-supported language classes are almost the only places in Canada where South Asian languages are taught. Only three universities in Canada teach Hindi, despite its being spoken by more people in the world than German or French; Punjabi and Urdu are taught at only two universities, and no other modern South Asian language is taught at all.

Beyond language instruction, associations do very little to support everyday South Asian culture, precisely because there is very little else they can do. Dance, music, language, and sometimes religion are amenable to formal instruction. In contrast, how does one teach cultural values or customary family relations? These have proven to be difficult and contentious areas for the Canadian educational system, which has far more resources available to it than any association. Such things are left to the family and religious institutions.

The federal multiculturalism program has had an enormous impact on the rise of South Asian associations. It is chiefly at an associational level that multiculturalism operates, and this alone has led many local communities to form associations or to break away from more inclusive ones in hopes of better access to funding. Multiculturalism and parallel provincial policies also generated a legion of South Asian spokespersons, some affiliated with associations, some not.[7] Multiculturalism and analogous provincial funding have been of great practical benefit to

195

South Asian associations. Government policy helped them develop a public forum to express their views and has made possible a wide range of programs aimed at cultural performance and preservation.

Another important role of the associations has been the establishment of bridging organizations between South Asian communities. In just about every city with many South Asians there now exist over-arching associations that tie together community-based South Asian associations for mutual co-ordination of cultural activities and liaison with government and to combat racism.

All ethnic and national communities have not yet been brought under one banner. There have been several attempts to establish a pan-Canadian association of all South Asian Canadians, but considering their widely varying backgrounds, this has been hard to achieve. The most successful attempt has been by the National Association of Canadians of Origins in India (NACOI). Founded in 1976 by Ranjit Singh of Ottawa, it has established branches, has affiliated local organizations across the country, and has put on a series of substantial annual conferences. Its objectives are very general: to provide a national voice for people of South Asian origin in Canada, to help protect their rights, to assist in the adaptation of people to Canadian life, and to make other Canadians more aware of South Asian contributions to the country. NACOI is still in the process of developing strong representative roots in local communities.

Specific ethnic and national groups have also tried to develop national associations with varying success. Ismailis already have a functional national organization. Pakistanis have founded an incipient national association, which has produced conferences and publications. Sikhs are attempting to do so but have been slowed by factional politics.

Perhaps the most significant force presently bringing together South Asians from various backgrounds is concern over racism and racial discrimination. South Asians are well aware that they are the potential victims of discrimination. Bettering ethnic and race relations has by now become a high priority of virtually every pan-South Asian organization and many local associations. Today it is a major force in bringing together South Asians of diverse origins.

ECONOMIC INSTITUTIONS

The overwhelming majority of economically active South Asian Canadians work for wages, salaries, or commissions much like everyone else. However, this has not necessarily been through choice. It may well be that there are more people with independent business experience within the South Asian population than in any other Canadian ethnic group of comparable size. Indeed, some groups, like the Ismailis and others from East Africa, concentrated heavily on entrepreneurship prior to coming to Canada. Throughout the South Asian world, being an independent businessperson, artisan, or craftsperson is highly valued. Many South Asians would therefore like to establish businesses here, but they find that the obstacles can often be profound. In fact, these constraints have had such a powerful effect on the growth and development of the economic institutions of South Asian communities that it is important to outline them here.

At the outset, all potential South Asian entrepreneurs face a key question: will they try to establish a conventional business or will they exercise the option of trying to provide some sort of service on a less formal basis. There are advantages and disadvantages to both. For example, many South Asian wage-earners and people who are presently unemployed have chosen the second option, chiefly as a way of augmenting their income. Often they see this as a first step into normal business life, though few actually make the transition. Typically informal business activities of this sort would include such things as auto body repair, carpentry, assistance with immigration troubles, and informally representing travel or real estate business within the community. Such informal business activities have the advantage of being cheap and easy to establish as well as being effectively tax-free. These businesses also tend to find a ready (though finite) market for their services within the community. The major disadvantage is that they are chiefly dependent on a self-limiting market – the local South Asian population. Even so, this form of small-scale entrepreneurship has proliferated in all large South Asian communities. Here are two successful examples:

I came from Fiji with my family in the early 1970's and was one of the lucky ones. I got a job as an auto body repairman almost immediately, and have been able to hold onto the job ever since. Even when I was in Fiji I wanted to own my own business. After all, most Indian businesses there were family affairs, and people were always starting new ones. Here, I soon realized that it took an enormous amount of money to get a normal business started. Why, the shop where I work must be worth at least half a million dollars.

What I did was to begin working on cars on weekends and after work. I did the work at home, and of course never told the city about it. I didn't advertise either, just let the word get out in the community that I was doing body work. It doesn't cost me anything near what it does for a normal shop to do the work, so I can charge people less. Now I have just about all the work I can handle, even with my brother helping out with the painting. I'd like to make it a full-time business, but can't see that it would be able to support the family well enough to try.

Being a little older than most and coming from a good family, I knew a lot of the people in the community before coming to Canada, and far more people than that knew me. After being here a few years I realized that a great many people who had settled here go back "home" very often, and that many new immigrants' plane fares were paid for by relatives here. There were already a number of [South Asian] travel agencies in existence, but many people didn't seem to be making good use of them to get the best fares. What I did was to make an agreement with one of those agents: I arrange ticketing for community people through his agency, and in return we split the commission. I think that this works well for all concerned. I get some income, the agent gets more business, and travellers get lower fares and better arrangements.

If an aspiring businessperson opens a regular business, he or she is still faced with an important decision: will the business deal primarily with South Asian clientele? It may seem sensible for a business to try to serve as wide a clientele as possible, but few South Asian business people have aimed their efforts at the general market. The chief constraint has been the established competition; open a small grocery store or a tire store and you must compete with the large chains. In such situations South Asians have few ethnic advantages and many disadvantages; they do not know the Canadian market well and often are under-capitalized. The failure rate in such businesses has been very high.

Businesses serving the general public have succeeded in a few key areas. Perhaps the most visible of these has been driver-owned taxis, an activity in which Sikhs and Pakistanis have become numerous. A majority of taxi drivers in Vancouver, Edmonton, Calgary, and Metro Toronto may be South Asian by the late 1980's. This small-scale business is well adapted to South Asian working-class needs because it is a fixed-cost investment offering flexible hours and the possibility of shared family utilization. Unfortunately, it is becoming more and more exploitative, as taxi companies presently encourage people to buy cabs and join their particular companies; taxi companies frequently gain their income primarily from fees paid to them by individual cab operators for the use of their name and their dispatching services, not from fares. As one Edmonton Sikh owner-operator put it:

> The companies today don't really care whether their cabs do any business or not. They will get their $400-a-month fee from each independently owned cab no matter what. The more cabs are on the street, the more money they make. I must pay for this cab, maintain it, fill it with gas, pay the cab company's fee and my taxes before I get a dime. Do you want to know why there are many Sikhs in the cab business? Because it takes at least two drivers to make a cab pay. I work twelve hours a day and then rent out the car to a relative. It's the only way I can make it.

In the Vancouver area many Sikhs went into business as independent dump truck owner-operators in the 1970's and some of these moved on to long-haul independent trucking; the recession of the early 1980's has effectively closed off growth in this direction.

These areas aside, South Asians have done best in situations where family labour predominates. Typical examples are restaurants and small janitorial, construction, transportation, and auto service companies operated by family labour. Many small firms have also been founded by South Asian doctors, lawyers, and accountants.

There are some exceptions to this general rule. Ismailis and other Gujaratis have taken great business risks in Canada and some of them have paid off.[8] Ismailis have been particularly active in real estate and development but are now sprinkled across the spectrum of manufacturing and wholesale and retail business. Some Sikhs have also become significant players in real estate and development. The importance of Sikhs in the Vancouver Island lumber industry remains undiminished.

Most South Asian entrepreneurs nevertheless have aimed their entrepreneurial activities toward a South Asian clientele. This decision has sharply reduced the range of such businesses. As a rule, South Asian community-based businesses succeed only when they offer required goods or services not easily duplicated by non-South Asian firms. They cannot automatically count on community patronage just because they are South Asian.

Perhaps the most significant operations are stores offering South Asian foodstuffs, which proliferated across the country in the 1970's. South Asians have maintained their many distinctive cooking traditions, the basic ingredients of which are not usually available in Canadian stores. Through the efforts of entrepreneurs, the whole range of these ingredients is now available – every imaginable lentil, grain, and spice from India; rice from Pakistan; frozen fish from Fiji, East Africa, and the Caribbean; fresh fruit and vegetables from Fiji, Mexico, and the Caribbean; *halal* meat. Such stores also typically stock cassette tapes and records of South Asian popular music, videotapes of Indian movies, cosmetics, and household items. Clothing is another such area. Although South Asians in public normally "dress Canadian," at home, when visiting, and at special events many women prefer to dress in "traditional" fashions. Their so-called traditional fashions change continuously, but they are nevertheless quite different from their Canadian counterparts. To fulfil this need, cloth and sari shops have been opened across the country. *Halal* butcher stores have also arisen in large cities. Several restaurants aimed specifically at other South Asians have been established in Vancouver and Toronto.

One other ethnic-specific type of business merits comment, even though it is a geographically localized phenomenon. This is farm-labour contracting in the Fraser Valley adjacent to Vancouver. Over the past ten years Sikhs have bought farms in this area long noted for its production of vegetables, berries, and dairy products. Like their neighbours, they have been faced with a shortage of farm labour – a shortage brought on chiefly by poor wages and working conditions. These farmers were able to turn to Sikh women, adolescents, and old people who were otherwise

199

unemployed. Sikh labour contractors soon arose to collect people, bring them to the farms, oversee them while there, and bring them back home. The practice was quickly extended to non-Sikh farms and by the late 1970's several thousand people were employed as farm labourers. The rewards of this system accrued primarily to farmers and contractors, not to the farm workers. Since 1976, a few socially conscious Sikhs have tried to change this system by organizing workers into a union – one of the first farm workers' unions begun in Canada in recent times. This has already led to a number of improvements in working conditions and wages.

Also common are businesses that tailor their service to a specific ethnic community. Because such business people operate as brokers and middlemen, there is always a risk that they might prey on their unsophisticated clientele. Such exploitation, though, is kept in check by virtue of the ever-present competition, both South Asian and otherwise. An entrepreneur who develops a bad name in the community can quickly suffer an enormous loss of business.

Economic exploitation is far more common where entrepreneurs do not have such competitive checks. For example, one of the ever-present frustrations of South Asians is the slow and imponderable working of the immigration machinery, chiefly in regard to the applications of their relatives. Immigration difficulties have given rise to entrepreneurs who claim to be able to resolve these problems. Some are above board but others exploit their clients through false claims to be able to "fix" the process. Still others occasionally concoct illegal immigration strategies. In a dramatic example of this latter practice, over 1,000 Sikhs arrived in Toronto in 1981 on one-way fares from Punjab. They had been instructed by unscrupulous travel agents to claim that they were political refugees. Travel agents and lawyers made millions from this one scheme alone. In the long term, a more serious situation has arisen where working-class South Asians secure work through South Asian intermediaries. The most obvious case has been Sikh farm labour in the Fraser Valley, as already mentioned. The exploitation of illegal immigrant labour has occasionally been common; fear of exposure has sometimes led to the acceptance of very poor working conditions by illegal immigrants.

In summary, South Asians have developed community-based economic institutions that are largely concentrated in a handful of retail trades and services. In those areas competition is fierce and the lifetime of many businesses is correspondingly short. The prevalence of small, diverse, geographically dispersed communities has made parallel economic institutions among South Asians much less extensive than among larger, more homogeneous, more localized communities such as those of Toronto Italians or Montreal Greeks that developed in the 1950's and 1960's. Conversely, the number and range of such institutions are only a bit less than those among the Chinese and are considerably more developed than those of most ethnic groups.

LITERATURE, THE ARTS, AND THE MEDIA

South Asian Canadian community involvement in the arts and literature is extensive. At the same time, there has arisen a collection of committed teachers, professional performers, artists, and writers. While obviously intimately linked to the overall rise of South Asian Canadian cultural development, their role is somewhat distinct. For one thing, such people have become important agents of cultural continuity and change in South Asian Canadian communities. To take one example, consider dance. Dance is without question the most highly developed South Asian Canadian artistic tradition, and all across the country, women (and a few men) have established themselves as professional or volunteer dance teachers; many have been professionally trained themselves and some have strong international reputations. They have established a number of schools of South Asian dance across the country and participate in dozens of community-based dance groups. In these capacities they are far from neutral bearers of community traditions. In fact, in the communities where they are active they often set the agenda for ethnic dance, determining style, technique, and the mix of folk and classical traditions. In this regard there is an increasing degree of experimentation in new forms and new ideas. Both as performers and teachers they have played an important role in introducing the dance traditions of specific South Asian communities to South Asians and other Canadians who are unfamiliar with them.

In contrast, professional musicians and singers have generally been able to command large audiences but comparatively few students. This may well be a function of the longer time it takes to become moderately proficient at singing or playing an instrument than it does for dance. An additional factor is the far greater likelihood of people's direct participation in dance prior to immigration. Nevertheless, there are a number of excellent musical groups in existence today whose performances in concerts and other events are enthusiastically supported. Although most of these musicians are either proficient amateurs or part-time professionals, a few have managed to earn their living solely through playing and teaching; they have also had a role in the establishment of several small schools of South Asian music in Canada.

South Asians have also been quite active as writers, an activity that in fact divides into two pursuits according to language and audience. On one hand, several hundred individuals presently are active writing poetry, stories, and social commentary in one or another South Asian language. These people tend to publish and seek their audience primarily in their countries of origin rather than Canada, where no community is really large enough to support their activities well. On the other hand, those who produce literature in English tend to aim their work at a general Canadian audience. Neither write primarily for South Asian Canadians.

Indeed, the very heterogeneity of South Asians in Canada makes them a difficult population for which to write. This is no more powerfully illustrated than by the erratic history of the South Asian periodical and newspaper press in Canada. Even though they were beset by interminable difficulties, before the First World War, immigrants were extremely active in the publication of newspapers and pamphlets. Yet, not one of those pioneer newspapers lasted more than two years. This was due to difficulties that no subsequent South Asian periodical has been able to surmount. Those printed in a vernacular language lacked financial support, for until recently no local community was large enough to make such an endeavour financially realistic. The alternative strategy has been to publish in English to aim at a wider audience. Such papers are inevitably seen to reflect no one's concerns very well and they, too, suffer from insufficient support. Although scores of South Asian Canadian newspapers have been started, none has yet achieved true financial stability. Those that have achieved the longest-term success have been English-language monthlies with an equal mix of news items on events in South Asia and South Asian Canadian happenings; most are chiefly supported by advertisements for South Asian Canadian businesses rather than through subscriptions or newsstand sales.

The rather weak state of South Asian Canadian print journalism contrasts with recent developments in the electronic media. Multicultural radio stations in Vancouver and Toronto have been presenting programs of popular music and talk in Hindi and Punjabi since the early 1970's. These have been followed by similar programs in other cities. More recently, access to cable television facilities has led to community-produced programs on a wide range of topics – music, dance, drama, precepts of South Asian religions, intercultural communication, community news and events, language training, and so on. These programs are most numerous and varied in Toronto and Vancouver but they are becoming more common elsewhere. Community-oriented television would seem to have a bright future.

COMMUNITY AND THE GENERATIONS

Today, community affairs affect South Asian Canadians in many ways. Useful to some, a hindrance to others, community social networks are at least to some extent a part of the lives of most adults. Even so, the present pervasiveness of community social organization and institutions does not necessarily portend a rosy future for them. Most adults are immigrants, but a growing number of their children are not. The future of South Asian community structure lies with those children.

It is not yet clear how much of what parents have built up will transfer to the second generation. Children are being acculturated to differing degrees but the overall rate is high. As the second generation matures, a weakening of informal community relations will be inevitable. The geographical dispersal of South Asian communities will augment this trend, especially for those groups where religious or sociocultural events do not frequently bring people together. Kinship will remain the major support for informal association, but those ties will be weaker than they were in the first generation.

The future of community organizations is also uncertain. Only now are many such South Asian institutions developing firm foundations, but the momentum toward organizational development of the late 1970's and early 1980's will likely carry through the rest of the decade as people who immigrated as adults between 1965 and 1975 grow older. Those who take their places in associations, leadership roles, and private business will have a crucial effect on "South Asianness," especially on who will be able to define what it is to be South Asian Canadian. It is possible that more recent immigrants will take control over these associations, for they have been created by immigrants and generally reflect their interests. If this occurs it may lead to an estrangement of the adult second generation and a decline in their participation in organizational affairs.

Already there is a considerable generational gap evident in some communities about the role of community organizations, as one second-generation South Asian explains:

> My parents are both quite active in our community's association, so I have seen quite a lot about what goes on in it. Frankly, I don't see much there for me. All the while I was growing up most of their association's activities were for adults – mostly dinners and other get-togethers. More recently they have been putting on language classes for children; I don't know the language very well myself, but can't see myself learning it in with a bunch of kids. They have also been bringing in movies, which I of course can't follow. There's little in that organization for me or for anyone else like me.

Save for some Sikh organizations, there are presently very few South Asian organizations where the second generation is well represented among active members. Should control over these associations eventually pass to the Canadian-born, they could be important vehicles for ethnocultural maintenance for a long time. For now, this must remain an open question.

Throughout this book it has been argued that South Asian ethnicity is grounded on identity. Assimilative and acculturative forces inevitably will have effects on the ethnic identities of the second generation. What it means to be Sikh, Guyanese, or Bangali to them will differ considerably from what it means to their parents. Their identity may not necessarily be weaker, but it will likely be more situationally restricted, more voluntary, and less culturally dependent, everything else being equal.

Everything else, however, may not be equal. Despite generally good relations between South Asians and others, negative stereotypes of South Asians remain quite prevalent across Canada. An inevitable effect of

203

prejudice and discrimination is to sensitize people to their ethnicity and to push them into association with each other. Insofar as the second generation is concerned, prejudice and discrimination may have a significant effect on their future participation in community affairs. It is already the impetus for considerable community activity on the part of immigrant South Asians. So important are intergroup relations to the present and future situation of South Asians in Canada that they are the central topic of the final chapter.

NOTES

1. D. Stasiulis, "A Sociopolitical Analysis of the South Asian Community in Toronto" (1979, mimeo.).
2. One sad outcome of this has been the sale of the historic Vancouver temple to raise funds for the present temple on Ross Street. The original Victoria temple has been destroyed to make way for a new one.
3. Fernando, "East African Asians in Western Canada."
4. Norman Buchignani, *Perceptions of Racial Discrimination in Calgary: A Situation Report* (Ottawa, 1982).
5. Appathurai, "The Sri Lankans," p. 101.
6. Ahmad Saidullah, "A Critique of Indian Music," in A. Mukherjee (ed.), *East Indians: Myths and Reality* (Toronto, 1977), pp. 317-23.
7. Stasiulis, "A Sociopolitical Analysis."
8. Fernando, "East African Asians in Western Canada."

TWELVE

South Asian Canadians and Others

Over the past twenty years the South Asian population has grown from insignificance to over 300,000. There is now a South Asian presence in virtually every town and city in the country. Canadians outside of British Columbia had little experience in dealing with South Asians or any other visible minority group prior to the 1960's, while some South Asian immigrants had even less experience in dealing with people like Canadians. We have seen that once this combination led to extreme racial polarization and to the systematic denial of South Asian rights and privileges; hostility engendered when only a few thousand South Asians arrived in British Columbia was to leave its mark on local race relations for forty years.

Fortunately, the great expansion in South Asian immigration over the past twenty years did not produce a similar result. Considering the short time they have had to gain an understanding of each other, both South Asians and other Canadians have responded in a flexible, generally positive fashion to the new situation. Most Canadians can be credited for the way in which they have accepted South Asians as friends, neighbours, and fellow citizens. For their part, South Asians deserve recognition for their willingness to adapt to Canadian society and culture. South Asians who have come to Canada in recent years have not had to face the kind of hostility and rejection that has greeted South Asian immigrants to Britain; there are no ghettos, no massive pools of unemployed among Canadian South Asians.

This is not to say that South Asian immigration and settlement have proceeded without any interracial problems. Canadians have inherited a long tradition of sensitivity to cultural and physical difference, and this sensitivity was activated when South Asian immigrants began arriving in large numbers in the early 1970's. Prejudice against South Asians rose steadily, apparently reaching a peak in 1977-78, a period characterized by a rash of violent attacks against South Asians and their property. In some places, name-calling became prevalent and there were indications

205

that discrimination against South Asians seeking work and accommodation was common. Prejudice and discrimination against South Asians appear to have decreased in more recent years, but they have by no means disappeared.

The consequences of racial prejudice and discrimination to South Asian Canadians are significant. Most South Asians are now intimately aware that they have been identified as racially and culturally different and are concerned about the degree to which this interferes with their life goals. Some people now believe that prejudice and discrimination against them are endemic, while others avoid the issue or claim that nothing can be done about it. Few South Asians remain untouched by the problem.

In this chapter we outline the pattern of South Asian relations with others as they have developed in the post-war period. The recent history of South Asian/Canadian relations exhibits both the best and the most reprehensible human qualities; they combine in such a way as to engender guarded optimism for the future place of South Asians in Canada. In the first section we review the post-war ideological and social context into which South Asians moved. Thereafter, we turn to the chronological development of relations between South Asians from the early 1960's to the present. The third section is devoted to a discussion of Canadian ideas about South Asians. The chapter concludes with a look at governmental, public, and South Asian efforts to increase harmony between South Asians and other Canadians.

THE CONTEXT

Race and ethnic relations are not entirely the product of interaction between the particular groups involved. Such groups come into contact with each other already holding ideas about culture and race; sometimes they hold well-developed stereotypes of the other groups in question. On occasion, one group has been able to shape in its own image the social and cultural context in which such interaction occurs. All these are precursors to relations between South Asians and other Canadians as they developed in the 1960's and 1970's. Canadians have been able to set up the basic social, cultural, and economic institutions of Canada in the image of the majority group, thereby incorporating their particular notions of ethnicity and race into the very fabric of the country. In doing so, they have been able to set the context in which intergroup relations have been carried out. While it is true that Canadian ethnic prejudices have never been especially extreme by world standards, they have often been a considerable impediment to the successful incorporation of new immigrant groups. It is now generally acknowledged that a chief cause of prejudice in Canada has been ethnocentrism – the comparison of immigrant culture with a British or French-Canadian ideal model. What is perhaps less well known is that the resulting stereotypes were not entirely cultural. Most contained racial elements as well.

Indeed, racial thinking has played a greater role in Canada than most people realize. To be sure, the prevalence, historically, of racial thinking in immigration legislation, in British Columbia, and in relations with native people are well known. But biological criteria were involved in virtually all nominally ethnic stereotypes of immigrant groups as well. Evaluations of ethnic culture, estimates of assimilation, and the stereotypic individual qualities of group members usually parallelled perceptions of how great the biological differences were between the group in question and the majority group. Although Canadian ethnic and racial prejudices have moderated over the past fifty years, attitudinal studies continue to show that Canadians still evaluate each other by these dual criteria of perceived biological and cultural similarity to the majority group.[1]

The increasingly diverse post-war flow of immigrants has served as a Canadian primer on ethnic tolerance. For example, stereotypes of Scandinavians, Germans, and Ukrainians became less prevalent as groups traditionally seen as more culturally and physically different, such as Italians, Greeks, and Portuguese, appeared on the scene in greater numbers. Even so, when the federal government removed the last racial and national restrictions from the immigration regulations in the 1960's, Canadians in most parts of the country as yet had little familiarity with racially different groups. Post-war immigration had increased their sophistication in dealing with cultural diversity but had done little to make them come to terms with their ideas of race. Then as now, most Canadians believed that people could be separated into biologically distinct "races" on the basis of the physical criteria of skin colour and facial features.

Racial thinking of this sort is a serious and potentially dangerous error, because it can easily lead to a conviction that there is a close association between "race" and cultural behaviour. Biological difference in turn suggests greater cultural difference between groups than actually exists and leads people into believing that such cultural differences are less changeable than they would be for an ethnic group. For some people, a wide range of social contacts with others seen to be racially distinct is in itself abhorrent.

The fact is that South Asians do not constitute a biological race in any scientific sense.[2] Just as South Asians stem from many cultural traditions, they derive from a range of physical types, mixed and remixed through thousands of years of conquest and migration. Furthermore, it would be impossible to find a scientific way to separate South Asians racially from Europeans. As individuals, it would not be possible to separate South Asians from a broad range of Mediterranean peoples such as Italians, Turks, and Greeks. Consequently, if one were to have to force South Asians into a racial category, it would certainly be one shared by Europeans.

This scientific perspective on race is slim comfort for South Asians in

Canada. Were Canada's population made up primarily of peoples from southern Europe and North Africa, most south Asians could not be distinguished from the mainstream. The ultimate origins of most Canadians, however, are in light-skinned western, northern, and eastern Europe. Because most Canadians have been drawn from the light-skinned end of the European spectrum, most South Asians are physically distinguishable. From the earliest days South Asians have been seen as racially distinct.

This has always been a liability for South Asians. Prior to World War II, the perception that South Asians were an inferior race legitimated an elaborate system of discrimination that would have been difficult to support on the grounds of cultural difference alone. Full civil liberties were granted to South Asians in British Columbia in 1947 and relations between them and other Canadians were quite good right through the 1950's. Even so, racial thinking lingered and even affected the acculturated second generation. As South Asians subsequently settled elsewhere in the country this Canadian sensitivity to biological difference was soon activated, with the consequence that South Asians have had to develop their relations with others who believe them to be far more culturally different than they actually are. The burden of contrary proof has always been on South Asians. The following account of an immigrant who arrived before the great expansion of the late 1960's typifies this kind of thinking:

> I arrived in Calgary as an engineer from India in 1964. At that time there were very few people from India in the city and just about all of them were professionals of one kind or another. I was lucky in that there wasn't really a strong stereotype of East Indians then, as there was later on. Even so, because I looked different people automatically assumed that I must be from somewhere incredibly exotic. When they found out that I came from India discussion inevitably focused on such things as Indian poverty, food aid to India, or the odd and "uncivilized" customs of the country. That I had been educated in English, studied in Britain, and had seen far more of the world than they made no impression. I was from the land of the Taj Mahal.

South Asians had one other significant group liability not shared equally by other post-war immigrants: they came from places with which Canadians have had little direct contact. Most of their impressions of South Asia must therefore come through literature, education, and the mass media. Each of these can be faulted for providing Canadians with a negative and unbalanced image of South Asia. This is particularly true of the news media. News of South Asia is almost exclusively of poverty, illiteracy, violence, flood, political repression, and other human calamities.[3] Few Canadians could become aware that, say, India is a major industrial nation whose urban population is seven times greater than all

Canadians together. Combined with literature and educational images that stress exotic culture and agriculturally based traditionalism, the overall effect is quite negative. Together they have made Canadians see South Asian immigrants as far more foreign and unusual than otherwise would be so. As a case in point, a careful Edmonton survey carried out in 1969 showed that those polled expressed a wish for more social distance from South Asians than from any other immigrant group.[4] There were so few South Asians then living in Edmonton that such attitudes could not possibly have arisen through direct contact. When South Asian immigration increased, this image of traditional South Asia was applied to South Asian immigrants. A Toronto high school student recounted that

> The few classmates [of mine] who tried to be friendly were patronizing and I couldn't stomach that. One girl asked me whether I went to school in India on elephants. Another asked me whether I ate grasshoppers. I became more Indian than ever before.[5]

THE RISE AND FALL OF PREJUDICE (1960-84)

By the early 1960's South Asian stereotypes in British Columbia had largely disappeared and most people there were unaware of the conflict over South Asian immigration that had arisen more than a half century earlier. At that time, only in British Columbia was the South Asian population growing rapidly, and press and public interest was very low. South Asian immigrants were usually able to settle without the complications of racial prejudice and discrimination.

Outside of British Columbia a similar pattern developed in the mid-1960's. Immigrants were geographically dispersed, which made their entrance less visible. Moreover, because so many were professionals who had been educated in English, they were able to get around any preconceptions that people might have had of South Asians being culturally foreign and unassimilable. Moreover, the skilled and educated Canadians with whom they primarily associated have been traditionally one of the less prejudiced elements of the population, and this also must have slowed the rise of anti-South Asian prejudices in the 1960's. The economy was expanding rapidly, especially in areas of professional employment, so South Asians were not seen as an economic threat.

Throughout the 1960's, South Asian settlement went smoothly. If we except for a moment the situation of Sikhs in British Columbia, it would be fair to say that most South Asian adults felt well accepted by other Canadians and could substantiate this with reference to an easy familiarity with a wide range of other Canadians. The personal social networks of many individuals were soon made up primarily of non-South Asians. Verbal abuse was rare and racially instigated physical violence against South Asians was almost unheard of. Relations with the police and government were good. Concern over prejudice and discrimination was focused on a very few things: the perceived aversion of some Canadians to a few South Asian cultural practices, the fairness of hiring and promotion, and access to rental accommodation.

The cultural practice that most commonly attracted the attention of other Canadians to South Asians in the 1960's was their heavy use of spices in the preparation of food; some dishes typically require several *ounces* of spices rarely used in European cooking. Then as now, some Canadians had a strong reaction to the associated smells. South Asians were well aware of this, and those who lived in apartments often consciously modified their cooking practices to avoid provoking their neighbours; others were reluctant to rent apartments in houses unless they were owned by other South Asians. By the end of the 1960's Canadians were beginning to become aware of other things marking South Asian cultural difference. The male Sikh turban, the sari, and other traditional female attire attracted some attention, and some sensitivity to South Asian "race" was becoming evident.

Between 1968 and 1972 these perceptions became considerably more developed in British Columbia than elsewhere. Starting in the late 1960's many Sikh men came to British Columbia as sojourners who envisioned making a lot of money there and returning to India; in this, they were following a similar pattern of sojourner immigration to Britain established somewhat earlier. As sojourners, they were loath to spend money and were unmotivated to learn much about Canada and Canadians. They chiefly found employment in the woods industries and lived and worked exclusively with each other. Many found accommodation in homes owned by other Sikhs, where on occasion they rented little more than a bed and cooking facilities. Few had anything to do with their non-Sikh workmates.

There soon arose a conviction that these Sikhs were taking away jobs in the mills from "real" Canadians and were making it more difficult for them to find work. These perceptions were not altogether spurious, for before the entry of immigrant Sikh workers in the late 1960's, mills in more isolated areas often had great difficulty keeping their employees. Woods workers could quit and find new work relatively easily. In contrast, Sikhs stayed and thus began to change the job ecology of the rural woods industries. Resentment against them quickly grew. As it did, it expanded from being an exclusively economic complaint to one including a range of real and imagined Sikh cultural practices. These included charges of Sikh aloofness and untrustworthiness, as well as a general critique of Sikh dress, food, and housing practices.

Employment was an issue elsewhere in Canada, but in a different fashion. From the earliest days of post-war professional immigration there was some concern as to whether being South Asian was a factor in getting work. In an indirect sense, this was clearly the case, for as immigrants from the Third World they found it harder than most to demonstrate their training and experience to prospective employers. Convincing employers that they had appropriate occupational qualifications was a particular problem, for neither employers, the government, nor the universities were equipped to evaluate adequately the educational and occupational qualifications achieved in South Asia. How was an employer to evaluate an M.A. degree from a university in India that he or she never before knew existed? What did it mean to be senior economic planner in Guyana? Employers frequently had no other way to answer these questions except through employing a person. Where there was high occupational demand this was often exactly what happened and it sometimes resulted in South Asians securing positions for which they were not fully qualified. In occupational sectors where there was less demand, South Asian qualifications were often severely discounted. Sometimes this led to tragic results:

> He came to Canada with B.A. and M.A. degrees from the University of Punjab. The Ontario Department of Education rated his B.A. as equivalent to Canadian Grade 13 and apparently overlooked his M.A. altogether. He unsuccessfully applied for over a hundred jobs in his occupation. The only work he could find was as a security guard. In 1971 he ended his life by jumping in front of a Toronto subway train.

South Asians with occupations not in demand also suffered from lack of Canadian experience, a selection criterion so frequently encountered that by the 1970's there were many jokes circulating among South Asians about it; most of them involved the Catch-22 theme of the problem – one needed Canadian experience in order to get some. Some enterprising South Asians began offering to work temporarily for nothing or for severely discounted wages to build up a Canadian work record.

By the early 1970's South Asians were spread throughout the economy, with the result that these problems affected them very unequally. Those who had found it easy to secure work thought little about direct discrimination against South Asians in the workplace. Unable to see clearly what criteria were relevant to getting a job, those who found the process difficult were more inclined to suspect discrimination. Then as now, there was little direct evidence of how pervasive job discrimination was. The only controlled test of anti-South Asian occupational discrimination ever done was carried out in 1972 in Montreal.[6] In it, white and South Asian actors provided with similar qualifications and dress applied for the same professional-level jobs. In thirteen of twenty-four instances, the white candidate was offered a position or was told to apply for a vacancy; this happened only two of twenty-four times when a South Asian candidate was involved. The South Asian actors were told there was no vacancy sixteen times; in contrast, their white counterparts received this reply only six times.

211

As South Asian immigration increased in the early 1970's, relations between South Asians and other Canadians continued to be quite good despite some apprehension on both sides. Prejudice against South Asians nevertheless began to increase. This was first seen in British Columbia, where Sikh men continued to enter the woods industries in large numbers. Building tensions between Sikhs and whites culminated in a serious brawl in Quesnel in mid-1971. This event seems to have made the Vancouver media aware of the news potential of local race relations, a topic they had rarely covered since the 1940's. Thereafter, the local newspapers made an increasingly strong stand against Asian immigration, which they equated with immigration generally.[7] Coverage of Sikhs increased, almost all of it to do with immigration or political disputes involving Vancouver Sikh temples.

By all accounts, incidents of verbal abuse and vandalism increased steadily in British Columbia during the early 1970's; this was certainly the perception of the Vancouver Sikh community. The period saw the rise of the Sikh-based Indian Workers' Movement, a political organization allied with the Communist Party of Canada (Marxist-Leninist) and the Communist Party of India (Marxist-Leninist). In late 1973 the IWM formed the East Indian Defence Committee to fight racial discrimination. Their political stance was to the left of the Vancouver Sikh population, yet concern over discrimination was already so great that the East Indian Defence Committee received strong support, especially from young working-class men. Because of the close-knit nature of the Sikh community each racial incident soon became known to a great number of people, and it did not therefore take very many of them to create the impression that they were endemic. Occasional violent conflicts between Sikhs and others broke out in Fort St. James and elsewhere in rural British Columbia in 1973.

Overt incidents of discrimination against South Asians spread across the country between 1974 and 1977. The increase was so sudden that it could not have resulted from a similarly quick rise in anti-South Asian prejudices. Prejudicial beliefs typically take longer than this to develop, especially when (as in this case) actual intergroup competition and conflict are low. Rather, the rise in discriminatory incidents must have been based on negative beliefs that had been developing for some time. As early as 1973, a study showed that Torontonians had developed a preference for more social distance from South Asians than any other group included in the survey.[8] By 1975 a fairly clear stereotype of South Asians had arisen; with it in British Columbia came the earlier term "Hindoo," which was later supplanted nationally by "Paki." This term was a direct borrowing from Britain, where South Asian immigrants were primarily Sikh and Pakistani; it surfaced first in Ontario and spread westward. This poem, widely distributed in the mid-1970's, represents the general stereotypic view of South Asians:

BLESS B.C.

I come for a visit – am treated regal,
So I stay . . . who cares illegal?
I come to B.C., poor and broke.
Get on bus, see Manpower bloke.
Kind man treat me really swell there
Send me down to see the welfare.
Welfare say, "Come down no more" –
"We send the cash out to your door"
Norman Levi make you wealthy,
Medical Plan make you healthy.
　　Six months on dole – get plenty money.
Thanks to working man – the dummy!
Write to friends in Pakistan
Tell them come as fast as can.
They all come – in rags and turbans
I buy big house in suburbans.
They come with me . . . we live together
Only one thing bad – the weather.
Fourteen families living in
Neighbors patience running thin.
Finally, whites move away
I buy *their* house too . . . I say!
Find more Paki's . . . house I rent
More in garden, live in tent,
　　Send for family – they all trash
They all draw more Welfare cash.
Everything is going good
Soon we own the neighborhood.
Now on quiet summer nights
Go to Temple – watch the fights.
We have hobby . . . it called *breeding*
"Baby Bonus" keeps us feeding.
Two years later, big bank roll
Still go Manpower, still draw dole.
Kids need dentist? Wife needs pills?
We get free, we got no bills.
White man good, he pay all year
To keep the Welfare running here.
Bless all white men, big and small
For paying tax to keep us all.
We thank B.C., damn good place
Too damn good for white man race.
If they no like colored man,
Plenty room in Pakistan.

The above poem is the British Columbia version. Variants were tailored for other provinces.[9]

Because the calculus of risk and reward involved in making a decision to discriminate can shift dramatically over time, so can levels of discrimination. This was the case with verbal abuse, vandalism, and physical violence, which were the most overt (though not necessarily the most significant) forms of discrimination faced by South Asians in the mid- to late 1970's. Contributing factors that shifted this risk-and-reward balance in the mid-1970's are not hard to find. Such incidents first attracted great attention to Vancouver in late 1974. House prices there had just made a strong upward move, which was widely attributed to immigrant activity in the market. The economy had suffered a downturn and jobs were becoming hard to find. Visible minority groups in particular were made the scapegoat, for their very visibility and the increase in their numbers made it easy to associate these ills with them. Antagonism to visible immigrants was increased by the government's then ongoing review of immigration policy, which culminated in the Green Paper on Immigration. Similar consequences were soon evident in urban Ontario as well.

In Vancouver, the way in which immigration issues were covered by local newspapers also became an important factor in the deterioration of race relations. Beginning in early 1975, the press in B.C. began to link a variety of social and economic ills with Asian immigration. The *Vancouver Sun* alone carried sixty-six items relating to South Asians between the beginning of January and the end of April; thirty-seven of them were on immigration.[10] In addition to making the general population more conscious of South Asian immigration, this coverage increased the concern of local South Asians about discrimination, particularly after a series of local incidents received prominent coverage. This culminated in a meeting of over 800 Sikhs on March 9, 1975. The general thrust of the discussion was that because the police had proved to be ineffective in stopping vandalism and physical attacks against South Asians, they should band together for self-protection. The two Vancouver dailies came up with the following front-page headlines the next day:

EAST INDIANS VOW TO FIGHT
A Vigilante Group Organized by Communist Party Plans to Retaliate Against 'White Racist Attacks' on East Indians[11]

VIGILANTES TO ACT AGAINST WHITE RACISTS
The leader of a Maoist Political Party Claims More Than 800 East Indians were Prepared to Meet Violence With Violence[12]

In this form the story made front-page news in Toronto, even though vigilantism was not mentioned at the meeting in question and the leftist political views of the principal speaker were not relevant to the central concern of the audience.

These events came at the time when the summary volumes of the Green Paper on Immigration came out. Within hours of its release, a *Vancouver Sun* headline claimed:

IMMIGRATION STUDY WARNS
Vancouver Faces Racial Tension[13]

The study did not make this claim. Even so, it was followed by several editorials and a speech by the mayor of Vancouver advocating a restriction of Asian immigration. Extensive press coverage of these issues further increased South Asian concern over discrimination. South Asian complaints about property damage went up sharply and only declined when press coverage did also; in the first half of 1975 the police received fifty-three complaints of damage to South Asian property from residents of southeast Vancouver alone; another fifty complaints were about interracial violence.[14]

Overt forms of discrimination were also on the rise in the Toronto area in 1975. Though somewhat more responsible than its Vancouver counterpart, the Toronto press began to associate visible minority groups with immigration and immigration-related difficulties. The Western Guard Party arose as a small but vocal extremist group explicitly devoted to stopping non-white immigration. The same factors contributive to a rise in discrimination were present: a large influx of visible minority group immigrants, rising house prices, and decreasing economic opportunities. Although slow off the mark, racial discrimination in the Toronto area soon became more prevalent.

This was particularly true of what can be termed a "youth culture" of anti-South Asian discrimination. Name-calling, vandalism against South Asian property, and physical attacks have rarely been carried out by adults above the age of twenty-five; most of them are perpetrated by adolescents and young adults, primarily by males.[15] Virtually all serious physical confrontations past and present have been initiated by young men. By 1976 the harassment of South Asians had become a socially acceptable peer-group activity among some Toronto and Vancouver area youth. In schools, graffiti denigrating South Asians, blacks, and Chinese became ubiquitous and visible-minority children became the frequent victims of name-calling and intimidation.[16] Children began to change schools to avoid racial conflict.

By 1976, "Paki-baiting" outside of the school context by small groups of youths was more frequent in Vancouver and urban Ontario and was on the rise in Edmonton, Calgary, and Montreal. Three or four youths would drive around areas where South Asians could be found on the streets and shout abuse from the safety of their cars; South Asian families would be similarly treated by neighbourhood youths. South Asian homes, cars, and places of worship were frequently vandalized. The following is a dramatic example from 1976:

> A regionally-based association rented a local hall in order to celebrate *Durga Puja*, an important Hindu yearly festival. The festival was to be carried out over five days beginning September 29th and involved several hundred individuals. Because of concern over possible vandalism and racial abuse which the celebration might attract the association requested increased police vigilance beforehand. On the second day local youths began to verbally abuse participants as they arrived. Verbal abuse subsequently evolved into a pattern of throwing things at the hall. The police were called, and attempted to 'negotiate' with the youths. An hour later a half dozen young men appeared with axes, baseball bats and sticks and attacked people near the entrance to the hall. One of the festival's organizers was seriously hurt. The police arrived only after two calls and well after the ambulance. Even though some of the youths were still in the area, none were charged. The pattern of verbal abuse and stone throwing continued and the celebration was terminated prematurely. [17]

So common did such attacks become that the list of those aimed at religious institutions alone is long. Hindu temples operated by the Hindu Prathana Samaj and Bharat Bavan in Toronto have been vandalized and their members have been abused; the same is true for Hindu temples in the West. Vandalism against Sikh gurdwaras became so prevalent that most are now surrounded by chain link fences.

Personal violence also increased, reaching a high point in a few incidents where the intent of the attackers was to kill or do serious harm to their victims:

> On January 3, 1976 a 49 year old Canadian of South Asian origin was returning home from a prayer meeting via the Toronto subway. While waiting for a train at the Islington station he was first verbally abused by two young men, then was pushed off the platform and onto the tracks. He could have been electrocuted or run over by a train. As it was, he was seriously injured by the fall. The two men were arrested and subsequently convicted of assault. This was only one of scores of racial incidents which occurred on Toronto public transportation that year. [18]

> In early 1976 a fifteen year old South Asian boy entered a Toronto area shopping mall. Without provocation, he was shot dead by a twenty-one year old man, who explained to police that "I just shot the nigger. For every one you shoot you leave a white girl with a broken heart." [19]

By 1977, harassment, violence, and vandalism against South Asians had become everyday occurrences in Metro Toronto and had spread across Ontario and the Prairies. In Thunder Bay, a municipal employee and two policemen were charged in connection with the severe beating of the South Asian assistant manager of a local hotel. A major riot broke out between sixty South Asian and white railway workers in Daysland, Alberta; other outbreaks of racial violence occurred in Calgary and Red Deer, Alberta, and in Prince George, British Columbia. The situation in Vancouver became only slightly less serious than it was in Metro Toronto.

The incidence of these forms of discrimination began to decrease in most parts of the country in 1979, but they continue to be frequent enough for concern. Acts of violence like the following continue to occur:

> On August 2nd, 1981, Khuspal Singh Gill, 21 years old, was beaten to death in Vancouver by four white youths. A witness in the courtroom reported that the attackers left after knocking Gill unconscious only to return later to further beat the body and clean the pockets. One of the murderers later proudly declared that "today, I've killed a hindu." Following the murder the victim's family repeatedly received threatening phone calls.[20]

> On March 5, 1982 a young Sikh was abducted while waiting for a bus in North Vancouver. The abductors, six whites, blind-folded the man and took him to a house where he was beaten, hanged by his feet, then shaven, put back into a vehicle, blind-folded again, and driven around. The young man managed to escape by jumping out of the vehicle while the abductors were at a stop light.[21]

Such violent actions are only one small aspect of intergroup relations between South Asians and others, but they are consequential. This is particularly so because many South Asians have used the real or imagined incidence of attacks on South Asians and their property to gauge the overall level of discrimination they face; based primarily on such evidence, some feel that discrimination in areas such as job selection, access to social services, relations with the police, and rental accommodation is profound. Their symbolic impact is also significant in another respect. Those individuals who have relatively little close contact with other Canadians tend to use the apparent frequency of racial incidents as an indication that most Canadians are racists. They consequently feel self-conscious in public and tend to avoid situations that might lead to racial victimization.

Although the visibility of discrimination of this sort has made it a continual subject of comment, this type is not of greatest concern to South Asians. Although they realize they are at risk, most are aware that the risk of involvement in violent incidents is low. South Asian immigrants usually have had considerable prior experience with highly polarized racial or ethnic situations and can therefore come to terms with living amidst prejudice. That same experience, however, has made them fearful of those types of discrimination that directly affect their economic, educational, and social opportunities. Much of this concern has always focused on prospects for hiring and advancement. Earlier immigrants nevertheless faced better economic and social conditions than today's immigrants with above-average educational and occupational resources.

Concern over job discrimination was always an issue. It became much more so in the mid-1970's when economic prospects worsened and overt discrimination increased. South Asian unemployment also increased, giving people more reason to be concerned; for example, in 1976 the unemployment rate for South Asians in Metro Toronto in all age categories was roughly twice that of the population as a whole.[22] No other ethnocultural population surveyed had as high an unemployment rate. In the far less buoyant economic conditions of the early 1980's these concerns have increased further. Attitudinal studies done across the country in recent years have shown that South Asians presently believe that racial prejudice plays an important role in their occupational careers.[23]

One should not be too highly critical of this reaction. Many recent immigrants – not only South Asians – have had great difficulty in becoming established in their prior lines of work, and an increasing number have found economically rewarding jobs of any kind hard to get. Lacking direct access to information on the availability of jobs, the prevalence of *pro forma* job advertisements, and the importance of personal connections in job selection, South Asians, understandably, consider discrimination an important factor. Moreover, in the face of how little definite information exists on the incidence of racial discrimination in Canada, no one can argue the opposite side with any greater certainty of being right.

South Asians harbour similar worries about discrimination in other areas of life. Immigrants continue to believe that their overseas educational and occupational qualifications are not being fairly evaluated. Again, little is known about the fairness with which government, industry, and educational institutions approach this process. Without doubt, the vast range of background experiences of South Asian immigrants and the fact that much of this has been achieved in areas of the world outside of Europe have resulted in the evaluation process being much more random than it would be for British or American immigrants. In a highly competitive occupational and educational market this must usually work against South Asians.

Job advancement is also a constant concern. Here, too, there are few hard data, but there is a mounting body of supportive ancedotal information. Perhaps the most frequent complaint comes from those with professional or business backgrounds, who claim that because they are South Asian their companies are reluctant to promote them into positions where they would deal with the public or with other businesses; the claim is that management personnel fear that prejudices held by their clients or the public will result in a loss of business. Few South Asians are presently in any kind of supervisory position where they are responsible for white workers. South Asian doctors (even some who are British-trained) have also had great difficulties in becoming re-established here.

Two other commonly voiced worries might be mentioned. One is a widespread feeling that South Asians do not have equal access to the process of immigration, particularly regarding their ability to support effectively the immigration of relatives. This perceived difficulty has been the cause of many petitions and personal representations to government. Once more, there is little hard evidence, but immigration rates and fluctuations in annual flows from the source countries of South Asian immigrants are such that some sort of governmental management seems evident; they certainly do not support the thesis that equally qualified immigrants from all countries have equal access to the process.

The other area might be generally characterized as a Canadian resistance to institutional change to accommodate the cultural and religious needs of South Asians. Until the rise of Asian immigration in the 1960's the only religions allowed full institutional status across Canada were Christianity and Judaism. In most provinces, for example, an individual could not officially become married in a Hindu, Muslim, or Buddhist ceremony, nor were these religions automatically recognized as such for tax and zoning purposes. Many of the first South Asian religious organizations were therefore incorporated as non-profit associations rather than charities. These difficulties were not entirely resolved until the late 1970's. Other religious difficulties come because the daily and calendrical observances of these religions do not correspond with those Christian ones incorporated into our work schedule. Most major ceremonies have thus been shifted to the weekends to accommodate those who work Monday through Friday. Muslims are constantly compromised, in that Friday is their traditional day of religious celebration. Even death is a little problematic, for Hindus have not been able to make use of the traditional funeral pyre and have had to opt for cremation. Muslims have had difficulty in carrying out interment within the traditional time after death, which is far shorter than here.

Other cultural constraints are perhaps less significant, yet are common. Many South Asian women are vegetarians, who have difficulty in finding something adequate to eat in public and on the job. Occupational dress codes have frequently discouraged Sikh men from continuing to wear turbans and South Asian women from wearing their traditional dress. Muslims can only eat *halal* meat, which has been butchered in a specific way, and this is never available in public eating places.

In overview, it is difficult to assess the impact of prejudice and discrimination on South Asians today. Looked at in objective terms, this depends much on what standard of comparison is used. Because Canadians had little experience with visible minority groups prior to the rise of South Asian, Caribbean, and East Asian immigration, some initial difficulties and misunderstandings were inevitable. However, government, business, and private organizations did little to prepare Canadians for dealing with "race," and little was done to mitigate race relations thereafter. Canadians and South Asian immigrants have had to come to terms with each other primarily on a one-to-one basis. Given this constraint, the development of intergroup relations went far more smoothly than one might have expected. Most Canadians neither actively discriminate against South Asians nor wish to do so. For their part, South Asians have made a successful attempt to integrate themselves socially and culturally into the mainstream of Canadian society. South Asians have not become a subordinate minority group, which could have become their lot if there had been less tolerance for them than there has been. One need only compare the Canadian situation with that in Britain, where greater levels of intolerance, a more class-stratified society, and worse economic conditions did lead to this result. The large increase in the rate of South Asian immigration in the mid-1970's without doubt was directly linked to the subsequent rise in racial incidents, which have gone down as Canadians have become more used to South Asians and as they immigrate in fewer numbers.

At the same time, it must be said that South Asian claims of discrimination have not attracted much public governmental attention until very recently. They have certainly received far less than would be the case if South Asians were a more politically influential population. To make this point one need only envision the public and governmental reaction that would occur if Canadian Jews or Ukrainians were to experience a similar wave of discrimination. For example, the Alberta government made no specific moves to address numerous South Asian representations about discrimination made to it prior to 1983. Even a widely publicized report on racial discrimination in Calgary produced by one of the authors led to no governmental movement.[24] In contrast, the anti-Semitism of a single small-town Alberta teacher led to the creation of a major provincial commission on intolerance, a full review of Alberta's curriculum materials for bias, and an aggressive media campaign by the Human Rights Commission.

No assurances based on good information can be given to South Asians that they presently enjoy equal access to jobs, housing, and the like to people of similar backgrounds and skills who are not South Asian. Viewed from the subjective point of view of South Asians, prejudice and discrimination continue to be important concerns that are only slowly being allayed as the 1980's progress. Although people are aware that overt racial incidents are on the decline, they are unsure that the same can be said of covert discrimination in employment, for example. This concern has lowered their psychological standard of living and has made their social world a very paradoxical place; on one hand, their relations with most Canadians are cordial and apparently unbiased, while on the other, South Asians fear discrimination from other Canadians who are not within their circle of friends and acquaintances.

STEREOTYPES OF SOUTH ASIANS

Considering Canada's historical prejudices against ethnic and racial groups, Canadians have become increasingly racially tolerant. One need only imagine the reaction that would have been provoked had South Asian immigration of the size that faced Toronto in the 1970's actually occurred in the 1950's. At the same time, South Asians do not interact with an average of all Canadians, but rather with specific individuals. Today, a significant minority of Canadians remains highly prejudiced against South Asians and other visible immigrant groups. What proportion of the population they represent is difficult to estimate. A study done at the height of interracial conflict suggested that about 15 per cent of Torontonians harbour strongly racist views.[25] Inasmuch as intergroup conflict was higher in Toronto than elsewhere, this may well approximate the maximum prevalence of highly prejudiced individuals in the population as a whole.

Whatever the proportion, it is clear that South Asians generally continue to be seen in more negative and stereotypical terms than any other widely distributed Canadian ethnic or racial group. For example, in a national survey in 1976-77 Anglo-Celtic individuals were asked to rank twenty-seven ethnic groups in terms of concurrence with "myself"; South Asians were placed twenty-third.[26] Among recent immigrant groups only Arabs were listed lower. South Asians were the category least mentioned as being "Canadian," "similar to me," and "likeable." South Asians were perceived to stick together and play by their own rules; 59 per cent of the sample in this study considered life in South Asia to be very dissimilar to life here.

In addition to this perception of cultural difference are more specific attitudes toward many supposed South Asian social and cultural practices. Condemned social practices include living in extended and overcrowded households, bringing over unqualified or illegal relatives, forming residential ghettos, and exploiting government services. South Asians have additionally been stereotyped as clannish, self-centred, arrogant, argumentative, and confrontational. These stereotypic ideas are given support by the almost universal belief that South Asians are a homogeneous ethnic and racial group.

Accounting for how these particular attributes were associated with South Asians and for why they so quickly came to prominence is difficult. It should be noted that in suffering a rise in prejudice in the 1970's, South Asians were not alone. Caribbean blacks in particular were subject to prejudice that, though different in conceptualization, was almost as strong. Like South Asians, Caribbean blacks were initially faced with racial prejudices stemming from race relations elsewhere, chiefly in the British Empire and the United States. Negative Canadian media coverage of American blacks in particular has continually involved violence, crime, poverty, unemployment, and family disorganization, and these attributes were soon applied to blacks in Canada.[27]

This comparison of blacks and South Asians suggests a simple association between high rates of immigration, prior Canadian ideas of analogous peoples, and consequent increases in the levels of prejudice against the groups in question. There is further support for this association in Canadian responses to Chinese immigration. Chinese immigration patterns have closely matched those of South Asians in numbers, rates of entry, class, occupation, age, and regional distribution. In earlier times anti-Chinese prejudices were as strong and were more widespread than those against South Asians. However, today Canadian prejudices against Chinese are nowhere near as strong as they are against South Asians (or people from the Caribbean). One clear difference is that Chinese Canadians have benefited from recent positive coverage of China to at least the extent that South Asians and blacks have suffered from negative stereotypes of South Asia and the Caribbean. In contrast to South Asians, Chinese Canadians have built up a reservoir of good will throughout their long history of work and struggle in Canada.

This does not, however, entirely account for why certain attributes have been negatively associated with South Asians rather than others. People who are anti-South Asian are also anti-black, and strongly prejudiced Canadians exhibit social and psychological characteristics found elsewhere; racism is more prevalent among those Canadians who are older, less educated, lower class, strongly religious, authoritarian, or politically conservative.[28] This still does not account for the attributes identified with South Asians.

Could it be that these truly are South Asian attributes? In some cases, this can be dismissed easily. For example, most South Asians identify strongly with Canada, in direct contradiction of the stereotype; after only three years in Canada, 70 per cent of Indian immigrants sampled in 1972 claimed such a commitment.[29] South Asians also pull their weight economically. South Asians typically earn incomes higher than the average immigrant arriving in the same year; German Canadians are stereotypically associated with hard work, yet the national study *Three Years in Canada* showed that German and Indian immigrant family incomes in 1975 were virtually identical.[30] In a recent Toronto survey no South Asian respondents had family incomes below $10,000 a year, whereas a third of Dutch, Chinese, and Caribbean respondents did.[31] In addition, there is no evidence that South Asians overuse social and health services.

It is perhaps closer to the truth to say that many of the stereotypic associations Canadians have made with South Asians are based on systematic misperceptions of South Asian behaviour. These misperceptions become negatively evaluated either because the observer is unaware of what South Asians mean by a given behaviour or because the observer is only able to get an unrepresentative exposure to it. There are, for example, some rather common cultural differences between South Asians and other Canadians that have irked the latter. Consider the context of work, where many South Asians come in contact with others. In most places from which South Asians come, work is not an end in itself as it traditionally was here; rather, work is a means to an end and tends to be valued chiefly for its results. Less affected than other Canadians by the work ethic, South Asian workers at low-pay or low-status jobs are sometimes perceived as unmotivated. In South Asia the responsibilities of an employee typically are rigidly defined and sharply constrained; innovation is sometimes seen as a threat to the status quo. The greater ambiguity of Canadian work roles results in some adjustment problems for South Asians unfamiliar with the Canadian work context, and adherence to South Asian notions of occupational responsibility has sometimes led to a belief among fellow workers that South Asians are too dogmatic and passive about their work.

There are similar but less common differences in how South Asians view their relationship to the state, especially among working-class South Asians, who tend to be suspicious of the role of the state and its officers, particularly police and bureaucrats; this chiefly comes from the fact that South Asian source country governments are more totalitarian and corrupt than Canada's.

Many Canadian misconceptions about South Asians concern family life and household practice – areas of South Asian life of which they are able to see very little. A frequent such perception is that South Asians are prone to overcrowding. Most South Asian immigrants lived in some form of extended household immediately prior to coming to Canada and would not be adverse to creating these family patterns here. As we have seen, long-term extended family units are actually rarely formed and South Asian Canadians normally live in nuclear families. Where does this perception of overcrowding come from? Is it pure illusion? Not entirely. An enormous number of temporary housing arrangements were made during the 1970's so that new immigrants stayed with friends or relatives until they got on their feet. From 1973 to 1977 a great many people were living in such situations, and by Canadian standards it did sometimes lead to overcrowding. Incessant visiting between one South Asian household and others must also have helped to convey this impression. As rates of immigration have decreased, so also has the proportion of South Asians in such living arrangements.

Other complaints are related to housing and residential settlement. House prices rose sharply across the country about the time that South Asian immigration rates were the highest, and as visible immigrants they were sometimes held responsible for it; their numbers, however, were never sufficient to have a determinant effect on house prices. Unaware of how much South Asians would sacrifice to buy a house, other Canadians sometimes found this as a cause for it was commonly believed that South Asians came to Canada well heeled or else manipulated the system to qualify for mortgages. Both are largely untrue. Another bias was that

South Asians allegedly did not keep up their homes; having never been in one, some must have imagined that South Asian Canadian homes come replete with mud floors and a cow. Actually, they look little different inside than anyone else's. Some of this misperception may well have come from two processes to which South Asians were prone in the 1970's. Many were willing to buy homes in disrepair rather than postpone purchasing a house until they could afford something better. Once purchased, the heavy financial commitment sometimes sent so many family members to work that there was little time to correct the situation. Complaints also arose that South Asians were forming residential ghettos, yet actual residential concentrations resulted chiefly from the local availability of appropriate houses. Many of these concentrations have dissipated as more established families have moved to better neighbourhoods at a rate faster than new immigrants have entered the old ones.

Most other stereotypic attributes of South Asians have to do with how they are perceived to interact with other people. Central among these is a conviction that South Asians are difficult to like. This is a clear impediment to future intergroup harmony, especially if (as we argue) person-to-person interaction is an important source of Canadian ideas about South Asians. Moreover, as long as such an impediment persists, other Canadians will likely be unwilling to join South Asians in a defence of their rights. This perception is so general that, one must conclude, it must be rooted in things South Asians actually do that appear to be unfriendly or uncivil. Such things are not hard to find. They result chiefly from incomplete cultural and linguistic fluency with Canadian idioms, with the consequent tendency to use South Asian models of interaction where they are inappropriate. Many of these difficulties stem from South Asian notions of social status and how status should affect interaction. Status criteria in South Asia may be sharper than anywhere else in the world, and the lines between status groups are very tightly drawn. How interaction proceeds therefore depends much on the respective statuses of the individuals involved; low-status individuals are expected to defer to those of higher status and there is much conversational jockeying around between two individuals of similar status to determine who will eventually be recognized to be of superior status.

Canadian status criteria, in comparison, are remarkably fluid and indefinite, and this initially confuses some South Asians. The confusion is compounded by the fact that low-status groups in India or Pakistan may not necessarily be so here. Downward occupational mobility makes some desperate to convey their pre-immigration status to others. The result is that, by Canadian standards, some South Asians have a tendency to be demeaning to people who are in roles they traditionally see as inferior to their own. A corollary is that many are unsure of whom to befriend; in South Asia, friends were drawn from a narrow range of social equals, but here there is great uncertainty as to who are their Canadian social equals. Unsure also of Canadian methods of decreasing social distance, they are sometimes seen as being aloof, unresponsive to overtures of friendship, and unwilling to participate in group activities. The following admission of one South Asian is a case in point:

> I must say that I really started off on the wrong foot when I came to Canada. In looking back, it's clear that I wasn't able to read Canadian signals very well; I knew English in a technical sense, but not in such a way as to be able to pick up things which indicated a wish for friendship. I also know now that I must have really hurt some of my first Canadian acquaintances with an approach that must have seemed very superior and standoffish. I fear some immigrants never learn to read these signals, but generally people today seem far better at it than they were ten years ago.

Another common belief is that South Asians are clannish and "stick together." In an overall sense, it would be impossible to argue that South Asians associate more with each other than do Canadians of European origin with themselves. After all, if one reverses the argument, it is clear that a high proportion of European Canadians also "stick together" in the sense that they have relatively few social relations with South Asians. Like those of European origin, the preference of South Asians for establishing relationships within their ethnic or national community varies dramatically, both individually and by group. What perhaps conveys this impression that South Asians wish to associate primarily with each other is actually a reflection of a greater overall desire for extensive social relations and feelings of responsibility toward kin and friends. This, however, is also prevalent among many other groups, such as the Portuguese and Italians. Relations with other Canadians remain weak because of factors other than individual preference; such factors include communication difficulties, initial unfamiliarity with the means to establish such relations, and some reluctance on the part of other Canadians to enter into them.

South Asians are also affected by their constant public association with immigration. Canadians often feel resentment against immigration and immigrants, especially when times become hard. The visibility of South Asians, blacks, Chinese, and others whose major phase of immigration began in the 1960's has shifted public consciousness about immigration to them, with the result that non-white immigration and immigration are now more or less linked in the public's eye. All South Asian cultural, religious, and national groups together have never made up more than about 10 per cent of the total immigrant flow, yet this is not the general perception.

The rise of these stereotypic ideas about South Asians was unfortunate and possibly unnecessary. Few private, public, or governmental attempts were made to head off the rise of anti-South Asian prejudices or to reduce them once their presence was felt. South Asians were given no initial guidance in the customs and social practices of Canadians, while other Canadians were left to come to terms with these new immigrants on their own. Considerable conflict and confusion resulted. Even so, two very positive points should be noted. First of all, relations between South Asians and others have improved despite the near total lack of programming aimed at achieving this result. Second, if, as it has been argued here, many of the prejudices against South Asians are the consequence of initial mutual misunderstanding and misperception, then the future looks somewhat optimistic. Using the incidence of racial attacks as an indicator, anti-South Asian prejudices have been on the decline since at least 1978. This hardly indicates a change of heart, but as South Asians reside in Canada longer their sophistication in dealing with other Canadians will increase; on the whole, their circle of non-South Asian friends will increase, bringing more people into multidimensional, prejudice-reducing contact with South Asians. This is particularly true for children, whose close interpersonal relations signify the eventual complete demise of South Asian stereotypes.

FOSTERING INTERGROUP HARMONY

Comparatively little has been done by Canadians to foster better intergroup relations actively and to assure that new immigrant groups have equal access to the rights and privileges they enjoy. This has been particularly true at the institutional level, few of which have been changed or developed to address this challenge. Consider those institutions aimed at protecting South Asian Canadian rights and privileges – the various human rights commissions, the police, and the legal system. South Asians share with other visible minority groups the conviction that provincial and federal human rights commissions are largely ineffective in addressing discrimination; they are almost certainly right. Human rights codes have been constructed in such a way that racial incidents like name-calling, vandalism, and physical assault are excluded; the latter two continue to be dealt with under the Criminal Code by the police. In the areas that are covered, such as job discrimination, housing, and access to services, the commissions move so slowly that cases take years to resolve. Few South Asians presently approach human rights commissions with their complaints about discrimination.

They are far more likely to go to the police, who unfortunately do not have a direct legal mandate to address discrimination; a complaint of racial assault must be approached no differently than any other assault case. The only types of discrimination covered by the Criminal Code presently are the distribution of hate literature and the catch-all of disturbing the peace. In contrast, the police are powerless to deal with job or housing discrimination, which are the preserve of the human rights commissions. Despite profound legal constraints, the police in some places have nevertheless tried to respond, chiefly to South Asian community complaints about discrimination by the police. Most police forces now have community relations officers whose duties focus on liaison with ethnic and racial communities; because they typically have been given a wide mandate, they are now constantly involved in informal mediation of intergroup conflict, even when such conflicts are not covered by the Criminal Code. However, while police administrators are now more sensitive to these issues, many rank-and-file police are not. Moreover, practical policy changes by the police have been scarce. By way of example, South Asian hiring by police has been insignificant, even though policing is a Sikh tradition.

Most municipal governments have been rather unresponsive to this issue, with the clear exception of Vancouver, Toronto, and North York. School Boards in these cities have introduced clear policies on racial discrimination in the schools and have tried to remove curriculum materials that portray South Asia stereotypically. Elsewhere, little has been done to date.

Something should be said in this context about the role of government multicultural policy in fostering intergroup harmony. Multicultural programs help ethnic groups preserve key, symbolic aspects of their culture and identity and demonstrate the government's recognition of the contribution they and their cultural heritages have made. Such programs have helped many South Asians feel comfortable about being Canadian and South Asian at the same time and have exposed many Canadians to South Asian culture for the first time. Multiculturalism has also been partially responsible for the rise of South Asian associations, which in turn have focused their concerns on their role in Canadian society. In addition, multiculturalism has had the effect of changing the sense of what it is to be a Canadian, shifting it away from a mechanical association with the two founding European groups.

Even so, because it has been primarily a policy directed toward cultural concerns, multiculturalism historically has tended to neglect racial ones. Growing numbers of people are completely Canadian in culture, have no strong identification with an ethnic group, yet are not white. Recognition of this led the Multiculturalism Directorate to include fostering racial harmony within its mandate as of mid-1981. This subsequently led to the production of race relations situation reports on eleven Canadian cities, which clearly illustrated the depth of South Asian concern about discrimination. In late 1982 the federal government announced the creation of a Special Parliamentary Committee on the Participation of Visible Minorities in Canadian Society, and briefs submitted to it by South Asian organizations across the country detailed a host of key problems concerning racism and its elimination; many of these concerns found their way into the committee's report, *Equality Now*. It is hoped that these government actions are a prelude to the creation of a distinct federal policy on multiracialism to parallel and augment multiculturalism.

Institutional responses to racism and racial discrimination have been scarce, but those of South Asian individuals and groups have not. Many associations have been developed to foster better intergroup relations or have included this objective within their charter over the past ten years. The first of these was the East Indian Defence Committee, which was formed in 1973. Its membership was almost completely Sikh. Its strong point was its ability to mount effective public demonstrations, which definitely led to improved Vancouver newspaper coverage of South Asians and to greater awareness on the part of the Vancouver and Metro Toronto governments of the need to act against racial incidents.

In most places, South Asian ethnic and national groups are too small to tackle this problem alone and have banded together to form pan-ethnic organizations whose principal goal is fostering intergroup harmony. Most of their effort has been directed toward responding to racial incidents or examples of bias. When they face an institution that does not want adverse publicity and does not have a vested stake in discrimination, they have been quite effective. Media coverage is a case in point. Until the late 1970's both local and foreign coverage of South Asians was quite negative, particularly in the newspapers. Even so, this only occasionally seemed to be the result of a conscious policy and a few well-aimed protests often resulted in significant changes. Similar tactics have forced the Toronto Transit Commission and construction companies in British Columbia to accept Sikh workers with beards and turbans. They have also led to somewhat greater police awareness of South Asian concern over racial assaults and vandalism.

Such protests have been much less effective when they directly challenge self-interest. For example, the media employ almost no South Asian or other visible minorities in the production of news. A study done in 1976 showed that in six Toronto newspapers only fourteen of 673 people involved in news production (or 2 per cent) were visible minorities.[32] This was in an area of Canada where visible minorities now make up about 11.5 per cent of the population.[33] Repeated calls for more news media hiring of visible minorities across the country have had little effect. Neither have South Asian objections to the almost exclusively white makeup of every police force in the country. Not a single police force has developed an effective program to seek out qualified minority applicants.

From the beginning it was realized that South Asian associations could themselves do very little to lessen discrimination in most areas of life. Discrimination in hiring, housing, and access to services was seen to be a problem better approached by government, whose resources are immeasurably greater. Consequently, a great deal of the energy of these associations and of community spokespersons has been directed not toward possible discriminators but to various levels of government.

There is presently an awareness that organizations devoted to the protection of South Asian Canadian rights have a long way to go before they have the power to influence readily government and public opinion.

While South Asians have been very active in representing their concerns about discrimination (to government in particular), they appreciate that they do not yet have sufficient political clout to command the attention they wish. In this respect the explicit goal is to achieve the level of political effectiveness of the Jewish community whose perceived abilities to speak out effectively against anti-Semitism have reached legendary proportions in the opinion of those South Asians involved in the fight against racism.

Important though organizational responses to increasing people's acceptance of South Asians are, it must be appreciated that the everyday ways in which South Asians and other Canadians interact are equally significant. As with so many other things about South Asian Canadians, there is presently a wide range of variation in how individuals and groups have responded to race relations. Sikhs, for example, are particularly at risk because their dress marks them, they often work in occupations where they receive racial abuse (e.g., taxi and truck drivers), and their strong sense of personal honour makes them reluctant to back way from a racial incident. In contrast, Ismailis learned the dangers of appearing different and apart in East Africa and try to keep a low profile here. More likely being in business or the professions, they are also less likely to be victims of racism than Sikhs. As we have seen, there is also a wide range of personal views on how seriously racism affects them and on what to do about it.

There is, however, one important perception spanning all South Asian groups and most individuals: a strong self-consciouness that others see them as physically different. Many South Asian Canadians feel this to be a stigma, which of necessity colours most relations they have with others. As such, it frequently has resulted in individuals feeling self-conscious in public and wishing to avoid new, untested social situations. For quite some time racial stigma was a key factor limiting the development of close relations between Asians and other Canadians. Though still prevalent, these feelings presently seem to be on the wane, as relations between South Asians and others grow progressively more rich and mutually rewarding.

INTERGROUP RELATIONS IN THE 1980's

The future course of relations between South Asians and other Canadians can be predicted with some confidence. Given the unlikelihood that Canada will ever see the high rates of South Asian immigration that marked the mid-1970's, an ever-increasing proportion of South Asian Canadians will be long-term residents or will have been born here. Settlement difficulties for them will either be behind them or irrelevant, and their knowledge of Canada will be deep and well grounded. Their concerns will be increasingly similar to those of other Canadians and their social relations will certainly reflect this. As the second generation matures they will be at the forefront of changes in South Asian Canadian relations with others; based on their present close relations with their non-South Asian student peers these will become increasingly multidimensional.

Changes such as these will certainly continue to erode stereotypic ideas about South Asians and make it less likely that such negative ideas are a factor in how others deal with South Asians. This should particularly be true of younger people, who are already more tolerant and whose ideas are more susceptible to change.[33]

This is not to suggest that all of today's racial problems facing South Asians will necessarily disappear quickly. Some may not disappear at all without active intervention. Those adults who harbour strong prejudices against South Asians are chiefly unreachable by any program designed to change their racist attitudes, yet it is exactly such people who are presently in positions where they can translate their prejudices into discriminatory behaviour. It is slim consolation for South Asians worried about the effect of discrimination on their lives today that it will pass with the coming of the next generation. Mechanisms to fight discrimination directly are at present not very effective, and it remains an open question whether governments or the public will be motivated to support stronger means. Relations between South Asians and other Canadians should continue to proliferate and improve over the years to the mutual benefit of all concerned. Hopefully, in the near future we can look for the full integration of South Asians into the fabric of Canadian life.

NOTES

1. Frances Henry, "The Dynamics of Racism in Toronto" (Ottawa, 1978, mimeo.); John Berry *et al., Multiculturalism and Ethnic Attitudes in Canada* (Ottawa, 1977).
2. For a discussion of the rise and demise of biological notions of race, see A. Montagu, *Man's Most Dangerous Myth: The Fallacy of Race*, 5th edition (New York, 1974).
3. Indra, "The Portrayal of South Asians in the Vancouver Press"; Indra, "Ethnicity, Social Stratification, and Opinion Formation."
4. M. Mackie, "Ethnic Stereotypes and Prejudice," *Canadian Ethnic Studies*, 6 (1974), pp. 39-52.
5. *Experiences of an Immigrant Youth*, collected by the Multicultural Resources Project, 1979, Cross Cultural Communications Centre (Toronto).
6. K.U. Chandra, *Racial Discrimination in Canada* (San Francisco, 1973).
7. Indra, "Ethnicity, Social Stratification, and Opinion Formation"; M. Rosenfeld and M. Spina, *All the News that's Fit to Print: A Study of the Toronto Press' Coverage of Racism, Immigration and Ethnic Communities* (Toronto, 1977).
8. Anthony Richmond, "Black and Asian Immigrants in Britain and Canada: Some Comparisons," *Journal of Community Relations Commission*, 4, 4 (1975), pp. 504-7.

9. For the Ontario version, see J. Rosenstock and D. Adair, *Multiculturalism in the Classroom: A Survey of Inter-Racial Attitudes in Ontario Schools* (Ottawa, 1976), p. 12.
10. Indra, "Ethnicity, Social Stratification, and Opinion Formation," p. 181.
11. *Vancouver Sun,* March 10, 1975.
12. *Vancouver Province,* March 10, 1975.
13. *Vancouver Sun,* February 3, 1975.
14. Dave Singh, *Some Factors in the Relationship between the Police and East Indians* (Vancouver, 1975), pp. 50, 31.
15. See Ubale, "Equal Opportunity and Public Policy"; W. Pitman, *Now Is Not Too Late* (Toronto, 1977).
16. Canada's 1980 junior bantamweight boxing champion, Asif Karam Dra, learned to fight in order to stand up to this intimidation (*Toronto Star,* November 14, 1980).
17. See Ubale, "Equal Opportunity and Public Policy," pp. 30-1; letter to Roy McMurtry, October 9, 1976 (Multicultural History Society of Ontario, MSR #597).
18. Ubale, "Equal Opportunity and Public Policy."
19. *Toronto Star,* April 14, 1976.
20. D. Jobidon, *Situation Report on the Current State of Race Relations in Vancouver, British Columbia* (Ottawa, 1982), pp. 20-5.
21. *Ibid.*
22. K. Lowe, *Race Relations in Metropolitan Toronto* (Ottawa, 1982), p. 66.
23. Head, *Adaptation of Immigrants*; Buchignani, *Perceptions of Racial Discrimination;* E. Tepper, *Is Ottawa Different? Perceptions of Discrimination and Race Relations in the Nation's Capital* (Ottawa, 1982); Jobidon, *Situation Report.*
24. Norman Buchignani, *Perceptions of Racial Discrimination in Calgary: A Situation Report* (Ottawa, 1982).
25. Henry, "The Dynamics of Racism in Toronto."
26. Berry *et al., Multiculturalism and Ethnic Attitudes,* pp. 94-100, 104.
27. Indra, "Ethnicity, Social Stratification, and Opinion Formation," pp. 418-27.
28. See, for example, Henry, "The Dynamics of Racism in Toronto"; Berry *et al., Multiculturalism and Ethnic Attitudes.* For an overview on the subject, see G. Allport, *The Nature of Prejudice* (Boston, 1954).
29. Canada, Department of Manpower and Immigration, *Three Years in Canada* (Ottawa, 1975).
30. *Ibid.*
31. R. D. Sharma, *Immigrant Needs in Metropolitan Toronto* (Toronto, 1980), p. 21.
32. Pitman, *Now Is Not Too Late,* pp. 243-4.
33. Sharma, *Immigrant Needs in Metropolitan Toronto,* p. 29.

231

Conclusion: A Continuous Journey

South Asians have been part of the Canadian scene since the turn of the century. For almost forty years, theirs was the history of an unwelcome minority group struggling to become established against the combined weight of public opinion and the government. The odds were all against them, and South Asian gains came slowly over four decades of hardship, conflict, and subordination. A dramatic fight against the ending of South Asian immigration led first to the rise of an Indian nationalist movement, then to important immigration concessions. The latter made possible the development of South Asian Canadian family life and resulted in an increasing commitment to life in Canada.

From the mid-1920's to 1947, life in Canada stabilized for South Asians and they became a culturally homogeneous, socially insulated community, where virtually everyone was a Sikh of similar class and life experience. Economic stability was achieved through an almost exclusive preoccupation with the woods industries. Relations with others improved, but the rate of assimilation was low; intermarriage was almost non-existent. They had become an encapsulated community, whose chief concerns remained the legal liabilities placed on them prior to World War I.

Little did members of this community know as they worked to eliminate the immigration ban and other restrictions that this would lead to an unalterable and explosive change in South Asian Canadian life. As immigration restrictions were swept away Sikh immigration resumed. But this was but the vanguard of a veritable explosion in the number and cultural scope of South Asians in Canada. Over 200,000 people of South Asian origin have come to Canada in the past fifteen years alone.

Unimpeded by the kind of legal and informal restrictions faced by the first Sikh pioneers, post-war immigrants have made a dramatic, swift, and successful adaptation to Canadian life. This is especially creditable, in that many were pioneers in their own right, founding new South Asian communities as they laid the groundwork for their personal and family

232

lives. Inasmuch as most South Asian Canadians are immigrants, adjustment and adaptation are ongoing. Also, they vary from one aspect of life to another. South Asian economic adaptation has more or less successfully stabilized, but family and community life continue to be under flux. Today, family and household are at once the principal reservoir of South Asian culture in Canada and the locus of dramatic intergenerational accommodation and change.

South Asians are nowhere so numerous as to be able to develop a full set of sociocultural institutions, nor is there much desire to do so. Rather, South Asian Canadians have chosen to maintain only certain valued aspects of their heritage. Perhaps the most important such element is the establishment and maintenance of large, interlocking networks of kin, friends, and acquaintances within their ethnocultural group. Community institutions such as associations, temples, businesses, and newspapers have typically followed. Attempts to maintain religion, language, and the arts have been substantial in more established communities, and a wide range of other functions are now being carried out by such institutions.

South Asian adaptations to Canada have not been exclusively in terms of their ethnocultural group. Most have achieved a firm integration into Canadian society. Historical Canadian and South Asian cultural and racial biases have been such that this integration was not achieved without some resistance and misunderstanding, and South Asian concern over discrimination continues to be significant. Nevertheless, such difficulties have not been so great as to prevent close and increasingly interdependent relations between South Asians and other Canadians.

The many South Asian ethnocultural, religious, and national groups are an important addition to the Canadian cultural mosaic. South Asians represent one-fifth of all humankind and a range of cultures as wide as that of all European Canadians together. As they have become more established, their cultural influence on Canada is increasing rapidly. Today, more and more Canadians are becoming exposed to South Asian food, music, and dance, and one sees the beginning of a greater and more realistic awareness of South Asia and the other places from which South Asians come.

Once stigmatized, legally restricted, and socially isolated, South Asians are now an integral and important part of Canadian society. The struggles of the first pioneers in British Columbia made it possible for those who have arrived more recently to enjoy this success. The latter in turn are now doing the same for their children and those immigrants who will arrive in coming years. The future direction of South Asian Canadian development will soon be with the second generation, whose responsibility it will be to continue this process to the mutual benefit of themselves, other Canadians, and those who come thereafter.

Bibliography

This bibliography is divided in two sections. The first includes all references cited in the text dealing specifically with South Asians in Canada, as well as a selection of other important references on this topic. This section comprises an essentially complete inventory of printed work and dissertations on South Asians in Canada. The second section includes references cited on other topics.

I. SOUTH ASIANS IN CANADA

Adams, B., *et al.* "Ugandan Asians in Exile: Household and Kinship in the Resettlement Crisis," *Journal of Comparative Family Studies*, 8, 2 (1977), pp. 167-78.

Ahmad, S.M. "Psychological Barriers in Adaptation to a Multicultural Society," in K.V. Ujimoto and G. Hirabayashi (eds.), "Asian Canadians: Regional Perspectives" (1982, mimeo.), pp. 316-28.

Ahmed, M. "Adaptation of Bangladeshis in Canada: A Case Study" (Toronto, 1978, mimeo.).

Akoodie, M.A. "Immigrant Students: A Comparative Assessment of Ethnic Identity, Self Concept and Locus of Control Amongst West Indian and Canadian Students," Ph.D. thesis, University of Toronto, 1980.

Ames, Michael M., and Joy Inglis. "Indian Immigrants in Canada," *Indo-Canadian*, 3-4 (1968), pp. 2-6.

———. "Conflict and Change in British Columbia Sikh Family Life," *B.C. Studies*, 20 (Winter, 1973), pp. 15-49.

Andracki, Stanislaw. "The Immigration of Orientals into Canada with Special Reference to Chinese," Ph.D. thesis, McGill University, 1958. (Reprint, New York: Arno Press, 1978.)

Angus, H.F. "The Legal Status in British Columbia of Residents of Oriental Races and their Descendants," in N.A.M. Mackenzie (ed.), *The Legal Status of Aliens in Pacific Countries* (London: Oxford University Press, 1937), pp. 77-87.

Appathurai, E.R. "The Sri Lankans in Eastern Canada." Ottawa: Secretary of State, 1980, mimeo.

The Aryan (Vancouver), vol. 1, no. 1 (1911) to vol. 2, no. 9 (1912). Sundar Singh, ed.

Awan, Sadiq. "A Study of the Problems Asociated with the Education of the People of Pakistani Origin in Canada, 1947-1970," M.A. thesis, Bishop's University, 1975.

_____. "The People of Pakistani Origin in Canada, Their First Twenty-Five Years," in K.V. Ujimoto and G. Hirabayashi (eds.), *Visible Minorities and Multiculturalism* (Toronto: Butterworths, 1980).

Beck, Brenda. "Perceptions des relations parentales entre parent et enfant chez des immigrants au Canada: Variations selon qu'ils proviennent d'Inde, du Japon et de Hongrie," in Ujimoto and Hirabayashi (eds.), "Asian Canadians," pp. 207-21.

Berry, John, Rudolf Kalin, and Donald Taylor. *Multiculturalism and Ethnic Attitudes in Canada*. Ottawa: Minister of State for Multiculturalism, 1977.

Bhatti, F.M. "East Indian Immigration into Canada, 1905-1973," Ph.D. thesis, University of Surrey, 1974.

Bopp, Franz, defendant: U.S. *v.* F. Bopp *et al*. District Court of the U.S., Southern Division of the Northern District of California before Hon. Wm. C. Van Fleet, 1917 (the Ghadr Trial). Microfilm (seven reels), University of British Columbia.

Bose, Arun Coomer. "Indian Nationalist Agitations in the United States and Canada till the Arrival of Hardayal in 1911," *Journal of Indian History*, 43 (1965), pp. 227-39.

_____. *Indian Revolutionaries Abroad, 1905-1922*. Patna: Bharati Bhawan.

Bristow, M., B. Adams, and C. Periera. "Ugandan Asians in Britain, Canada and India: Some Characteristics and Resources," *New Community*, 4, 2 (1975), pp. 155-66.

British Columbia, Department of Labour. *Annual Report*. Victoria: Queen's Printer, 1917-1946.

British Columbia, Legislative Assembly. *Report on Oriental Activities within the Province*. Victoria: Charles Banfield, 1927.

Broad, Isabella Ross. *An Appeal for Fair Play for the Sikhs in Canada*. Victoria: Victoria Society of Friends of the Hindu, 1913.

Brown, Emily C. *Har Dayal: Hindu Revolutionary and Rationalist*. Tucson: Arizona University Press, 1975.

Brown, Giles T. "The Hindu Conspiracy and the Neutrality of the United States," M.A. thesis, University of California, Berkeley, 1941.

_____. "The Hindu Conspiracy, 1914-1917," *Pacific Historical Review*, 17 (1948), pp. 299-300.

Buchignani, Norman. "A Review of the Historical and Sociological Literature on East Indians in Canada," *Canadian Ethnic Studies*, 9, 1 (1977), pp. 86-108.

____. "Immigration, Adaptation, and the Management of Ethnic Identity: An Examination of Fijian East Indians in British Columbia," Ph.D. thesis, Simon Fraser University, 1977.

____. "Social Identity Formation and Interpretation: Recent East Indian Immigration to British Columbia," in J. Elliott (ed.), *Two Nations, Many Cultures* (Scarborough: Prentice-Hall, 1979), pp. 325-37.

____. "The Effect of Canadian Immigration on the Political Economy of Fiji," in O. Mehmet (ed.), *Poverty and Social Change in Southeast Asia* (Ottawa: University of Ottawa Press, 1979), pp. 265-83.

____. "Culture or Identity? Addressing Ethnicity in Canadian Education," *McGill Journal of Education*, 15, 1 (1980), pp. 79-93.

____. "South Asian and the Ethnic Mosaic: An Overview," *Canadian Ethnic Studies*, 11, 1 (1980), pp. 48-68.

____. "The Social and Self Identities of Fijian Indians in Vancouver," *Urban Anthropology*, 9, 2 (1981), pp. 75-97.

____. "South Asians in Alberta," in H. and T. Palmer (eds.), *Generations: The Peoples of Alberta* (Calgary: Western Producer, 1985).

____. *Perceptions of Racial Discrimination in Calgary: A Situation Report*. Ottawa: Secretary of State, 1982.

Buchignani, N., and D. Indra. "Intergroup Conflict and Community Solidarity: Sikhs and South Asian Fijians in Vancouver," *Canadian Journal of Anthropology*, 1, 2 (1981), pp. 149-57.

____. "The Political Organization of South Asians in Canada," in J. Dahlie and T. Fernando (eds.), *Ethnicity, Power and Politics in Canada* (Toronto: Methuen, 1981), pp. 202-32.

Button, R.A. "Sikh Settlement in the Lower Mainland of British Columbia," B.A. essay, University of British Columbia, 1964.

Canada, Board of Review (Immigration) on Charges Concerning Illegal Entry of Aliens into Canada. *Interim Report and Supplement*. Vancouver, 1938.

____. *Report*. Ottawa: King's Printer, October, 1938.

Canada, Department of the Interior. *The East Indians in British Columbia: A Proposal to send some to British Honduras*. Dominion Archives, pamphlet 3413, 1908.

Canada, Department of Manpower and Immigration. *The Immigration Program*. Ottawa: Information Canada, 1975.

____. *Three Years in Canada*. Ottawa. Information Canada, 1975.

Canada, Department of Manpower and Immigration/Department of Employment and Immigration, *Annual Immigration Statistics*. Ottawa: Government Printer, 1966-1982.

Canada and India (Toronto). Kartar Singh (ed.), 1915-1916.

Canada India Committee. *A Call for Canadian Justice*. Toronto, 1915.

____. *The Hindu Case*. Toronto, 1915.

____. *India's Appeal to Canada or: An Account of Hindu Immigration to the Dominion*. Toronto, 1916.

Canada Pakistan Association of Ottawa-Hull. *A History of People of Pakistani Origin in Canada.* Ottawa, 1976.

Cassin, A. Marguerite, and A. Griffith. "Class and Ethnicity: Producing the Difference that Counts," *Canadian Ethnic Studies*, 8, 1 (1981), pp. 109-30.

Chadney, James G. "The Joint Family as Structure and Process," *Journal of Social Thought*, 7, 1 (1975), pp. 17-22.

____. "The Vancouver Sikhs: An Ethnic Community in Canada," Ph.D. thesis, Michigan State University, 1976.

Chandra, K.U. *Racial Discrimination in Canada.* San Francisco: R & E Research Associates, 1973.

Chawla, Saroj. "Indian Children in Toronto: A Study of Socialization," M.A. thesis, York University, 1971.

Cheng, Tien Fang. *Oriental Immigration in Canada.* Shanghai: Commercial Press, 1931.

Corbett, David C. *Canada's Immigration Policy: A Critique.* Toronto: University of Toronto Press, 1957.

Dadabhay, Yusuf. "Circuitous Assimilation among rural Hindustanis in California," *Social Forces*, 33 (1954), pp. 138-41.

Darlings, Malcolm Lyall. *The Punjab Peasant in Prosperity and Debt.* London: Oxford University Press, 1928.

Das, Rajani Kant. *Hindustanee Workers on the Pacific Coast.* Berlin: Walter de Gruyter, 1923.

Das, Taraknath. *An Open Letter to Count Leo Tolstoy in Reply to his "Letter to a Hindoo."* New York: Free Hindustan, 1909.

Dhami, Sadhu Singh. "Discovering the New World," *Queen's Quarterly*, 76 (1969), pp. 200-12.

Dignan, D.K. "Hindu Conspiracy in Anglo-Indian Relations," *Pacific Historical Review*, 40 (1971), pp. 57-77.

Dodd, Balbinder Singh. "Social Change in Two Overseas Sikh Communities," B.A. honours essay, University of British Columbia, 1972.

Dodd, W.D. "The Hindu in the Northwest," *World To-day*, 13 (1907), pp. 1157-60.

Dusenbery, V. "Hierarchy, Equality and the Assertion of Sikh Identity in North America," paper presented at the annual meeting of the Central States Anthropological Association, 1980.

____. "Canadian Ideology and Public Policy: The Impact on Vancouver Sikh Ethnic and Religious Adaptation," *Canadian Ethnic Studies*, 8, 3 (1981), pp. 101-20.

Ferguson, Ted. *A White Man's Country: An Exercise in Canadian Prejudice.* Toronto: Macmillan, 1975.

Fernando, Tissa. "East African Asians in Western Canada: The Ismaili Community," *New Community*, 7, 3 (1979), pp. 361-8.

Free Hindusthan (Vancouver, Seattle). Taraknath Das (ed.), 1908.

Gill, Kuldip. "A Canadian Sikh Wedding as a Cultural Performance," M.A. thesis, University of British Columbia, 1982.

Grace, Elizabeth Ross. "East Indian Immigration," *Westminster Hall Magazine*, 3 (1908), pp. 10-12.

237

Grant, Kenneth James. "Among the Hindus of British Columbia," *Missionary Messenger* (1915), pp. 106-09.

____. *My Missionary Memories.* Halifax: Imperial Publishing Co., 1923.

Hallet, Mary E. "A Governor General's View on Oriental Immigration to B.C., 1904-1911," *B.C. Studies*, 14 (1972), pp. 51-72.

Harkin, J.B. *The East Indians of British Columbia. A Report regarding the Proposal to provide Work in British Honduras for the Indigent Unemployed among Them.* Ottawa: Minister of the Interior, 1909.

Hawkins, Freda. *Canada and Immigration: Public Policy and Public Concern.* Montreal: McGill-Queen's University Press, 1972.

____. "Uganda Asians in Canada," *New Community*, 2 (1973), pp. 268-75.

Head, Wilson. *Adaptation of Immigrants: Perceptions of Ethnic and Racial Discrimination.* Toronto: York University, 1981.

Henry, Frances. "The Dynamics of Racism in Toronto" (Ottawa: Secretary of State, 1978, mimeo.).

Hilliker, J.F. "The British Columbia Franchise and Canadian Relations with India in Wartime, 1939-1945," *B.C. Studies*, 46 (1980), pp. 40-60.

The Hindustanee (Vancouver). H. Rahim (Chagan K. Varma) (ed.), 1914-1915.

Holland, Sir Robert. "Indian Immigration into Canada: the Question of Franchise," *Asiatic Review*, 39 (1943), pp. 167-71.

Hunt, James. *Gandhi in London.* New Delhi: Promilla, 1978.

Husaini, Zohra. "Social Networks: A Factor in Immigrant Economic Success," Ph.D. thesis, University of Alberta, 1981.

Ijaz, Mian. "Ethnic Attitudes of Elementary School Children and East Indians and the Effect of a Cultural Program on these Attitudes," D.Ed. thesis, University of Toronto, 1980.

India, Government of. *Report of the Komagata Maru Commission of Inquiry.* Calcutta: King's Printer, 1914.

India and Canada (Vancouver). Kartar Singh (ed.), 1929-30.

Indra, Doreen. "The Production & Legitimation of East Indian Stereotypes in the Vancouver Press" (1977, mimeo.).

____. "The Portrayal of South Asians in the Vancouver Press: 1905-1976," *Ethnic and Racial Studies*, 2, 2 (1979), pp. 164-87.

____. "Ethnicity, Social Stratification, and Opinion Formation: An Analysis of Ethnic Portrayal in the Vancouver Newspaper Press, 1905-1976," Ph.D. thesis, Simon Fraser University, 1979.

____. "The Relationship Between Canadian Immigrant Flows and Source Country Populations, Wealth and Trade," in Ujimoto and Hirabayashi (eds.), *Visible Minorities and Multiculturalism*, pp. 163-80.

Jensen, Joan M. "The 'Hindu Conspiracy': A Reassessment," *Pacific Historical Review*, 48, 1 (1980), pp. 65-84.

Jobidon, O. *Situation Report on the*

Current State of Race Relations in Vancouver, British Columbia. Ottawa: Secretary of State, 1982.

Johnson, Hugh. The Voyage of the Komagata Maru: The Sikh Challenge to Canada's Colour Bar. Delhi: Oxford University Press, 1979.

Josh, Sohan Singh. Hindustan Gadar Party: A Short History. 2 vols. New Delhi: People's Publishing House, 1977, 1978.

Joy, A., and V. Dusenbery. "Being Sikh in British Columbia: Changing Definitions of 'Self' and 'Others,' " paper presented at the annual meeting of the Canadian Asian Studies Association, 1980.

Kanungo, Rabindra. "South Asian Presence in the Canadian Mosaic: Impact and Potential," in Ujimoto and Hirabayashi (eds.), "Asian Canadians," pp. 297-316.

Khalsa Diwan Society of Vancouver. Report of correspondence and Documents relating to Negotiations between 1939-47, culminating in Domiciliary Rights being Accorded to 210 Members of the Indian Community by the Dominion Government. Vancouver, 1947.

Khalsa Herald (Vancouver). Kartar Singh (ed.), 1911-1912.

Khosla, Renu. "The Changing Familial Role of South-Asian Women in Canada: A Study in Identity Transformation," in Ujimoto and Hirabayashi (eds.), "Asian Canadians."

King, William L. Mackenzie. Report of the Royal Commission appointed to inquire into the Method by which Oriental Labourers have been induced to come to Canada. Ottawa: King's Printer, 1908.

_____. Report by W.L. Mackenzie King on his Mission to England to confer with the British Authorities on the Subject of: Immigration to Canada from the Orient and Immigration from India in Particular. Sessional paper no. 36a, A 1908 Edward VII. Ottawa: King's Printer, 1908.

_____. Confidential Memorandum accompanying Report of W. L. Mackenzie King on his Mission to England, May 2, 1908. Gov. Gen. File, vol. 2(b), G 21, #332, 1908.

Lal, Brij. "East Indians in British Columbia, 1904-1914: A Historical Study in Growth and Integration," M.A. thesis, University of British Columbia, 1976.

Laut, Agnes C. Am I My Brother's Keeper? A Study of British Columbia's Labour and Oriental Problems. Toronto: Saturday Night Publishing Co., 1913.

Lockley, Fred. "The Hindu Invasion," Pacific Monthly (1907), pp. 584-95.

Lowe, K. Race Relations in Metropolitan Toronto, 1982. Ottawa: Secretary of State, 1982.

Lowes, George H. "The Sikhs of British Columbia," B.A. honours essay, University of British Columbia, 1952.

Manitoba Organization of South Asians in Canada (MOSAIC). "A Socio-Demographic Survey of South Asians in Manitoba" (Winnipeg, 1979, mimeo.).

Mathur, Laxman Prasad. Indian Revolutionary Movements in the

United States, 1922- . Delhi: S. Chand, 1970.

Mayer, Adrian C. *A Report on the East Indian Community in Vancouver.* Vancouver: University of British Columbia, 1959.

McDonough, B. "A Study of South Asian Immigrants in the Montreal Metropolitan Region" (1978, mimeo.).

Minde, K., and R. Minde. "Children of Immigrants: The Adjustment of Ugandan Asian Primary-School Children in Canada," *Canadian Psychiatric Association Journal,* 21, 6 (1976), pp. 371-81.

Mittal, S.C. *Freedom Movement in Punjab (1905-29).* Delhi: Concept Publishing Co., 1977.

Morah, Benson C. "The Assimilation of Ugandan Asians in Calgary," M.A. thesis, University of Calgary, 1974.

Morse, Eric W. "Immigration and Status of British East Indians in Canada: A Problem in Imperial Relations," M.A. thesis, Queen's University, 1935.

Moudgil, Ranvir. "From Stranger to Refugee: A Study of the Integration of Ugandan Asians in Canada," Ph.D. thesis, SUNY, Buffalo, 1977.

Munday, Jennifer G. "East Indians in British Columbia: A Community in Transition," B.A. honours essay, University of British Columbia, 1953.

Muthanna, I.M. *People of India in North America (Part First).* Bangalore: Lotus Printers, 1975.

Naidoo, J.C. "The East Indian Woman: Her Potential Contribution to Canadian Society" (1977, mimeo.).

____. "The East Indian Woman in Canadian Context: A Study in Social Psychology" (1977, mimeo.).

____. "Women of South Asian and Anglo Saxon Origins in the Canadian Context: Self Perceptions, Socialization, Achievement Aspirations," in C.S. Adam (ed.), *Sex Roles* (Montreal: Eden Press, 1979).

____. "South Asians in the Canadian Mosaic," paper presented at the annual meeting of the Canadian Ethnic Studies Association, 1981.

____. "The South Asian Experience of Aging," in Ujimoto and Hirabayashi (eds.), "Asian Canadians," pp. 84-95.

Nasser-Bush, Merun H. "Differential Adjustment Between Two Indian Immigrant Communities in Toronto: Sikhs and Ismailis," Ph.D. thesis, University of Colorado, 1973.

O'Dwyer, Sir Michael. *India as I Knew It, 1885-1925.* London: Constable, 1926.

Owaisi, Lateef, and Z. Bangash. *Visible Minorities in Mass Media Advertising.* Ottawa: Canadian Consultative Council on Multiculturalism, 1977.

Pannu, R.S. "A Sociological Survey of Teachers from India Teaching in Alberta, 1958-65," M.Ed. thesis, University of Alberta, 1966.

Pardeshi Khalsa (Vancouver). Hira Singh (ed.), 1910.

Patel, D. *Dealing with Interracial Con-*

flict: *Policy Alternatives.* Montreal: Institute for Research on Public Policy, 1980.

Pereira, Cecil Patrick. "East Indians in Winnipeg: A Study of the Consequences of Immigration for an Ethnic Group in Canada," M.A. thesis, University of Manitoba, 1971.

Pereira, C., B. Adams, and M. Bristow. "Canadian Beliefs and Policy Regarding the Admission of Ugandan Asians to Canada," *Ethnic and Racial Studies,* 1, 3 (1978), pp. 353-64.

Pidgeon, G.C., and E.D. McLaren. "East Indian Immigration," *Westminster Hall Magazine,* 7, 8 (1912), pp. 23-8.

Pitman, W. *Now Is Not Too Late.* Toronto: Metro Toronto, 1977.

Qureshi, R.B. "The Family Model as a Blueprint for Social Interaction Among Pakistani Canadians," in Ujimoto and Hirabayashi (eds.), "Asian Canadians."

Raucher, Alan. "American Anti-Imperialism and the Pro-Indian Movement, 1900-1932," *Pacific Historical Review,* 42 (1974), pp. 82-110.

Richmond, Anthony. "Black and Asian Immigrants in Britain and Canada: Some Comparisons," *Journal of Community Relations Commission,* 4, 4 (1975), pp. 504-07.

Rosenfeld, M., and M. Spina. *All the News that's Fit to Print: A Study of the Toronto Press' Coverage of Racism, Immigration and Ethnic Communities.* Toronto: Cross Cultural Communication Centre, 1977.

Rosenstock, J., and D. Adair. *Multiculturalism in the Classroom: A Survey of Inter-Racial Attitudes in Ontario Schools.* Ottawa: Department of Manpower and Immigration, 1976.

Saidullah, Ahmad. "A Critique of Indian Music," in A. Mukherjee (ed.), *East Indians: Myths and Reality* (Toronto: Indian Immigrant Aid and the Indian Students' Association at the University of Toronto, 1977), pp. 317-23.

Sandhu, Sukhdev Singh. *The Second Generation: Culture and the East Indian Community in Nova Scotia.* Halifax: Ethnic Heritage Series, 1980.

Sansar (Victoria). Sundar Singh and Kartar Singh (eds.), 1912-1914.

Sharma, R.D. "Trends in Demographic and Socioeconomic Characteristics of the Metropolitan Toronto Population" (1980, mimeo.).

____. *Immigrant Needs in Metropolitan Toronto.* Toronto: Ontario Council of Agencies Serving Immigrants, 1980.

Siddique, C. "Changing Family Patterns: A Comparative Analysis of Immigrant Indian and Pakistani Families of Saskatoon, Canada," *Journal of Comparative Family Studies,* 8, 2 (1977), pp. 179-200.

____. "Structural Separation and Family Change: An Exploratory Study of the Immigrant Indian and Pakistani Families of Saskatoon, Canada," *International Review of Modern Sociology,* 7, 1(1977), pp. 13-35.

Siddique, Muhammad. "Patterns of Familial Decision Making and

Division of Labour: A Study of the Immigrant Indian and Pakistani Community of Saskatoon," M.A. thesis, University of Saskatchewan, 1974.

Singh, Dave. *Some Factors in the Relationship between the Police and East Indians.* Vancouver: B.C. Police Commission, 1975.

Singh, Baba Gurdit. *Voyage of the Komagata Maru or: India's Slavery Abroad,* 1st edition. Calcutta: Arya Press, n.d.

Singh, J.B. "Perceptions of Prejudice Experienced by International Students," M.A. thesis, University of Toronto, 1980.

Singh, Kushwant. *A History of the Sikhs,* 2 vols. Princeton, N.J.: Princeton University Press, 1966.

Singh, Kushwant, and Satindra Singh. *Ghadar 1915: India's First Armed Revolution.* New Delhi: R & K Publishing House, 1966.

Singh, Saint Nihal, and J. Barclay Williams. "Canada's New Immigrant: The Hindu," *Canadian Magazine,* 28, 4 (1907), pp. 383-91.

Sirha, Nand Singh. "Indians in Canada," *Modern Review,* 14 (1913), pp. 453-6.

Srivastava, Ram P. "Family Organization and Change Among the Overseas Indians with Special Reference to Indian Immigrant Families of British Columbia, Canada," in G. Kurian (ed.), *Family In India: A Regional View* (The Hague: Mouton, 1975).

Stasiulis, D. "A Sociopolitical Analysis of the South Asian Community in Toronto" (1979, mimeo.).

Subramaniam, Indira. "Identity Shift:

Post-Migration Changes in Identity Among First-Generation East Indian Immigrants in Toronto," Ph.D. thesis, University of Toronto, 1977.

———. *The East Indian Child in Toronto Schools: A Cultural Background and Psychological Profile.* Toronto: Toronto Boards of Education, 1977.

Sugimoto, Howard H. "Japanese Immigration, the Vancouver Riots, and Canadian Diplomacy," M.A. thesis, University of Washington, 1966.

Swadesh Sevak (Vancouver, Seattle). Guru Dutt Kumar (ed.), 1910.

Tepper, E. *Is Ottawa Different? Perceptions of Discrimination and Race Relations in the Nation's Capital.* Ottawa: Secretary of State, 1982.

Ubale, B. "Equal Opportunity and Public Policy" (Toronto, 1977, mimeo.).

Wakil, P.A. "The Immigrant Indo-Pakistani Family: A Case Study Research Note," paper presented at the VIIIth World Congress of Sociology, Toronto, 1974.

Ward, William Peter. "White Canada Forever: British Columbia's Response to Orientals, 1858-1914," Ph.D. thesis, Queen's University, 1973.

———. "The Oriental Immigrant and Canada's Protestant Clergy," *B.C. Studies,* 22 (1974), pp. 9-19.

Wood, John R. "East Indians and Canada's New Immigration Policy," *Canadian Public Policy,* 4, 4 (1978), pp. 547-67.

———. "A Visible Minority Votes: East Indian Electoral Behavior in the

Vancouver South Provincial and Federal Elections of 1979,'' in J. Dahlie and T. Fernando (eds.), *Ethnicity, Power and Politics in Canada* (Toronto: Methuen, 1981), pp. 177-201.

Woodsworth, James S. *Strangers within our Gates*. Toronto: Missionary Society of the Methodist Church, Canada, 1909.

Wynne, Robert E. "American Labour Leaders and the Vancouver Anti-Oriental Riot," *Pacific Northwest Quarterly,* 42, 4 (1966), pp. 172-9.

Yasmin, M. "Retention of Ethnic Identity for the Bangladeshi Immigrants in the Toronto Census Metropolitan Area," M.A. thesis, University of Guelph, 1982.

II. ADDITIONAL REFERENCES

Adachi, Ken. *The Enemy That Never Was*. Toronto: McClelland and Stewart, 1979.

Allport, G. *The Nature of Prejudice*. Boston: Beacon Press, 1954.

Benedict, Burton. *Indians in a Plural Society: A Report on Mauritius*. London: Oxford University Press, 1967.

Bolt, C. *Victorian Attitudes to Race*. Oxford: Oxford University Press, 1973.

Brereton, B. *Race Relations in Colonial Trinidad*. Cambridge: Cambridge University Press, 1979.

Brooks, E. *Apartheid: A Documentary Study of Modern South Africa*. London: Routledge and Kegan Paul, 1968.

Cole, W.O., and Piara S. Sambhi. *The Sikhs: Their Religious Beliefs and Practices*. London: Routledge and Kegan Paul, 1978.

Dillon, Anup S. *Nehru: The Rising Star of India*. New York: J. Day, 1939.

Farmer, B.H. *Ceylon: A Divided Nation*. Oxford: Oxford University Press, 1963.

Fisk, Earnest K. *The Political Economy of Independent Fiji*. Canberra: Australian National University Press, 1970.

Gillion, K.L. *Fiji's Indian Migrants: A History to the End of Indenture in 1920*. Melbourne: Oxford University Press, 1962.

Helweg, Arthur W. "A Punjabi Community in an English Town: A Study in Migrant Adaptation," Ph.D. thesis, Michigan State University, 1977.

_____. *Sikhs in England: The Development of a Migrant Community*. Delhi: Oxford University Press, 1980.

Hopkins, J.C. *The Life of Edward VII*. London: W. Scull, 1910.

Jayawardena, C. *Conflict and Solidarity in a Guyanese Plantation*. London: Oxford University Press, 1963.

_____. "Culture and Ethnicity in Guyana and Fiji," *Man* (September, 1980).

Kearney, R.N. *The Politics of Ceylon (Sri Lanka)*. New York: Cornell University Press, 1973.

Lee, Carol F. "The Road to Enfranchisement: Chinese and Japanese in British Columbia," *B.C. Studies*, 30 (1976).

243

Lemon, A. *Apartheid: A Geography of Separation*. London: Saxon House, 1976.

Mackie, M. "Ethnic Stereotypes and Prejudice," *Canadian Ethnic Studies*, 6 (1974), pp. 39-52.

Marenco, E. *The Transformation of Sikh Society*. Portland: Hapi Press, 1974.

Majumdar, R.C. *History of the Freedom Movement in India*, vol. 1. Calcutta: K.L. Mukopaohyay, 1963.

Mayer, Adrian C. *Peasants of the Pacific*, 2nd edition. London: Routledge and Kegan Paul, 1973.

Montagu, A. *Man's Most Dangerous Myth: The Fallacy of Race*, 5th edition. New York: Oxford, 1974.

Morris-Jones, W.H. "Language and Region Within the Indian Union," in P. Mason (ed.), *India and Ceylon: Unity and Diversity* (London: Oxford University Press, 1967).

Nasenko, Y. *Jawaharlal Nehru and India's Foreign Policy*. New Delhi: Sterling, 1977.

Nelson, John. *The Canadian Provinces*. Toronto: Musson, 1924.

Niehoff, A. and J. *East Indians in the West Indies*. Milwaukee, 1960.

Phillips, Paul A. *No Power Greater: A Century of Labour in B.C.* Vancouver: Broadway Printers Ltd., 1967.

Sahni, Ruchi Ram. *Struggle for Reform in Sikh Shrines*. Amritsar: Sikh Ithas Research Group, n.d.

Singh, Harbans. *The Heritage of the Sikhs*. New York: Asia Publishing House, 1964.

Singh, I. *The Philosophy of Guru Nanak*. New Delhi: Ranjit Publishing House, 1963.

Singh, Teja. *The Religion of the Sikh Gurus*. Amritsar: Shiromani Gurdwara Parbardhak Committee, 1963.

Tandon, Yash. *Problem of a Displaced Minority: The New Position of East Africa's Asians*. London: Minority Rights Group, 1974.

Tinker, Hugh. *A New System of Slavery: The Export of Indian Labour Overseas, 1838-1920*. London: Oxford University Press, 1974.

_____. *Separate and Unequal: India and the Indians in the British Commonwealth, 1920-1950*. London: Hurst, 1976.

_____. *The Banyan Tree: Overseas Emigrants from India, Pakistan, and Bangladesh*. Oxford: Oxford University Press, 1977.

Trades and Labour Council (Canada). *Proceedings* (1930-1941).

Twaddle, M. (ed.). *Expulsion of a Minority: Essays on Ugandan Asians*. London: Athlone, 1975.

van den Berghe, P. *South Africa: A Study in Conflict*. Berkeley: University of California Press, 1970.

Wilson, A.J. *Politics in Sri Lanka, 1947-1979*. London: Macmillan, 1980.

244

Index

245

GENERATIONS: A HISTORY OF CANADA'S PEOPLES